BEING THE OTHER

Also by Saeed Naqvi

The Last Brahmin Prime Minister (1996)

Reflections of an Indian Muslim (1993)

BEING THE OTHER

The Muslim in India

Saeed Naqvi

ALEPH

ALEPH

ALEPH BOOK COMPANY
An independent publishing firm
promoted by *Rupa Publications India*

First published in India in 2016
by Aleph Book Company
7/16 Ansari Road, Daryaganj
New Delhi 110 002

ISBN: 978-93-84067-22-9

6

Printed in India

For Aruna, always

Contents

Introduction

This book, which had been germinating in me for nearly six decades, first came into focus because of an act of betrayal. On 9 November 1989, my mother Atia Naqvi, wife Aruna, daughter Zeba and I drove down to Ayodhya to watch the shilanyas ceremony. Bricks to build a Ram Temple where the Babri Masjid stood were being consecrated. As we watched the rituals, the violent kar sevaks, I grew increasingly despondent. Even though the Babri Masjid still stood, I knew that it was only a matter of time before it would be brought down. And with its fall, the whole charade of secularism and protestations that all was well with our country's politics and attitudes towards minorities, especially Muslims, would come to be seen for what it was. As an Indian Muslim who loved his country and was fully invested in it, I felt betrayed. And angry, because it could all have been so different.

I was born and brought up in Awadh, in the heart of the Hindi heartland, a land of exquisite culture and creativity. Most of all, it was a region where lines between Hindu and Muslim (despite the best efforts of the colonial ruler) were seldom drawn, and where syncretism was a way of life. (I describe all this in the first two chapters of the book. It is also where I discuss the first signs of disharmony between the communities that began to show up as Independence neared.) However, from the time the subcontinent was partitioned, an alarming phenomenon began to manifest itself in the country. There had been periods of conflict between Hindus and Muslims, usually at the behest of whichever ruler was the most powerful during the period in question, but this was the first time that a systematic 'Othering' of Muslims started taking place. Much of the time it was by design, at other times it was because of the bungling of political and religious leaders, but the result was the same—the minorities, especially Muslims, became increasingly alienated and insecure. Both the Congress, which was in power for the majority of the period since Independence, and the BJP were responsible for this phenomenon to a greater or lesser degree. Those who profited the most from the phenomenon were hard-core Hindu fundamentalists, who felt that it would only be a matter of time before they achieved the Hindu Rashtra that had been denied them at Independence by India's far-sighted founding fathers, who, unlike Muhammad Ali Jinnah who secured an Islamic state for his countrymen, refused to pander to sectarian demands. But as the founding fathers passed on, and as new political realities began to emerge—the 'Othering' of India's Muslims began, alarmingly, to proceed apace.

⁓

The Oxford Dictionary defines the 'Other' as 'that which is distinct from, different from, or opposite to something or oneself.' In the late twentieth century, the Palestinian scholar Edward Said analysed this phenomenon. From this issued his seminal work, *Orientalism*, on the 'affiliation of knowledge and power'. This is how the West created an image of the East as the 'Other'. The supremacist ideology of imperialism is structured on this platform. Looked at through this lens, it helps us see how, in India, an entire community, which comprises over 14 per cent of the total population, has come to be seen as the Other, as something exotic, backward, uncivilized, even dangerous.

⁓

When I began writing this book I intended it to be a memoir. However, in its final form, a part of it is a procession of images, 'scratches on my mind'. The rest of it comprises my observations and eyewitness accounts of various seminal events in contemporary Indian history that have had a bearing on Muslims. *Being the Other* is also a lament for the vanished syncretic Hindu–Muslim culture, especially in that crucible of tolerance, the qasbah of Mustafabad near Lucknow, where I grew up. Ours was a Muslim home. But the cultural derivatives of the Islam we lived were set against a broad Hindu civilizational framework. It was not something we talked about. It was something we lived.

I have had an eventful life, rich with experiences gleaned from this country and a hundred other countries. In that sense, I am the 'other' within the Other. I was fortunate in that the liberal, secular outlook gifted to me by my environment turned out to my advantage. In 1966, Pran Chopra, the first Indian editor of *The Statesman* and the paper's political correspondent, Inder Malhotra, sent me as special correspondent to Jaipur when I was still in my twenties. They were not Hindus with marks on their forehead; I was not a Muslim wearing the elder brother's outsized shirt and the younger brother's pyjamas that dangled above the ankles. We grew out of different faiths but had a common social meeting ground. This was the early promise of Nehruvianism. It was soon to be belied.

Not only was my career as a journalist not adversely affected by Partition, but I found myself cruising ahead of my competitors. The Punjabi Hindu found my Urdu background attractive. In 1977, Ramnath Goenka, despite his right-wing Hindu leanings, appointed me the principal political reporter of his newspaper, the *Indian Express*. In time, I would go on to become the editor of the six southern editions of the newspaper. In other words, I have never had the experience of tens of millions of Muslims in this country—of being treated with suspicion and disfavour because of my faith. In a way, that has helped me, if anything, to see the reality of the situation clearly and even objectively.

As I have said, the deliberate 'Othering' of the Indian Muslim that would have long-term repercussions first took shape in 1947:

after all, the decision to divide the subcontinent on religious lines was inherently communal. Muslims were all given the 'option' to go to Pakistan by a specified period—1956. Many senior Muslim civil servants, officers in the police and the armed forces proceeded to Karachi, the initial capital of Pakistan, to help the new country stand on its feet. Many stayed on in India because it appeared to them to be tolerant and they didn't feel under threat. It didn't take long for Muslims who had stayed on in India to realize that they were being treated differently. Politicians, officials and a largely Hindu police force would work progressively against them, decade after decade, especially in communally charged situations.

In the early nineties, my journalistic experience enabled me to realize that these trends had reached dangerous levels. External and internal conditions were reinforcing each other. After the Babri Masjid was demolished on 6 December 1992, communalism spiralled out of control, especially during the Bombay riots, one of the worst the country had seen; these took place when a Congress chief minister was in charge.

Around this time, Prabhash Joshi, a distinguished Hindi journalist, invited me to be the main speaker at a seminar held in New Delhi's India International Centre (IIC). I disappointed him that evening because I failed to live up to his expectations. I said something that was close to blasphemy—that in the decades since Independence, under the supervision of the Congress party, the national mood was nothing but soft saffron. Remember, there was no Narendra Modi even on the horizon then and the Congress was in power in Delhi. In that context, mine was a scathing observation.

I remember arriving late for the seminar because an unusually large number of road blocks obstructed my way. Attendance at the auditorium had exceeded expectations—there was standing room only. The mood in the room was anxious because of the the country's latest round of communal trauma.

Prabhash had organized the evening on just that theme. When

he saw me enter, he immediately gestured to me to make my way to the stage 'to save the day'. The 'day' was being lost because the packed hall, which a decade ago would have been eating out of his hand, had turned upon him like the Romans upon Cinna the poet in Shakespeare's *Julius Caesar*. His secularism was so much cant, they said. It was the usual Congress appeasement of 'anti-national' elements. The earlier accusation used to be that Muslims were being 'appeased'. Now they were being described as 'anti-national'. (Yes, this was about a quarter century before Narendra Modi became prime minister.) They had gone up a notch on the hate chart. This response from an IIC audience, generally educated and restrained, was something of a new trend. Prabhash did not know how to rein in the new soft saffron tendentiousness that was being mounted by those who would normally have been very much part of the middle ground that had, not very long ago, been under the sway of the Congress party. I decided to speak some home truths.

Middle India was not shifting towards the BJP, I said, it had already gone over to that camp. It had become more 'Hindu' in its core. There now existed a national consensus shaded in saffron. Individuals in this IIC audience may or may not have been BJP supporters. They may have been Congress sympathizers. It did not matter. In the metropolitan centres, the BJP and the Congress had become indistinguishable. The false screen that had existed between the two since 1947 had started lifting a while ago, and now it was all quite stark. A disturbing sectarian uniformity had descended on the collective attitude of those belonging to urban India, irrespective of political affiliations. With each passing day, the Muslim retreated more into his shell. The non-communal Hindu was equally bewildered. I tried to avoid the term 'secular' where I could, because the word had been profaned too often.

This saffron uniformity, which I was referring to, was an evolving reality because neo-liberal economic policies had provided the burgeoning middle class with Maruti plus aspirations.

This Indian sensibility had no elements of the high cultural avant garde. Rather, it sprang out of an imitative consumerism, it belonged to avaricious accumulators, it was more tinsel than true—an Indian with a different balance—Lakshmi minus Saraswati. This class had become very fearful of the new caste politics which sought to transfer power and wealth to the ever expanding lower caste-base of the pyramid. Until the nineties, all chief ministers in North India were Savarnas, mostly Brahmins. The emergence of Mulayam Singh Yadav and Mayawati in Uttar Pradesh, Lalu Prasad Yadav, and Nitish Kumar in Bihar frightened the Savarnas. Was the caste pyramid being upturned? But how had something that started out as caste conflict become communal? Because of the upper caste appraisal that Muslims were being mobilized by the Avarna or the lower castes to topple the age-old caste system and the privilege that went with it. This largely intra-Hindu tussle worked to the disadvantage of Muslims. A frightful thought germinated: target the Muslim as the 'Other' to affect greater Hindu consolidation.

A new disconcerting truth over the past two decades since the 1990s has been one that most Indians, including friends like Prabhash Joshi, appeared not to have grasped. The deepening of the Hindu–Muslim divide is now also being determined by external factors. The external stimulus had always been there, but after the fall of the Soviet Union and 9/11 it became pronounced. Gradually, the West, nudged by Israel, identified political Islam, Islamic fundamentalism, Muslim militancy, call it what you will, as its target in the nineties, and we joined the war on terror in 2001. Over time, this coloured matters within our country as well. The tolerance and syncretism that had marked over a thousand years of Hindu–Muslim equations began to give way to bitterness and hostility. I am not suggesting that communalism was never there, but now it gathered velocity.

᠊

Being the Other

This book does not claim to be a comprehensive history of the Muslim in India, nor is it a political history of Islam in the subcontinent. Rather, it is a chronicle of my growing disillusionment and disappointment with the direction in which the country is heading, filtered through my own experiences and observations of key events in recent Indian history.

With the exception of Partition and its aftermath, which I was too young to personally have a view on, every other event I discuss I have reported on myself or experienced in one way or another. I have tried to devote individual chapters to seminal events but as a single chapter is scarcely sufficient to go into the enormous complexity of all these events, I have often teased out a single strand to illustrate the whole. For example, to offer a new perspective on the Babri Masjid, I have relied on a long and extraordinarily clear-sighted interview with the top RSS leader of the time, Bhaurao Deoras. Again, to shine a different light on the problem of Kashmir, I have showed how it was viewed by the great British editor, Ian Stephens of *The Statesman*—Stephens was prescient in more ways than one and if his counsel had been heeded, things may well have turned out differently. In the chapter 'Unholy Riots', I write about all the riots I have reported on, and the insights they afford on the communalizing of India.

When the reader has finished reading the book, I hope he or she will have gained a measure of understanding of what is being lost to communalism. Muslims aren't the only ones who will lose, every Indian will. It doesn't matter if you are Hindu, Buddhist, Sikh, Christian, Jain or atheist—a country divided by sectarianism or shaped along communal lines will no longer be India. It will be a different country, a retrograde nation ruled by belief, superstition and authoritarian impulses, a replica of failed states and religious dictatorships around the world where tyranny has displaced democracy, human rights, justice and liberty for all.

ONE

Growing up in Awadh

AS I HAVE said in the Introduction, the urge to write this book grew on me from the day my mother, wife, daughter and I drove from Lucknow to Ayodhya to witness shilanyas, the bricklaying ceremony of the Ram Temple on the perimeter of the Babri Masjid.

The existence of a mosque in a patently Hindu environment was not all that surprising given the complex relationship that has existed between the two faiths for centuries, especially in medieval times. What was surprising was that Muslims in the twentieth century were digging in their heels to prevent the destruction of a mosque where prayers were not being held. If they hadn't done so it is unlikely that the Babri Masjid would have assumed the symbolic importance it has had in modern times. What we saw in Ayodhya was not two belief systems in conflict, but rather the use of religion to expand territories. It was about status. As far as the Muslim was concerned, it was status reversal all the way.

After Partition, Emperor Babur's name got attached to a controversial mosque built during his reign. Yet there is no credible proof whatsoever that he built a mosque on the spot where Lord Ram was supposed to have been born. In fact, there is no evidence to suggest that Babur built a mosque anywhere in the region. If a mosque was at all built, it was by a nobleman called Mir Baqi. Mir Baqi is patently a Shia name. It is unlikely that the founder of the Mughal Empire, a Sunni Uzbek by birth, would send out a Shia courtier to proselytize on his behalf. Babur was a pleasure-loving adventurer, not a bigot. A verse attributed to him goes:

Babur ba aish kosh ki aalam dobara neest

(Enjoy yourself because this world will not repeat itself.)

Be that as it may, my mother's bewilderment was on another count. 'The bricklaying ceremony was sanctified by Jawaharlal Nehru's grandson, Rajiv Gandhi,' she pointed out with a sense of déjà vu. For wasn't it on Nehru's watch that the Hindu idols under the central dome of the mosque had first 'appeared'?

Nehru was a sensitive subject within the family. Abbajan, our great grand-uncle, had built up Nehru as some sort of a family icon. We saw him as one of us—as an embodiment of Awadh's composite culture. Mir Wajid Ali, my paternal great-grandfather and a distinguished lawyer in Rae Bareli, was a friend of Jawaharlal Nehru's father, Motilal Nehru. When the Nehrus stayed with Mir Sahib, the instruction to the kitchen was, 'khana for Motilal; bhojan for his son Jawaharlal'. This was because the latter had taken to vegetarianism under Gandhi's influence. The house Mir Sahib lived in, Khali Sahat, had been reduced to rubble in 1857. His grandfather, Mir Baqar, a landed Sayyid, was arrested by the British for supplying men and weapons to Rana Beni Madhav who fought alongside Begum Hazrat Mahal against the British during the Revolt of 1857. Mir Baqar (along with a dozen companions) was then hanged from a tamarind tree outside the Collectorate. The bodies were left to rot for a week. A battery of cannons brought down his house.

His son, Mir Waheed, lived in penury. Houses of close relatives were open for him only at night. He had to leave before daybreak just in case the police found out. Mir Wajid Ali had to study under lanterns at the railway station. Through his efforts and labour he became the lawyer in Rae Bareli who forwarded cases for the High Court in Allahabad to Motilal Nehru. The two joined the

Congress party at the same time and spent years in Naini Jail.

Following in Mir Sahib's footsteps were my father and my uncle, Wasi Naqvi, who became the first Congress MLA from Rae Bareli during the general elections of 1952. The constituency was made famous subsequently by the 'Gandhi-Nehru' family. Indira Gandhi's husband, Feroze Gandhi, was asked to weave his parliamentary constituency around Wasi Naqvi's assembly seat in the 1957 elections. I was ten years old at the time and have a recollection of PL 480 ghee cans arriving from Delhi in trucks to be distributed among district officials, panchayat members and other influential people. My uncle's house was the election headquarters, and the cans that were stacked up to the ceiling provided my dadi (paternal grandmother) with the incentive to churn out copious amounts of halwa for the family twenty miles away in Mustafabad even as they were beginning to suffer the pangs of zamindari abolition in 1951.

During the election campaign, Feroze Gandhi lived in a small windowless room in the nearby Laxmi Hotel where his Parsi parentage was occasionally the subject of some whispered exchanges. Supposing his surname was not Gandhi but, say, Batliwala or Screwvala, would the history of India have been different?

ſ

In the heart of the modern Indian state of Uttar Pradesh (UP) lies the erstwhile region of Awadh—or Oudh as it was known in British historical texts—an independent state that rose to prominence in the early eighteenth century as the power wielded by Mughal emperors was on the wane. The first ruler of Awadh, and the progenitor of the Nawabs of Awadh, Saadat Khan, laid the foundation of the capital city, Faizabad, on the outskirts of Ayodhya in 1722 CE. Awadh was truly God's own country with the Ganga, Jamuna, Sarayu and Gomti flowing through it. It was circumscribed by the Triveni at Prayag (Allahabad), Kashi

(Varanasi), Vrindavan (Mathura), Haridwar and Rishikesh—the core of Hindu civilization. The reign of the nawabs gave rise to what is known as the Ganga–Jamuni tehzeeb—a multiculturalism particular to this area of the central plains of northern India, a fusion of Hindu–Muslim elements. And it is here, in the qasbah of Mustafabad—near Rae Bareli and Lucknow—in the heart of Awadh's syncretic culture, that my early years (the 1950s) were spent.

My mother, like her mother before her, always wore saris, of which a varied, and steady, supply was maintained by her daughters-in-law. Her sartorial preference for the sari would by itself not be a matter of interest if she were from some other part of the country. But because these women were born and raised in Bara Banki and Mustafabad, both in the Awadh region, the cultural motifs they adopted in the course of growing up deserve mention. Their faith was Islam but the culture they exuded had strands in it which were Hindu, not in a religious sense but in its broader cultural connotations. Take, for example, the rituals that surrounded birth. As soon as we received news of someone being in the family way, the mood in our house in Mustafabad became electric, especially with the arrival of Aseemun, the family songstress, her harmonium and dholak following behind her. Festive music, especially Sohars—a song sung in the Awadh region when a woman is in confinement and has been carrying for seven months—would rend the air. My mother's favourite Sohar was:

Allah mian hamray bhaiyya ka diyo Nandlal

(Oh my Allah, bestow on my brother a son like Lord Krishna.)

These were the strands which made up the tapestry we call our composite culture, the fruit of hundreds of years of cultural interplay. I am reminded here of a cultural snippet from my childhood. Hazrat Bibi, the Prophet's daughter, asks Sugra the parrot to go in search of her husband, 'Ali Sahib', who has not returned from battle. 'If you cannot find him, go to Vrindavan, where Krishna is. Look for him there.' We lived in this culturally Hindu ambience with a tremendous sense of participation and pride. Neither in Mustafabad nor in Lucknow was one exposed to Hindu–Muslim antagonism. It was an article of faith with the people of the region that life would be lacklustre without the enormous cultural enmeshing between the two communities which bound them together. So, Hindus and Muslims participated in each other's festivals. This, in turn, generated a two-way traffic in the arts: from the highest to the popular level and the other way around.

✓

There was great uncertainty on how we arrived in the qasbah. An impressive family tree was occasionally unwrapped and spread out on the settee in our home. But it was just that: a tree. It had no geographical mapping of the regions the clan had traversed. This created room for mythmaking: Princess Mah Parvar, a niece of Aurangzeb, fell in love with an ancestor, a chakledar or an officer in the Mughal protocol department. Her barge, it is said, landed one day on the banks of the Ganga, three kilometres from Mustafabad. She fell in love with the place and decided to stay on. But there were several holes in this rather implausible story. For instance, no one could explain how the Princess made the journey from Delhi, through which the Jamuna flows. How did she switch to the Ganga? When did she make the switch from one river to the other? The late Professor Nurul Hasan, architect of Aligarh Muslim University's History Department, in his conversational drawing room style, helped me trace our history from Mashad, Nishapur (in Iran) and Gardez in Afghanistan. Some years later, protected by an armed escort, I was driven to Gardez in search of my roots. This was thanks to Afghanistan's president, Hamid Karzai. My search, I must add, was not without its share of drama—en route our convoy came under fire from Pacha Khan, a warlord fiercely opposed to Karzai.

The windswept settlement of Gardez was divided between Sunni and Shia quarters. The Shias lived in a colony of Sayyids, which means descendants from the family of the Prophet through one of the eleven Imams. The name Naqvi is a giveaway: Naqvis are supposed to be the children of the tenth Imam, Ali Naqi. But how did my ancestors happen to make the journey via Gardez and Multan, to Mustafabad? To understand this, one has to place their migration in its historic context. Sultan Iltutmish (he founded the Delhi Sultanate and reigned from 1211-1236) had barely consolidated power when the advance of the Mongols led by Genghiz Khan in the 1200s caused the panicked migration of various groups including Sayyids in large numbers from Khorassan, particularly Nishapur (today part of Iran), to what they hoped would be safer territory. Similar migrations began from the Arab world. The route they took has not been mapped, but large numbers settled in Gardez until the next upheaval.

I savoured a banquet, seated cross-legged on a blazing red Afghan Fiel Paa (elephant feet, a carpet design), in one of the homes in Gardez. The master of the house, who wore a black turban, declared me a cousin. My search revealed that from Gardez, groups migrated to Multan and thence to the Indo-Gangetic qasbahs like Kara, Manikpur, Patti, Mustafabad, Bilgram in Awadh, and larger townships like Amroha. These habitations were arranged differently from anything else that then prevailed in northern India. Traditional townships would have the raja or big landlord living in his fort or haveli on an elevation or ridge in the centre or at a prominent spot in the township. The lane below would lead to a bazaar, and then branch out to where washermen, milkmen, barbers, butchers and grocers plied their trade, as well as a sprinkling of unplanned neighbourhoods segregated according to caste, community and profession. The north Indian qasbah

Being the Other

was bigger than a hamlet or a village but it was smaller than a township. The dominant residents were not folksy or rustic; they were genteel. We described ourselves as 'qasbati shurafa' or country gentlemen. In a sense we had an edge over our cousins in Lucknow because we were part of their urbane Urdu culture but were also entirely at home with folksy Awadhi traditions. Women of my grandmother's generation spoke Awadhi at home.

Mustafabad, like most Sayyid qasbahs, was settled horizontally, unlike the vertical pattern of most Indian enclaves of the time. By vertical, I mean a top-down feudal hierarchy. Ours was the largest haveli, at one end of the qasbah, overlooking what was once a pond and has now been reduced to a shrunken waterbody, overgrown with hyacinth. All other pucca houses belonged to cousins from our own tribe. Our ancestor must have been selected the head of the clan at the time of the 'founding' of Mustafabad, hence our possession of the biggest haveli.

It was a settlement of equals in descent and hierarchy. All the surnames were Naqvi. Only some, like my maternal uncle, Sayyid Mohammad Mehdi, suffixed their names with Gardezi. My uncle tracing his ancestry to the tribes of Gardez was rather surprising because he was, in his younger days, a card-carrying member of the Communist Party of India. The Sayyids of Mustafabad actually settled in two contiguous villages separated by a mud path. Bhitri Gaon or the Inner Village was one settlement. Our part was called Phatak Bhitar (inside the gate). It was like a gated colony of Sayyids, not very different from the one I had seen in Gardez.

Like all settlements, Mustafabad too needed barbers, bakar qasabs (butchers), ghosis (milkmen), dhobis (washermen), and sundry others, the majority of them weavers. These were Sunnis. There clearly was a system outside the Shia/Sayyid nobility where conversions were effected.

ᴠ

Our haveli in Mustafabad was divided into three courtyards surrounded by arched double verandas, backed by long rooms. There were no caparisoned elephants at the gate, no cavalry, not even infantry. There were no cars, only a phaeton. Next to the mosque there was a stable for a solitary horse which doubled up as a Zuljenah or a replica of Imam Hussain's horse during Muharram, the annual observance of the Battle of Karbala. It was known as Abbajan's horse, which made us feel grand because owning a horse had princely connotations.

We were not maharajas, nawabs, taluqdars, not even big landlords. The key characteristic of our family was being genteel rather than grand, more literary, musical and low-key than wealthy and entitled. There were no swimming pools, polo or tennis in our lives. Nor did we possess what had been made fashionable in the cantonments, civil lines and the gymkhanas as hallmarks of the colonial high life.

One of the few things that our elders made much of was their caste. Sayyids extracted a premium in the marriage market. For instance, the Nawab of Rampur was a Rohilla Pathan who converted to Shiaism under the influence of the Awadh court. But in the marriage market for his daughters he searched for Sayyid grooms. The transaction was mutually beneficial. Professorial grooms gained access to princely lifestyles; brides climbed up the caste hierarchy. Their progeny would now be Sayyids.

Mustafabad was the centre of our universe. It was accessible by train from Allahabad at one end and Rae Bareli and Lucknow at the other. Railways had come to Mustafabad in 1905 when the Unchahar Railway Station was built on land owned by Nabba Mian of Bhitri Gaon. Mustafabad was two miles from the railway station and took ten minutes to reach by tonga, or twenty minutes by bullock cart. The train from Allahabad steamed in at 12.45 p.m. The one from the opposite direction of Rae Bareli and Lucknow arrived at 1.15 p.m. Since Unchahar was a junction where the steam engines replenished their water tanks, each engine would blow its whistle before departing. Abbajan would sit cross-legged at the 'dastarkhwan' (a yellow cloth spread on the floor for service of food) and wait fifteen minutes after the second whistle just in case an unexpected family member arrived.

The Persian inscription on the dastarkhwan was apt:

Shukr baja aar ke mehmaan e tau
Rozi e khud mi khurad az khwan e tau

(You are fortunate and you must thank god that your guest is eating 'his food' at your dastarkhwan.)

Hospitality was a habit not a function of prosperity. We shared what we had. There was always something extra in the pot by deliberate design. Just in case someone turned up. Any visitor was invited to the dastarkhwan. This did not mean the visitor automatically settled down to a meal. It was part of the culture of 'takalluf' or formality that the visitor would hesitate, decline and would only partake of the meal when persuaded by the elders. It was part of our training as children.

Mutton curry, a vegetable, dal, chapatti, rice and a sweet dish like kheer or halwa was common fare. Families borrowed to keep up levels of hospitality and were occasionally reduced to penury.

To survive in post-Partition Mustafabad meant practising some austerity. The thriftiest woman of the family was chosen to manage the kitchen. At the arched door of the kitchen would sit Amman Apa on a broad low stool, her ample gharara, like a split dress, spread on the jute mattress. She held a large copper ladle. During breakfast, it served as a frying pan to fry eggs sunny side up. Amman Apa would quickly slide the fried eggs onto our plates when our turn came in that long queue of cousins. At lunchtime, another ladle was used to measure out gravy and two pieces of mutton. By the side of the main cooking vessel was a smaller one, into which all the 'asli' ghee from the gravy had been siphoned off. A spoon of this masala ghee was dropped into our plates as seasoning. It added richness to the rather bland gravy. The elders, who ate more formally outside, had dollops of this ghee dropped into their korma.

The system was open to some favouritism. If she liked, Amman Apa could always fry an extra egg for you or give you four pieces of mutton instead of the rationed two. It was all more than adequate and a great deal of fun but we were always aware that life was being lived in the shadow of austerities.

None of these austerities deterred the weekly or monthly appearance of miriasans (professional singers)—Kalvi or Aseemun with their respective harmoniums, and tabla or dholak accompanists. Aseemun, in fact, was an inexhaustible source of musical forms, particularly those popular in Sufi gharanas.

One of the infinite hierarchies of India is that which exists among singers, dancers and composers. The Devadasi system in South India threw up geniuses like Balasaraswati and M. S. Subbulakshmi. In the courtesan culture of the north, there were outstanding talents like Akhtari Bai Faizabadi, who became Begum Akhtar when she married the aristocratic Ishtiaq Abbasi.

There was a subculture of songstresses like Aseemun who had been trained in the Maihar Gharana by Baba Allauddin Khan, Ustad Ali Akbar Khan's father. Aseemun had been sponsored by the local grandees to this high-powered coaching system. It reflected on the general decline of the feudal order in Awadh that a singer like her who may once have had a special attachment to a particular house, had become something of a freelancer during the years soon after Independence. That said, she was a regular at our Mustafabad house, where there was always a ready audience.

It was mandatory for everyone in the family to be in Mustafabad for the ten days of Muharram, to remember the Battle of Karbala and Imam Hussain's martyrdom. We were also required to assemble for the mango season during the summer holidays. Aseemun was a permanent fixture for all family get-togethers. When the joint family dispersed to various locations with the passage of time, other women of Aseemun's family became the occupants of the haveli to keep Abbajan entertained with classical music. Abbajan was not alone at these soirees as his close friend Babboo Mian from Bhitri Gaon was usually at them as well.

Abbajan, the fifth of ten children, was born in 1889 (the same year as Jawaharlal Nehru) to Mir Farzand Hussain and Kaniz Fatima. The eldest of his siblings was a sister called Barki Amma or the Eldest Amma. The festivities during her marriage yielded stories that became part of family lore. Half a dozen singing and dancing troupes from Lucknow, Varanasi, Allahabad, Kanpur and Pratapgarh had to be hidden in a godown kept for cattle feed because their arrival coincided with that of Maulana Sayyid Nasir Hussain Qibla, the senior-most Shia aalim (scholar) from Lucknow. It was situation comedy at its slapstick best, when one of the dancers, unable to cope with the suffocating atmosphere of the godown, walked past the Maulana, covered with hay, the bells in her anklets tinkling!

Given our harmonious existence and free cultural intermixing, the pain of Partition in 1947 cut rather deep because closely knit families were abruptly divided. It is one of life's painful ironies that our wonderful great-aunt, Naani Ammi, who always dreamt of being buried in Mustafabad, died in Lahore. Her body could not be brought back to India, and we could not attend her funeral. In these days of growing nuclear families, a great-aunt might seem a distant relative, but it wasn't that way in our family, modelled as it was on the traditional joint family system. My mother's mother was the eldest in her family; Naani Ammi, the youngest. She was particularly attached to my mother who grew up in her care. This did not lead to any neglect of Naani Ammi's children;

they were taken care of by others in that highly interdependent system. In fact, as I've said earlier, our house in Mustafabad was filled with cousins, aunts and uncles (sometimes up to a hundred at the time of Muharram, births, deaths and marriages).

Right up to her dying day, Naani Ammi had great difficulty understanding the document called the passport. She had grown up with the knowledge that to travel from one place to another all one needed was a railway ticket. This made immense sense because all her earlier journeys were confined to Awadh in UP. She was born in Barabanki, married in Bilgram, and visited my parents either in Mustafabad or Lucknow. Then Partition came, followed by the abolition of zamindari and the death of her husband, a minor aristocrat. The houses in Barabanki and Bilgram were in ruins. Naani Ammi moved in with us, commuting between Mustafabad and Lucknow.

The need for a passport arose because two of her daughters got married and settled in Pakistan. Her dilemma was every bit as acute as Toba Tek Singh's (Saadat Hasan Manto's great fictional character), who could not understand how his village could 'go' to Pakistan when Partition took place; Naani Ammi similarly could not understand how her daughters could 'go' to another country. How can anybody give up home for good? In an attempt to console her, she was told that her daughters, Sughra and Sakina, were not really leaving home. There were two 'very good boys' for her daughters in Bombay, but Lahore was infinitely closer to Lucknow. Moreover, 'the boys' (who some cousins in Pakistan had chosen) were of impeccable 'caste'. (The impact of the Hindu caste system on the subcontinent's Muslims should never be overlooked. Sayyids, Sheikhs, Pathans are still upper caste while Julahas (weavers) and all those similarly professionally denominated are supposed to be lower in the pecking order.)

A map of India was pulled out. Naani Ammi was shown how Trivandrum, Madras, Bangalore, Hyderabad, Bombay were all in India but much more distant from Lucknow than Lahore or even

Karachi. She was also told that the India–Pakistan border was only an artificial boundary hastily drawn up in a matter of weeks by an 'angrez', Sir Cyril Radcliffe, who headed the two commissions set up for demarcating the boundary between India and Pakistan. With time, this boundary would dissolve—she should only see it as a temporary inconvenience.

So Naani Ammi agreed to Sughra and Sakina getting married to 'boys' in Pakistan. But very soon she came face to face with her first doubts, the beginnings of disenchantment. She wished to visit her daughters and was asked to acquire a passport. If Lahore and Karachi were closer to Lucknow than all the major cities of India, why was she being asked to obtain a 'ticket' in addition to the one that would get her onto a train? Attempts were made to explain the reasons for this 'strange' requirement, passport forms were then obtained and she, in a daze, filled them up in her tidy Urdu hand. Then came the second disenchantment. My father's munshi told her that she would get her passport faster if the form was filled in Hindi or English. Was Urdu at a discount? she asked.

Naani Ammi's attachment to Urdu was because it was the only script she had been taught, although the language she spoke was undiluted Awadhi or Dehati, the village dialect. In fact, there was a gender divide when it came to the spoken word. Most of the ladies spoke in Awadhi or Dehati but could speak Urdu or Hindustani on formal occasions. The gentlemen conversed in Urdu or Hindustani but could lapse into Awadhi or Dehati on informal occasions.

There may be some symbolism in the fact that Naani Ammi died without a passport, a document that was always anathema to her. She had been with her daughters in Lahore, ailing for six months. Her Indian passport had expired. She wanted it to be renewed because she wished to be buried in Mustafabad. Her daughters told her that her passport would be renewed before long. But that unfortunately never happened. I remember that as being a particularly painful time. We had barely recovered from Naani Ammi's death, when the newspapers informed the world of the ghastly communal riots in Moradabad (UP) in 1980 which left hundreds dead, and the usual 'thousands' homeless. We will look at the phenomenon of communal riots in greater detail later on in the book.

Naani Ammi is not the only pain I carry. My dearest aunt, Alia Askari (later Alia Imam), is another. We received news about her circumstances just the other day. Her husband, Kazim Imam, whom I called Raja Sahib Bhatuamau in jest, died in a Karachi hospital recently. This mock elevation of Kazim Bhai's status to Raja was actually somewhat ironical. His father really was the ruler of that awkward sounding principality in Awadh. The status reversal for the gentry of that region was considerable (after the zamindari abolition) but the enormity of it apparently did not touch Kazim Bhai who drowned out the blues at the Lucknow Club, danced the foxtrot in buckskin shoes, and escorted Anglo-Indian ladies from the Maqbara to the weekly 10 a.m. English movie at Lucknow's Mayfair Cinema. Heaven knows how he ended up in Sweden from where, armed with a degree in structural engineering, he landed on his feet in Karachi and built a few buildings.

Alia Askari, my youngest aunt, communist after a fashion, proceeded to lead the Lucknow University union and became the first woman in the family, indeed in Lucknow of the fifties, to obtain a highly acclaimed PhD. She was my favourite aunt, and for her many idiosyncrasies, I addressed her as Aunt Agatha, straight from Wodehouse. Given the gender biases of the period, Aunt Agatha's education, her exceptional oratorical skills, her equation with the finest minds of the day became her greatest handicaps. 'How to find a husband for such an educated girl?'

There were other handicaps: she was a Sayyid too. A feudal landscape in a state of collapse was singularly bereft of postgraduate Sayyids. Word was sent by another aunt that Karachi was crawling with 'postgraduate' Sayyids. So Aunt Agatha was placed on a

Karachi-bound Dakota and received in Pakistan with fanfare by relatives who were active members of the Pakistan Communist Party. Before she had opened her bags, she was whisked off to a large public meeting which Aunt Agatha kept spellbound with her oratory and sharp 'anti-imperialist' invective. General Ayub Khan lost no time. She was picked up from the meeting by some of the General's officers, her bags collected from her sister's house, and put on a Delhi-bound Dakota within a day of her arrival.

But the Karachi aunt would not give up. She scoured the city until someone drew her attention to a tall engineer from Sweden, always in a flashy suit and, of course, those trademark buckskin shoes. He could not measure up to Aunt Agatha's intellect, but he was a Sayyid all right. Aunt Agatha was recalled. Books were scoured on whether an Awadh taluqdar could be a Sayyid? Sayyids, like Brahmins, were theologians and generally respected for their minds. Distinguished historian Professor Nurul Hasan had a theory. Since Sayyids descended from the family of the Prophet, and came to India as refugees after the Mongol hordes ransacked Khorasan and Central Asia, Mughal Emperor Jehangir gave them the title Lashkar-e-Dua (Army for Prayer) and grants of land for their upkeep. Nurul Bhai's drawing room history lesson was certainly plausible so far as the Sayyid settlement of the qasbah of Mustafabad is concerned. Jehangir was a fugitive from the royal court in Fatehpur Sikri for a brief spell in Kara-Manekpur, not far from Mustafabad. Around him were a number of settlements of Shia Sayyids which became recipients of his munificence.

The first phase on Aunt Agatha's part was one of acquiescence. She was all too conscious of what to her, in the beginning, seemed an unbridgeable chasm: two people from the same region, Awadh, living in completely different intellectual zones. Most of those who had migrated from India, the Mohajirs or refugees as they are called to this day, would see them as an unlikely pair. The trick was to escape to an alien culture where people would not spot the nuances.

Aunt Agatha proceeded to teach Urdu Literature at Beijing University until the Cultural Revolution of the sixties made it difficult to live in China. In China, too, Kazim Bhai was her perfect escort, even to the Great Hall of the People. Returning to Karachi, she immersed herself in her favourite literary groups. Kazim Bhai, clad in his suit and buckskin shoes, fixed his gaze on her with unwavering adoration. She became an in-house intellectual to Begum Nusrat Bhutto, a fact which further elevated Aunt Agatha in Kazim Bhai's doting eyes. After Begum Bhutto's death they proceeded to waste themselves in mutual adoration bereft of any inspiration—a very feudal decay. But they were, by now, totally inseparable.

There was always in Kazim Bhai something of a Walter Mitty, daydreaming, lost in reveries, including one of a day in paradise. I called him from Delhi: 'I believe life in paradise is terrific. Would you like to go?' 'No,' he said in his frail voice. 'A bird in hand is worth two in the bush.' He was a lovable man. If we tried we would have got visas to attend his funeral. But we did not. The sheer habit of living in different countries with obstacles in travel increases distance exponentially. Dearest relatives take up residence only in the mists of memory. So I sent an email: 'Look after yourself, Aunt Agatha!'

∽

Our home had ceased to be a house of plenty long years ago, but it remained the enchanting place we cousins loved returning to from whichever school we were attending in Lucknow, Kanpur, Allahabad, Pratapgarh or Fatehpur. The breaking up of our joint family had been hastened by Partition and the calamitous abolition of zamindari that followed a few years later.

After the zamindari abolition of 1951, for which UP Chief Minister Pandit Govind Ballabh Pant was hailed by the majority community, all the elders of the family fell into a deep silence, their faces sullen, brows furrowed. For with their lands would go their means of livelihood, the only one they had. These country gentlemen were not landlords in the classical sense who exploited the peasantry by harsh methods. For this reason they had the affection of the largely Hindu peasantry. Land revenue collections were almost voluntary.

Landlordism was for the genteel folk of Mustafabad not a means of ostentatious living but a way in which they could survive respectably. I never saw in my elders a rasping desire to improve their lot at the cost of the poor. They never had any ambition to create investments for which it would have been essential to cultivate politicians who had the power to sanction the construction of roads and canals, or fix bus and truck routes. To the Awadhi gentry, 'money making' was an impulse to be curbed. They were out of sync with the times. When the prospect of penury loomed, all they could think of was to direct their progeny to professions like law and teaching.

Western education would have given them some advantage. But the Awadhi Muslim gentry's addiction to their tehzeeb, culture, poetry, music, diction, intonation, cuisine and the courtliness of Urdu held them back from Western education and, therefore, new means of livelihood.

All of this was art for art's sake. Social accomplishments could not provide livelihoods, except as undeclared courtiers in the newly emerging ministerial durbars in Lucknow which was the 'markaz' or the centre for all of Awadh, including our family, eighty miles away in Mustafabad.

Courtiers were the earliest form of life who gave birth to an industry which over several decades ballooned into modern public relations. Manzar Bhai (Saiyid Manzar Hussain) and Safdar Bhai (Saiyid Safdar Hussain), memorable wits, were regular fixtures in Lucknow's Hazratganj of the sixties. Safdar turned up at Kwality's or Royal Café for breakfast. Occupants of every table implored him to join them. The table he graced was always of his choice. Having exploited his very high level of popularity at Lucknow's other restaurants, coffee houses, clubs, and paan shops, when Safdar eventually got home, near Aminabad, past midnight, his father would have closed his pavement bookshop and gone to sleep. Safdar nursed his hangovers till breakfast, by which time his father had already spread out his books on the pavement outside. Safdar once famously confided to us that even though they slept under the same roof he had not met his father for over a decade.

My school friend, Vinod Mehta, the famous editor, almost jealous of Safdar's leisurely lifestyle, once remarked: 'The fellow doesn't know where his next meal is coming from. All he knows is that it is going to be a terrific one.'

A thin line divided a leisurely lifestyle and rank decadence, exactly the milieu in which most twentieth-century Urdu poets also wallowed. Sharab or liquor was an essential part of their lives but they could seldom afford rum, gin, whisky. Country liquor was the usual fare. Scotch whisky was within their reach only after P. C. Joshi, Secretary General of the Communist Party, launched the Progressive Writers' Association in Bombay. It was as song writers in Bollywood that Sahir Ludhianvi, Majrooh Sultanpuri, Ali Sardar Jafri and Kaifi Aazmi first had regular access to Scotch. Ghalib, a century earlier, had fared better. After the upheavals of 1857 he complained in a letter: 'Life in Delhi has become impossible; Scotch is selling at Rs. 16 a dozen.'

ᕲ

In India, the largest concentration of Shia Sayyids is in Lucknow. They are spread out in qasbahs like Mustafabad. In the vicinity of these qasbahs, sometimes in them, are dotted the khanqahs or ashrams of Sufi saints who were Sunnis by birth but also believers in Ali. These places are superb centres of syncretism in song, verse, devotional poetry, cuisine, aphorisms, comical stories, all sensitively preserved and processed, in a rural, pastoral ambience.

The Muslim in, say, West Bengal, where he happens to constitute 30 per cent of the population, has Bengali as his mother tongue, a language he shares with the residents of Bangladesh. Rabindranath Tagore and Kazi Nazrul Islam, both enriched Bengali literature in equal measure. Likewise, the Mappila Muslims in Kerala are at home in Malayalam and the Labbais in Tamil Nadu are immersed in Tamil culture and so on.

Yet I'd say that among the Muslim communities to be found in India, while ours did not always have a common tongue with those of other religious communities who were native to the region, there was no let or hindrance to the way we mingled most effortlessly with the multiple cultural streams of the region we lived in. Culturally, as I have said earlier, we were creatures of the Urdu composite culture synonymous with Ganga-Jamuni tehzeeb. The label is self-explanatory. It carried the lilt of Brajbhasha, Bhojpuri, Awadhi, the flavour of life in the stretch between two great rivers which enclose the spaces where the legends of Radha, Krishna, Rama lived.

Syncretism as a way of life was more or less institutionalized under the Nawabs of Awadh from the beginning of the eighteenth century. They happened to be Shias. This explains why an overwhelming majority of the Awadh elite were Shia. A section of the elite, which may not have been Shia, came under Shia cultural influences. The Shia spell was not confined to Awadh alone. Contiguous cultural zones like those of Delhi were equally affected. Mirza Asadullah Khan Ghalib, the great poet, was by birth a Mughal Sunni. But he found the personality of Ali so compelling that he declared himself 'Ali's slave'. Whether he was technically Shia or not became irrelevant. Culturally, he was.

In the heart of Awadh, Shabbir Hasan Khan Josh Malihabadi, perhaps the greatest wordsmith of Urdu poetry, was born a Sunni Pathan but found Ali irresistible and converted to Shiaism. His long poem 'Tulu e Fikr' or the 'Dawn of Reason' is a eulogy to the Prophet's son-in-law.

Urdu was the crowning glory of India's composite culture. What would happen to it after Partition? True, the contribution of Muslims to this language was considerable. Was that the logic for it to be made the national language of Pakistan? There were going to be almost as many Muslims in India. What would be their language? Those who partitioned the subcontinent had concluded in great haste: Urdu should be the language of Muslim Pakistan and Hindi the language of Hindu India. Yes, Hindu India, in that sense, was in the minds of everyone, even senior Congress leaders. A puerile simplicity was sought to be imposed on a subcontinent of great complexity.

People in West Pakistan were familiar with Urdu but their mother tongue was Punjabi, Pushto, Saraiki or Sindhi. Allama Iqbal (Pakistan's national poet) and Faiz Ahmad Faiz are two of the greatest Urdu poets from the Punjab. Urdu was the language in which they wrote poetry, but their mother tongue was Punjabi. Ahmad Faraz was a fine Urdu poet whose mother tongue was Pushto.

In East Pakistan, it was the passionate evolution of Bengali nationalism against a Punjabi-Urdu amalgam which resulted in the birth of Bangladesh. I was quite surprised to find nearly a hundred schools in Dhaka in 2001 teaching Rabindra Sangeet. Why, then, should Dhaka have been distanced from Vishwa Bharati, indeed from Kolkata? A liberal, secular Brahmo like Tagore was virtually accorded the status of India's National Poet. But a firebrand poet, whose verses are soaked in references to Kali, Shakti, Durga, Shiva was popularly recognized as the national poet of Bangladesh. Why? Because his name happened to be Kazi Nazrul Islam? It was absurd arbitrariness.

In India, influential Urdu poets and writers were paranoid about another matter dear to their heart. They were worried not just about their language but also about the future of the exquisite culture connected with their language. Since Urdu had been made the official language of Pakistan, and Hindi of India, it was likely that Urdu would be neglected in the land of its birth. This was their nightmare: Urdu would be demoted. The culture associated

Being the Other

with it would wither away.

Sahir Ludhianvi was scathing in his criticism of the Congress government on the hundredth death anniversary of one of Urdu's great poets, Asadullah Khan Ghalib.

Sau saal se jo turbat
Chadar ko tarasti thi
Aaj uspe aqeedat ke phoolon ki numaaish hai,
Urdu ke taalluq se yeh bhed nahin khulta
Yeh jashn, yeh hungama khidmat hai ki saazish hai

(For a hundred years there was no cover on the grave which
Today is loaded with flowers of adoration,
But from Urdu's point of view, I am intrigued.
Are these celebrations of sincerity or a trick for Muslim votes?)

Jin aihle siyasat ne ek zinda zaban kuchli
Un aihle siyasat ko barbadi ka ghum kyon hai?
Ghalib jisse kehte hain, Urdu hi ka shayar tha
Urdu pe sitam dhaakar, Ghalib pe karam kyon hai?

(Politicians who crushed a language,
Why are they distraught at the death of that language
Ghalib, after all, was a poet of Urdu.
Having killed his language, why this celebration of his anniversary?)

True, the culture Urdu spawned had feudal, courtly roots. Poetry, diction, the art of conversation, manners, the food associated with that culture—all these might possibly have been unfamiliar to the aspiring new Hindi elite rooted in the mofussil. They did not have, in sizeable numbers, access to the cosmopolitan urbanity of Lucknow. They were also at some distance from the folksy lyricism of Awadhi and Brajbhasha. It must be noted here that

Awadhi, Brajbhasha, Bhojpuri and Maithili were vehicles for some of India's greatest literature. Malik Muhammad Jayasi and Tulsidas enriched Awadhi and Surdas and Sayyid Ibrahim (Raskhan) wrote in Brajbhasha. But none of this was enough reason for Urdu to have been cast aside in India, as would happen in the years following Independence.

Lucknow's Urdu elite consisted of Muslim residents of Chowk and Nakkhas, Kashmiri Pandits and Kayasthas, who were either professionals or who specialized in Mughal and Nawabi bookkeeping. This was an urbane elite, headquartered in old Lucknow. There was another Urdu elite, which had its core in the qasbahs—Malihabad, Kakori, Rudauli, Mustafabad, Pratapgarh, Mehmoodabad, and so on. Because this elite lived in the midst of rural Awadh, it had imbibed the inflections of Awadhi and the more rustic Dehati with its musical lilt. Poet Josh Malihabadi was the foremost example of this integrated elite. It was this supple group which patronized and helped evolve Thumri, Dadra, Kajri and Sohar.

Awadh's Urdu culture enriched our way of life in unique ways, sometimes too obvious to be noticed. For instance, Awadh's secularized norms of greeting. The universal Islamic greeting is 'Assalam alaikum' (may Allah's peace be upon you), and its response 'Waalaikum salaam' (peace on you too). In Awadh the accepted form of greeting became 'Aadaab', which means 'respects'. This was accompanied by bowing and raising the right hand towards the head. One could even say 'Tasleem' or 'I bow' or 'I submit'. This took out 'Allah' or any religious connotation from the culture of greeting each other. When women in Pakistan greeted Josh with 'Assalam alaikum' he found it strange. 'We are all familiar with a cock crowing,' he said, 'but in Pakistan I heard hens crowing.'

For a time, evidence of Urdu's all embracing culture served to reassure the new, emerging Hindiwallahs. Ali Sardar Jafri translated Bihari, the seventeenth-century Shringhar Rasa poet, possibly the most romantic in Hindi literature. Jafri was trying to provide an example of Urdu's compatibility with Hindi literature. Arzoo Lucknavi, the remarkable Ghazal writer of the early twentieth century, had already proved the point. He said of his collection of poems, *Surili Bansuri* or 'Melodious Flute': 'There is not a single word of Persian or Arabic in my collection.' And there wasn't.

Urdu poets were understandably shattered by the divisions Partition had created. Some tried to collect the broken bits and weave them into tapestries. Kaifi Aazmi was at his optimistic best when he wrote:

> Naye Hindostan mein hum nayi jannat basayenge
> Wafoore justjoo mein kaise apne kaise begaane
> Alag hokar rahenge muttahid tasbih ke daaney
>
> (We shall make a paradise out of our new India
> There's no 'us' and 'them'
> when we are in a common struggle
> Like rosary beads, we shall be together.)

These positive efforts were interrupted by negative propaganda. It was alleged that we Urdu-speaking Awadhis were captivated by Muhammad Ali Jinnah and the Muslim League. Both were remote to our experience. Jinnah did not speak Urdu and those who used the English idiom were non-existent in our circle. Membership of the Muslim League was a bargaining tactic used by taluqdars and big landlords. They did not want to give up their palaces and their lifestyle. Pakistan was never the goal; it was a bargaining chip. I know it because I was privy to such discussions in my family in Mustafabad, Rae Bareli, Lucknow, Kanpur.

In this twilight era, the Urdu-speaking Muslim elite was financially embarrassed. It had withdrawn and distanced itself from both the expanding Hindi elite as well as the new English-speaking middle class. Those who came from a Hindi background had stolen a march over Muslims by taking to Western education in large numbers.

The Muslim aversion to Hindi and English had simple roots. Hindi, they thought, was being promoted for communal reasons because Urdu, in its simplest form, is quite as easily accessible. They never digested the untruth that Urdu was the language of Muslims. Why, Raghupati Sahay (better known by his pen name Firaq Gorakhpuri) was the finest Ghazal writer of the twentieth century and a Hindu! Muslims, therefore, feared that Hindi zealots with their newly acquired political clout, would eventually harm Urdu.

As early as the 1950s (much before Aurangzeb Road was renamed Dr APJ Abdul Kalam Road) Lucknow street poets had shrewdly anticipated the future:

> Unki yeh tamanna hai har ek naam badal jaaye
> Bigrey jo zubaan, zehniat e aam badal jaaye

> (It is their desire to change words and place names,
> Once language is debased, the popular outlook will change.)

The punchline of this satirical ghazal was:

> Kulhar ko ijazat hai chaley, jaam badal jaaye

> (The crude earthen pot will be promoted,
> the crystal wine cup replaced.)

To preserve their beloved language, the Urdu camp was open to compromises. Supreme Court lawyer Danial Latifi actually produced *Diwan-e-Ghalib* in a variant of the Roman script. Poet Ali Sardar Jafri translated the great Braj poet, Bihari Lal Chaubey, into Urdu. Bekal Utsahi's 'Hindi geets' became hits at Urdu mushairas or poetry recitations.

Mustafabad's Urduwallahs even accepted the proposition that Devanagri was much the more scientific and phonetic script and the attachment to the Urdu script was largely for sentimental reasons. Oh, the compromises that were made! The Urduwallahs were willing to contemplate life without the script which has produced some of the world's greatest calligraphy. It was an article of faith with almost everyone in the family—indeed, in our entire environment—that Urdu and Hindi were more or less the same language. The only difference was in the script.

My maternal grandfather Saiyid Mohammad Askari's passion for Urdu, without any prejudice against Hindi, was shared by the entire community:

Hai dua yeh ki mukhalif jo hain dharey mil jaaen
Aaj phir Kausar O Ganga ke kinarey mil jaaen

(It is my prayer that the streams of Hindi and Urdu must join, like the Sangam;
Kausar, the river of paradise, must mingle with the holy Ganga.)

This was my maternal grandfather's chant.

∿

In Awadh, with Lucknow as the centre, the Shia liberal streak became the base on which a huge monument of multiculturalism was erected. In this endeavour Shias were not alone. Sufism of the Chishti order adorned otherwise prosaic Islamic practice with high culture. Everything that Amir Khusro contributed in music and literature became available to the common secular cultural pool.

In urban areas like Lucknow the reservoir of composite culture was augmented greatly by Kashmiri Pandits too. A pioneering Urdu prose writer, the author of the sixteen volumes of *Fasana-e-Azad* was a Kashmiri Pandit, Ratan Nath Sarshar. Kayasthas, bookkeepers for the Awadh kings who had risen on the cultural scale, were also participants in this great cultural efflorescence. Any number of Brahmins, Kayasthas, even the Lalas or the more cultured Banias wrote Urdu and Persian poetry.

The tradition of organizing Urdu mushairas was maintained

on a grand scale even after Partition by the prominent Delhi family of Lala Charat Ram and Bharat Ram. Their ancestors, Sir Shankar Lal and his nephew, Lala Murli Dhar, were competent Urdu poets themselves. Sir Shankar Lal's takhallus or pen name was Shankar while Murli Dhar adopted the pseudonym 'Shaad'. Shankar-o-Shaad mushairas in New Delhi remained the high point of the celebration of Urdu poetry in the subcontinent until the 1960s. Gradually, Hindi nationalism and the declining ranks of Urdu enthusiasts reduced these grand soirees to mere tokenism.

Cultural syncretism and the Urdu language aside, there are some other aspects of Awadhi Islam that deserve a mention. In the feudal system, the percolation of culture was always from the top. However, before these cultural impulses took root among the masses, the mullah had with alacrity shepherded them to the mosque. The mosque remained their 'markaz', the meeting place, the ultimate rendezvous, the enclave that was skewered by Urdu's greatest satirical poet Akbar Allahabadi's 'Jumman'.

Akbar Allahabadi succinctly summed up the Muslim social hierarchy in the late thirties:

Council mein bahut Sayyid;
Masjid mein faqat Jumman

(The Viceroy's executive council is full of Sayyids,
But the mosques are packed only with the Jumman.)

It is a sensitive social detail to dilate on.

Jumman is a common name for a low-caste Julaha or weaver. It is also shorthand for the largest number of converts at the hands of proselytizing groups. At the heart of it all was the tension between the liberal Muslim, Persianized and broadminded and the majority of Indian Muslims, the newly converted 'Jummans', Arabized and focused on the mosque. A basic rule of thumb was: culture came from Persia, Islamism from Arabia. The Persian stream had tributaries of Sanskrit, Awadhi, Brajbhasha flowing into it, enriching it to a point that it became something organically new. It came to be known as Urdu culture, totally independent of religion. Arabic remained the language of the Quran, and, therefore, the language of prayer and of religious reform.

The title of the Shah of Iran was 'Arya Mehr', or 'Light of the Aryan'. When Aryan tribes arrived from Persia and Central Asia and settled in the Indo-Gangetic plains, they called it Aryavarta or the Land of the Aryans. Persia's Shia Islam did not erase Zoroastrian culture but absorbed it. Navroz, the Persian New Year, is celebrated by sprinkling saffron colour in all countries which were once part of the pre-Islamic Persian Empire. This tradition has been preserved by the Shias of Awadh and the Parsis of India. Awadh, after all, is the undisputed 'markaz' or centre of Shia culture in India, indeed in South Asia.

Akbar Allahabadi's mischievous play on 'Jumman' was actually a commentary on hierarchies in Muslim society that I have briefly touched upon earlier. These divisions were as rigid as those in the Hindu caste system. Of course, there was a difference between the two. The varna or caste-based system was the social architecture designed by Brahmins. Muslim hierarchies evolved under the feudal system. When Sir Syed Ahmad Khan laid the foundation of Aligarh Muslim University (patterned on Cambridge) in the late nineteenth century, he was quite firm that it was a campus for the 'Ashraf' or genteel, the well-bred elite. Below the Ashraf were 'Ajlaf' or the Julahas (weavers) and 'Arzal', the menial class.

The Prophet's immediate family was called 'Panjatan' or 'The Five'. The five were Prophet Muhammad, his cousin and son-in-law, Ali, the Prophet's daughter, Fatima, and his grandsons, Hasan and Hussain. The extended family is called Ahle Bait, or the fourteen 'Masoom', the 'Pure Ones', consisting of the twelve Imams, Ali being the first. The other two in this galaxy are Prophet

Muhammad and his daughter Fatima, Ali's wife.

Sayyids prided themselves on being direct descendants of the family of the Prophet. In the list of the Muslim elite, which consisted of landowners and other upper-caste Muslims like Shaikhs and Pathans, Sayyids were the most influential. Their status in Muslim society was similar to that of Brahmins among Hindus. A reform movement to expand the list of fourteen masooms was initiated by some women in the family, led by our mother, Begum Atia Naqvi. She quoted a Persian verse:

Kitab e ish do baab ast—Karbala o Damishq
Yake Hussain raqam kard, deegare Zainab

(The great book of love has two chapters—Karbala and Damascus.
One was written by Hussain and the other by his sister Zainab.)

There are numerous ways to describe the dividing line between Shias and Sunnis. One of them, which applies to the Shias and Sunnis of India, is simple: Shias are in agreement with the followers of the family of the Prophet on the issue of succession after the Prophet's death in 632 CE. By their reckoning, Ali should have succeeded him as the first caliph. He was the first convert to Islam, an outstanding soldier who led most of the Prophet's military campaigns. He was, at the same time, an exceptional administrator and scholar.

Did the Prophet nominate him as his successor? Shias cite the incident at Ghadir Khumm as clinching proof that the Prophet had indeed announced that Ali should be accepted as his successor.

Returning to Medina after his last Haj at Mecca in March 632, three months before his death in June that year, the Prophet halted at a place called Ghadir. He lifted Ali's hand and proclaimed: *Munkunt O Maula, Haza Ali Maula* (They who consider me their Maula or leader appointed by God, must also consider Ali their Maula). This line has become an essential declaration of faith at the start of every Qawwali session, the form of spiritual music based on Hindustani ragas initiated by Amir Khusro. Qawwals go into ecstasy singing the 'Qaul' or declaration of Ali's prophethood. No Samma (qawwali sessions in Sufi shrines) can be held without the Qaul. Interestingly, a large percentage of the audience at a Samaa is usually Sunni. This is ample evidence of Sufi influence on Sunni Islam in India. Also, as I have shown elsewhere in this chapter, there was a blurring of the boundaries between Shia and Sunni in the cultural sphere.

The 'Qaul' or the proclamation of Ali as the Prophet's successor constitutes the basic fault line dividing Shias and Sunnis. Ali's primacy is the very antithesis of Sunni belief: Sunnis believe the Prophet's real successors were the 'Sahaba' or his companions— Abu Bakr Siddiq, Umar ibn al-Khattab, Uthman ibn Affan. This decision was endorsed by the elders at a meeting place called Saqeefa. Basically, Shia–Sunni differences have their origins in tribal divisions within the overarching clan, the Quresh.

The first three caliphs, one after the other (from 632 CE to 656 CE) are claimed by Sunnis to have been the chosen ones. Sunnis cite a signal supposedly given by the Prophet when He was seriously ill. The Prophet asked Abu Bakr to lead the prayers. Does this event supersede the announcement at Ghadir Khumm? Somewhere here is the central dispute between Shias and Sunnis. Sunni theology follows the decisions taken by tribal elders in Saqeefa. The Prophet's senior companion Abu Bakr Siddiq was named the first caliph to succeed Muhammad. Shias challenge the validity of the Saqeefa meeting and regard the twenty-six years of Abu Bakr, Umar and Uthman as 'usurpation'.

Since the 1979 Islamic Revolution in Iran, the Shia–Sunni divide has been a growing feature of international politics. This, in turn, began to influence Shia–Sunni relations everywhere and to a small extent even in India. For the first time, government appointments of, say, university vice chancellors in this country began to be conditioned by electoral considerations. That Sunnis had the numbers began to matter.

In India, more particularly in Awadh, Shia–Sunni were social categories. As we have noted, the Sunnis form the majority, while the elite Shias form nearly 20 per cent of the Muslim population in India. The proportions in Pakistan are similar.

All Muslim rulers in the medieval period, from the Delhi Sultans right up to the Mughals, were Sunnis. But there was a large sprinkling of Shias in their courts, and they had a prominent role to play in the fields of education and administration. This elevated status accorded to Shias by the emperors and kings of large kingdoms explains the presence of Shia satraps and regional rulers in such diverse places as Awadh, Deccan and Bengal.

The first Islamic probe into India was Muhammad bin Qasim's arrival in Sindh in the same year as the Muslim arrival in Spain—711 CE. But it can be argued that Islam's contact with India predates Muslim invasions. We know this because of clues like the Cheraman Juma Mosque in Kerala, built by Malik bin Dinar—a disciple of the Prophet, and named after Cheraman Perumal, a nobleman—at a time when the Prophet was still alive. This is not surprising if one looks at a map. Only a stretch of water separates the Arabian Peninsula from the coast of Kerala. Trade links across the oceans predated Islam by thousands of years.

When two civilizations mingle, they also clash. At the time that Pope Urban II ordered the First Crusade in 1095, the temple of Somnath in Gujarat was under attack by Mahmud of Ghazni. No desecration of a temple by a Muslim invader has left such a scar on the Hindu psyche. The persistent image of the 'Muslim invader' derives from these raids. If Mahmud had been interested in setting up an empire in India, he would have been as careful as the Delhi Sultans and Mughals were in dealing with the local populace.

Somnath was no ordinary temple. Even making allowance for the mythology surrounding it, it was an extraordinary piece of architecture and engineering—the main idol was said to levitate without any support from below or suspension from above. It was apparently a superb management of powerful magnets that accomplished this feat.

According to historian Romila Thapar, Mahmud's raids were primarily for 'the wealth exceeding 20,000 (twenty thousand dinars) worth of jewels and gold'. But the shock and awe they produced were designed to intimidate the population. There are divergent versions. H. M. Elliot and J. Dowson's *The History of India* records the event almost as a call for revenge: 'When the Sultan...went to wage religious war against India, he made great efforts to capture and destroy Somnath in the hope that Hindus would become Mohammedan... The Indians made a desperate resistance. They would go weeping and crying for help into the temple and then issue forth to battle and fight till all were killed. The number of slain exceeded 50,000.'

Romila Thapar contests this history: 'There is much fantasy in these accounts.' It is a fact that there is no contemporary account of the trauma experienced by Hindus because of Mahmud's raids. There is superficial mention of Somnath in some Jain texts. Apparently, in the thirteenth century, a wealthy merchant from Hormuz was given permission by the town authorities to build a mosque indicating that things were normal. According to Thapar, 'it was soon back to business as usual between temple priests, the local Vaghela administration and visiting Persian and Arab merchants'.

In his wayward life, Mahmud also pillaged Shia mosques and then, in a mood swing, proceeded to fall in love with Persian culture. One of the greatest epic poems ever written, the *Shahnameh* by Firdausi, was in fact commissioned by him. But the great poet left Mahmud's court in some disgust because of the Sultan's miserliness.

Bad publicity given to the 'Mussalman in India' by Mahmud was made worse by Muhammad Ghori (1175), Timur (1398) and, about five hundred years later, by Nadir Shah (1739) and

Ahmad Shah Abdali (1748). That the victims of the raids by these conquerors were mostly Muslims has been lost in the popular narrative. After Abdali's raid, for example, Meer Taqi Meer, the great poet, became homeless. However, selective amnesia began to colour the discourse. Babur founded an empire after defeating the Pathan ruler of Delhi, Ibrahim Lodhi, in the first battle of Panipat in 1526. It was a Muslim–Muslim conflict. But in the popular imagination it has been allowed to persist as a Hindu–Muslim conflict.

By the time Shamsuddin Iltutmish ascended the throne in Delhi in 1211, a great Sufi saint, Hazrat Moinuddin Chishti, had put down anchor in Ajmer where he lived until his death in 1236. All Sufi schools, with one exception, derive spiritual inspiration from Hazrat Ali, the Prophet's cousin and son-in-law. Ali was married to Fatima Zehra. They were the parents of Imam Hasan, Imam Hussain and Zainab.

Therefore, it is not surprising that among those moved to write poetry on Hussain's sacrifice in Karbala was Hazrat Moinuddin Chishti:

Shahast Hussain, Badshahast Hussain
Deen ast Hussain, Deen panahast Hussain
Sar daad na daad dast dar daste Yazid,
Haqqa ki bina e la Ilahast Hussain

(Hussain is King and Emperor
He is the faith and faith's protector
He sacrificed his life
But didn't endorse Yazid's evil rule,
Thus He saved and preserved the Prophet's faith.)

Hazrat Moinuddin Chishti is among the earlier examples of a Sunni steeped in admiration not just for the Prophet but also for

Hazrat Ali and the Prophet's family, Ahle Bait. Even before Shiaism evolved as a theological school, there were growing numbers who came under the spell of Hazrat Ali and the Prophet's family, without necessarily describing themselves as Shia. In a manner of speaking, they had all developed the same aesthetics of Islam, read the same books, without formal affiliations with the Shia seminaries of Najaf in Iraq and Qom in Iran. Those with these affiliations are today called the 'Twelvers', ones who believe in the Twelve Imams. This is the dominant stream of Shiaism in Iran, Iraq, Lebanon and the Indian subcontinent.

And, as I have said earlier, one of the most important centres of Shiaism in the subcontinent was the Awadh region, of which I've attempted to give the reader a flavour.

TWO

The Mangoes of Mustafabad

WAJID ALI SHAH (1822-1887), the last ruler of Awadh, was indisputably one of the country's most spectacular rulers. Besides being a popular leader, his contribution to music, Kathak, poetry and theatre was enormous. He wrote plays in which he acted. *Indersabha* or 'The Court of Lord Indra' is one of them. He danced the Kathak with professional aplomb.

Unfortunately, it is the clichéd view of him and his capital, Lucknow, that survives. And so we have Lucknow, the city of nawabs, portrayed as laid-back and decadent—its hubble-bubble smoking aristocracy passed away because it had to. This picture of a debauched, sensuous elite was largely the work of the British who used it to undermine Nawab Wajid Ali Shah before dispatching him to exile at Matia Burj near Calcutta in 1856.

The great filmmaker Satyajit Ray has, in his 1977 film *Shatranj ke Khilari* (The Chess Players), contrasted the Lucknow style of kingship with that of Queen Victoria's. General Outram is explaining to Wajid Ali Shah the excellent aspects of Queen Victoria's rule. A puzzled Wajid Ali Shah asks him, 'Does your queen do anything other than rule?'

When the British wanted to annexe Awadh, they realized that Wajid Ali Shah was much loved, and hence, an obstacle. He had to be removed. So they caricatured him and then exiled him. The exile of the king of Awadh was in some ways even more traumatic than the last Mughal emperor Bahadur Shah Zafar's exile to Rangoon a year later.

Kathak maestro Birju Maharaj is full of stories of his legendary ancestor, Bindadin Maharaj, founder of the Lucknow school of Kathak and the latter's association with the Awadh king. During Krishna-Leela performances, Bindadin played Krishna while the portly Wajid Ali played a rather unlikely Radha.

In the period after Partition, the 1940s and the 1950s, historians mostly ignored this remarkable king. There is a simple reason for this oversight. Early post-colonial historians were so overwhelmed by the phenomenon called the 'victor's narrative' that they did not have the time or the inclination to make fresh enquiries into the past. They saw little profit in being contrary. These worthies took their cue from such events as Nehru's toning down the centenary of India's First War of Independence in 1957. Why rake up an issue with anti-British connotations while Lord Louis Mountbatten, the last British Viceroy, was still alive? Mountbatten had, after all, facilitated the transfer of power on terms acceptable to Nehru. Mountbatten had been invited by Nehru to stay on as the first Governor General of independent India. This was not without consequences (which I discuss later). The new historian was either in the English mould or had acquiesced in the new Hindi nationalism that was gaining strength. Consequently, the brilliance of the eccentric Wajid Ali Shah did not find much mention in historical works authored in the 1950s.

Wajid Ali Shah lived in exile for thirty-one years and died circa 1887 in Matia Burj, fifty miles from Calcutta. Given his past as a fervent patron of the arts, there's little doubt that he would have influenced the music, cuisine and lifestyle of the region had the colonial power not sought to extinguish his influence. He is absent from the contemporary literature of the Bengali bhadralok, to cite just one example of how thoroughly he was sought to be discredited by the British. Even his masnavi, or long poem, describing the circumstances of his exile has remained unnoticed though it is a revealing document about the culture of the period. It should have been a primary source of information on how the British captured power. Because of the growing British stranglehold on Calcutta, after the Battle of Plassey in 1757, the metropolis was well on its way to becoming the second city of the empire, next only to London. A little after Wajid Ali Shah's death, India came directly under Queen Victoria's rule in 1858 and Calcutta became an imperial metropolis with a Bengali ambience.

The imambara Wajid Ali Shah built is now part of a ghetto in Matia Burj. It must have been an elegant building even up to the time of Independence. Today, a fair sprinkling of the people lounging in the verandas of the imambara could be descendants of the king's courtiers. In fact, I spoke to a man who claimed descent from Wajid Ali Shah's sarangi player, that sonorous instrument which, as accompaniment, enhances the melodic line in classical singing. On one column hangs a quatrain Wajid Ali Shah composed on his departure from Lucknow.

Andoh o alam ka dilpe ghera hoga
Ai bazm ajeeb haal tera hoga
Ek shama kya, bujh jaayenge ghar ghar ke chiraagh
Chhup jaayega Akhtar to andhera hoga

(A deep sadness encircles the heart
Stillness engulfs this gathering
Darkness descends when Akhtar, the most shining star, is eclipsed.)

It was a tradition for Persian and Urdu poets to adopt a pen name or 'takhallus'. Wajid Ali Shah's pen name was 'Akhtar' which means a shining star. Here the king has punned on his pseudonym.

⌁

The impact of the 1857 Uprising on Awadh should never be underrated. The British saw in the revolt seeds of a national movement for independence that would eventually question their authority. As a member of the Parliamentary Select Committee on India, Prime Minister Benjamin Disraeli had studied the country in some depth. He was sharply critical of his government's handling of the events which led to the Uprising. Although the British called it a 'mutiny' (a canard that persists to this day, especially among British historians), Disraeli saw it for what it was—a 'national uprising', something Nehru himself disputed, strangely enough, when he called it a feudal uprising in his *Discovery of India*. Was Nehru adjusting to the revised British appraisal at the turn of the twentieth century which was at variance with Disraeli's considered view?

In his famous speech in the House of Commons on 27 July 1857, Disraeli described the annexation of Awadh as one of the principal causes of the uprising. With that one faulty step, 'you alienated the most powerful class of Mohammedans in India, the Shiites', he observed. Shias were identified by the British ruling class as India's most respected aristocracy. This is important in the understanding of the British view of Muslim rule in India. Disraeli lamented the fact that the British made 'war upon an Oriental monarch whom the Mohammedans regarded as the head of their religion'. This elevated perception of the Awadh king in London is not reflected in the history handed down to us.

My maternal uncle, Sayyid Mohammad Mehdi, who, as I have mentioned, was a young card-carrying communist in Lucknow University, was my source for details about 1857 and how the political elite in London in the decades after the event read the traumatic developments. The colonial authority had no interest in dwelling on the theme, but communists at Oxford, like Dr Z. Ahmad and Syed Sajjad Zaheer, had been sensitized by English communists like Rajani Palme Dutt to the initial appraisal of 1857 by the British establishment as a national uprising.

As we've seen, Disraeli's conclusion was that it was a consequence of the annexation of 'Oudh' that the 'Mohammedan princes felt they had a similarity of interest with the Hindoo Rajahs'. The British mishandling of Wajid Ali Shah caused

'Hindoos, Maharattas, Mohammedans' to secretly feel 'a common interest and a common cause'. After this diagnosis at the highest level, one fact must have been made amply clear to the English—the struggle of 1857 cut across creeds and castes to be truly 'national' in nature.

It was indeed the first major pan-Indian uprising in which Hindus and Muslims, landlords and peasants, united in a war under one banner with Mughal Emperor Bahadur Shah Zafar as their symbolic leader. This was the secularism of common aspirations, which mainstream Congress leaders in independent India chose to ignore. Perhaps they ought to have remembered Disraeli's lament that the situation was brought about because Britain deviated from its time-honoured policy. To quote: 'Our Empire in India was, indeed, founded upon the old principal of divide et impera (divide and rule).'

In fact, after the experience of 1857, Britain would, with redoubled vigour, promote its policy of divide and rule to consolidate its hold. This should have been expected and resisted. To the contrary, the Congress during 1940-47 appears to have found these divisions advantageous, considering the alacrity with which its leadership accepted partition. Did the nationalist leadership, right up to Partition in 1947, realize that communal tensions did not evolve naturally because of a divide between communities and faiths? It was what the British had made of Hindu–Muslim equations. Disraeli's 1857 address to the House of Commons is only one proof of this reality.

✧

'Angreziat' or westernization crept up on the Naqvi family imperceptibly, after the abolition of zamindari in 1951. This was the fourth body blow Muslims had taken in under a hundred years—first, there was the annexation of Awadh, then the brutal suppression by the British of the 1857 Uprising, followed by the Partition of India in 1947 without any reference to the people directly affected by it, and finally the abolition of zamindari. In the previous chapter, I have explained in some detail how all of these cumulatively broke the back of the landed gentry which had not compromised with the English.

Nehru assured Muslim rajas and taluqdars that zamindari abolition would not follow so soon after the trauma of Partition. Even the smaller landlords felt reassured by this promise, only it turned out to be false. How could he have made such promises, standing as he did on the Congress party's socialist plank? This was the key difference between the Congress and the Muslim League. Indeed Muslim landlords held up the Muslim League's status quoist stance on land tenures as a model for the Congress to follow. The League did not touch the issue of land reforms. How could it, when its support base was the landed gentry, exactly the class which dominates the Pakistan National Assembly to this day?

Given this backdrop, Muslim youth found themselves in a cul-de-sac. Those who had access to income from land prior to the zamindari abolition now faced a peculiar kind of penury: a huge shell of a haveli remained, but in disrepair, and the residents were uncertain of their next meal. Cousins whose parents had travelled to Najaf and Karbala in Iraq for pilgrimage with an entourage of twenty now lived in hovels quite literally without a roof over their heads. Food was quietly smuggled in by better-off relatives to keep the recipients' 'thin skins' from being bruised. If you brought the food in trays through the door, the master of the house would dismissively growl. 'We don't need it, thank you.' Both sides had to pretend that food descended like the Biblical manna from heaven. Households which once hosted descendants of Mir Anis to recite marsias during Muharram, now had sons seeking employment as security guards specifically on night duty so that no one would recognize them.

It was because of these circumstances that we Naqvis were pushed into Western education. A compromise was made which, in a manner of speaking, created an intellectual divide in the very heart of our family. Of the seven Naqvi siblings, four happened to be boys, three girls. The four boys were admitted to Lucknow's La Martiniere College, the finest school my parents knew. It truly is a great institution. Of my three sisters, the two older ones were admitted to Karamat Hussain Girls College, where they imbibed all the austerities considered essential for the preservation of Muslim culture. By the time our youngest sister, Naheed, was of schoolgoing age, the family elders having been defeated by circumstances, made a U-turn. She was admitted to La Martiniere. But my other sisters bore the brunt of the self-imposed domestic apartheid.

The boys and the girls returned home from their schools with a different set of books, different plans for the evening, different friends, interests, dress, food preferences and a different attitude to sex and religion. Above all, we, the boys, began to converse in English. It became a bilingual home. Our sisters became the preservers of tradition and we, its agnostics.

My Hindu friends, even the ones in Lucknow, had thrown in their lot unequivocally with English education. Many of them had parents who had been uprooted from what was now Pakistan after Partition. They were not going to be burdened by the past. The choice had been made for them—move forward with English. My circumstances were vastly different. I had seen three generations of my family grapple with the choice that was being offered: move ahead with Western education, as Sir Syed Ahmad Khan had prescribed for the community, or stay rooted and confined to the past and our traditional language. The resistance to English was at two levels—an extraordinary pride in Urdu and the reluctance to surrender to everything that our elders had resisted this far. With English would come aspects of Western civilization which were considered debilitating for our culture.

After my Senior Cambridge examinations, the question arose on the kind of college I should attend. Father, unhappy that I was drifting away from the gentlemanly sherwani to a dark suit, felt more comfortable sending me to Aligarh Muslim University for graduate studies rather than to Christian College, Lucknow, Christ Church College, Kanpur or St. John's College, Agra. These were the choices within UP that my father was familiar with. His college of choice would have actually been Lucknow's Shia College where most of my cousins studied.

At Aligarh University's MacDonnell Hostel, I had to share a large room with three god-fearing boys. They were different from me because they earnestly followed Tableeghi Jamaat (Muslim version of the Salvation Army) instructions to congregate in the large mosque next to the cricket ground for Friday prayers. For the first time in my life, I became aware of my Shia upbringing which separated me from the majority in the university. Of course, there must have been many Shias in the university. There were, after all, distinct theological departments under Shia and Sunni professors. The two Shias I met on the campus were from Bangalore and Srinagar. It dawned on me that a Shia from Awadh was a category unto himself.

There were sharp differences between me and the rest of the students. Congregational prayer on Friday afternoons was an article of faith with all Muslims but it was optional in Shia practice. At least, that was the culture in our house. I must state here that my understanding of Shia practice is extrapolated from my family and their friends. If in my exuberance I have tarred more solemn Shias I apologize in advance.

Namaz or prayers five times a day, fasting during the month of Ramadan, planning for pilgrimage to Mecca and Medina as the high point of one's life were serious Muslim priorities. These observances were in the Shia book too but they were not enforced. Sufis of the Chishti School had so internalized the divine experience that namaz to them was sometimes a superfluous ritual. This had influenced Shia thinking too.

Josh Malihabadi wailed about this circumstance in Karachi:

Sab se zyada khauf hai is baat ka mujhey
Dum tor dein kaheen na meri waza darian
Aisa na ho ke aihle suboo se bigar kar
Aale wuzoo se gaanthna par jaaen yaariyan

(I dread the day my way of life is compromised
Will I have to break ranks with my friends in the tavern?
I shudder to think that I may have to line up with
supplicants in prayer.)

Namaz was important but it was not the highest priority. The Shias of Awadh, distinct from Shias elsewhere, had learnt to live with this paradox. Here are a few lines often recited at Muharram:

Bulbul ko gul pasand, gulon ko hawa pasand
Hum butaravion ko hai khaake shifa pasand
Yeh apni apni taba hai ai khaazine behisht
Tujhko Iram pasand, hamein Karbala pasand

(The bulbul loves flowers; flowers love the gentle breeze
We love the divine dust from Imam Hussain's tomb
We have our own preferences;
You like paradise, I am in love with Karbala!)

My grandfather, Mohammad Askari, was a friend of Sayyid Waris Shah, the high priest of Dewa Sharif, the Sufi shrine outside Lucknow. When Grandfather asked him. 'Why don't you say your namaz regularly?' Waris Shah's response was succinct: 'Where is the space for me to kneel and go down in prayer?', in other words—'He is in me', the very essence of Advaita monotheism.

Notionally, Mecca and Medina are equally holy to both Shias and Sunnis, but in practice, Shias have different priorities—Najaf, Karbala, and Damascus, where the shrine of Zainab (Imam Hussain's sister) stands, are the most sacred pilgrimage centres. Zainab, incidentally, was the one who witnessed the Battle of Karbala in which Imam Hussain, the grandson of the Prophet, was martyred and recounted it to the people in her eloquent sermons.

Without Zainab the tragedy of Karbala would have been buried in Karbala. For Shias, the ten days of Muharram, mourning the Battle of Karbala, trumped everything else.

I am personally aware that the Sunnis, as a collective, or during congregations like Friday prayers, may in jest make the charge of apostasy against Shias, but these divergences do not make a difference in personal relationships. Shias and Sunnis consider the Haj to Mecca the highest form of worship.

⁓

The grandeur of Lucknow's architecture is in its imambaras, the elegant halls and palaces built in memory of Imam Hussain. Numerous tazias (replicas of Imam Hussain's tomb in Karbala), and Zuljenahs (horses that represent Imam Hussain's horse) are taken out in decorative processions several times a day during Muharram. Zuljenah or 'dul dul' in common parlance is admired for its equine feats, of course, but particularly because it returned to the tent of Zainab and other ladies without its rider, Imam Hussain. The Zuljenah is, therefore, the first bearer of the news of what Shias consider the greatest tragedy to have overtaken them. Lucknow, the headquarters of India's Shias, was known for these Zuljenah processions.

Because every activity connected with Muharram was patronized by the Shia ruling class since the installation of Nawab Saadat Ali Khan in 1680, the Shias continued to dictate the tempo of Lucknow's cultural life despite the abolition of the nawabi after the Uprising of 1857. The Uprising brought them down several notches economically but their status vis-à-vis the general population was not immediately reversed. It took considerable time to fade away.

⁓

My grandfather, like Dryden, always maintained that 'priests of all religions are the same'. But some he respected, even befriended, for their scholarship and conversation. The difference between the mullah and ulema was marked. The mullah kept the mosque clean and led small congregations. Ulemas were theological scholars. I remember sitting through many a theological discourse, with Maulana Nasir-ul-Millat holding court. A permanent fixture among the participants was Brij Mohan Nath Kachar, a Kashmiri Pandit who frequented Mustafabad at Muharram. His sermons from the pulpit on the Battle of Karbala were riveting.

When I was growing up, a maulvi of little distinction was hired to ostensibly brush up my arithmetic, but actually to put me through my first paces in namaz. His efforts at proselytization were supplemented by my mother's; she augmented our meagre library with biographies of the Prophet and the great Imams. I believe the maulvi left in some disgust because he complained that there was too much music, which he found distasteful, in our house, even on Eid.

Eid for us was never Eid without Babu Mahavir Prasad. We changed into our new clothes and waited at the doorstep for Babuji (as he was referred to) to arrive. He would walk in, clad in a black 'achkan' and Gandhi cap, meet my father, settle down to large helpings of 'sewai' (sweet noodles prepared traditionally for the celebration) and then hand us a one rupee coin each—a handsome amount in those days when two rupees a week was good pocket money. On Raksha Bandhan, my mother would send out rakhis to my father's close friends. Babu Kameshwar Prasad's rakhi went out with a plate of kebabs. These were delivered to his office. His family was vegetarian but he had worked out this surreptitious deal with my father.

There was a quaint little mosque in the compound of our house in the village. Since, by now, we visited Mustafabad only during school holidays, marriages, deaths and births, it was not difficult to maintain a certain discipline and be seen in the mosque with reasonable frequency, if only to please Grandfather. He expressed his pleasure either by making additions to our pocket money or taking us out on shikar.

⌇

We were groomed into believing that Islam was the most dynamic of religions but we found it equally easy to accept that it was Islam's interaction with an older civilization that resulted in Dara Shikoh, Rahim, Kabir, Amir Khusro, Raskhan, Nazeer Akbarabadi, Ghalib and Anis. As I have pointed out, the merging of Urdu culture with Awadhi and Brajbhasha was something we learned very early in life and it is sad that this syncretism is now under siege. These days people are ignorant of the eighteenth-century poet Nazir Akbarabadi's poem, *Kya kya likhoon main Krishna Kanhaiya ka baal pan* (How should I write about the beautiful childhood of Lord Krishna), or Mohsin Kakorvi's *Samte Kashi se chala janibe Mathura badal, jab talak Braj mein Kanhaiya hai yeh khulne ka nahin* (The clouds are moving ecstatically from Kashi to Mathura and the sky will remain covered with dense clouds as long as there is Krishna in Braj). These lines about Lord Krishna were written by a Muslim poet to celebrate not Krishna's birthday but that of Prophet Muhammad!

Several events had a part in breaking the syncretism of Awadhi. The decline of the feudal order exacerbated the division between the Hindus and the Muslims. It was the self-confident Muslim feudal elite which found it easy to accept the beautiful aspects of Hindu culture. Dhrupad, Khayal and Kathak evolved in the Muslim courts. So tenacious is the grip of clichés, that most people have difficulty associating such music (and dance) with Muslims. This despite the fact that Ali Akbar Khan, Vilayat Khan, Amir Khan, Faiyaz Khan were all Muslims.

With the decay of the feudal hierarchy, the lower middle class, always more religious in every society, gained upward mobility. It is around this class that religious groups like the Jamaat-e-Islami formed clusters. These clusters were 100 per cent Sunni. No Shia was ever a member of Jamiat Ulema-i-Hind of Deoband, Tableeghi

Jamaat, Ahle Hadith, or what is known as the Bareli group. The various militant groups—Lashkar-e-Taiba, Jaish-e-Mohammed, Al Qaeda, Taliban, Jamat-ud-Dawa, Jabhat-ul-Nusra—are Sunni without exception. Sensible Sunnis will have their own take: jihadis are not proper Muslims at all.

Now the ground realities in Mustafabad have changed. Three-fourths of the house where our family assembles is in ruins. Half the relatives can barely make ends meet. Does all of it reflect on the declining socio-economic condition of Muslims as reported by the Sachar Committee? In the first flush of the 2004 electoral changeover from the BJP-led National Democratic Alliance (NDA), some Congress leaders allowed the Sachar Committee to be set up to study the socio-economic reality of the world's second largest Muslim population. By good luck, or bad, an energetic scholar and processor of data, Dr Abusaleh Shariff, drove the research. The dismal findings of the Sachar Committee did not get a sympathetic response from the Congress-led United Progressive Alliance (UPA). Perhaps that is why Sachar Committee recommendations are still in cold storage. Likewise, no follow-up has taken place on the Ranganath Misra Commission recommendations, published in 2007, to help improve the pitiable condition of Indian Muslims. Dr Abusaleh Shariff, who had got his teeth into the subject, confided later that he, like others in the know, was convinced that 'the UPA had no intention to implement the committee's findings for fear of losing Hindu support'. Before I move on to other matters, a final paean to the Awadh I've lost.

It was my father's firm belief that Awadhi culture was partly defined by mangoes grafted in the region. And thereby hangs a tale. Our grove in Mustafabad once produced boutique mangoes. In the summer each year, friends and relatives would turn up at our house in South Delhi with the 'king of fruits' wrapped in newspapers, gunny bags, even in discarded bedsheets. There are problems with this ritual. Good mangoes have to be separated from the bad. There are subtleties involved in this separation of the ripe from the stale. The seasoned mango carrier takes care not to travel with ripe mangoes. They will get pulpy in passage. The untrained will make just this mistake and arrive with pulp so smelly as to turn you off mangoes for a few seasons.

It is relatively simple to differentiate good mangoes from bad. What requires expertise of a high order is to establish a hierarchy of flavours from excellent to the barely tolerable within each genre of the fruit: Langra, Chausa, Dussehri, Malihabadi Safeda. And, if you cast your net nationwide, there's Malda from Bengal, Hemayat and Benishan from Hyderabad, Alphonso from Mumbai, and scores of others.

Our Awadhi chauvinism is bruised when we are reminded that the finest Langras—the king of mangoes with a tang in its sweetness—come from areas east of Awadh—Varanasi, for instance. Langra means lame and it is well possible that this most delicious of fruits was grafted or developed by a mango enthusiast who did not have a leg or who limped like the Turco-Mongol conqueror Timur who was called Timur the lame (Tamerlane to the European world).

In 2013, mango trafficking from our catchment area of Awadh was hectic because there were many more visitors to see my mother who, at ninety-seven, was trying to conquer an oesophageal malignancy with radiation therapy. One day, my sister turned up from Mustafabad, with the ritual bagful of mangoes, greatly pleasing my mother. Even though she could not swallow, she did hold a mango in both her hands, sniffed it like a wine expert, and lay back having approved of the quality.

'Where are these mangoes from?' I asked.

'From Mustafabad.'

'You mean you bought them in Mustafabad?'

'From our house in Mustafabad.'

When I heard this, I was suddenly transported to summer

holidays during my childhood in Mustafabad. Our adorable grandfather, Abbajan, who, after graduating from Aligarh, had settled in the sprawling family house as something of an anchor, would prepare himself for visitors. In anticipation of our arrival—some twenty or thirty cousins from Lucknow, Kanpur, Allahabad, Fatehpur, Pratapgarh, Rae Bareli, Kara, Patti—Abbajan would arrange for raw mangoes of varying lineage to be piled up in the four corners of a godown meant for foodgrains. A waterproof sheet would be placed on each pile which was then plastered with a thick paste of mud to ripen the mangoes. Each pile thus treated was called a 'paal'.

It required expertise to know which pile would ripen first and which last. This was essential to space out the opening of each paal so that a steady supply of mangoes lasted throughout our holidays. The suspense that preceded the opening of each 'paal' was nail-biting as we sat outside Abbajan's veranda in small circles around buckets filled with water to cool the mangoes which had been steaming inside the caked mud before it was cracked open. The orgy of mango eating followed Ghalib's dictum: 'they should be sweet and in plenty'.

Abbajan had kept up the illusion that the mangoes we ate came from groves in one village or the other, all part of the property under his supervision. But the truth was that most of the groves had been sold, particularly after the abolition of zamindari. So every summer, during the holidays, he would lease trees from groves that had already been sold.

That is why the ritual gift of mangoes my sister brought from Mustafabad surprised me. Yes, beyond the pond outside our house, in a small patch of land stretching up to the railway tracks, there was one tree with an exquisite mango called Kalua. But over the years the Kalua had withered away and the wood from it had been sold. So, where did my sister's gift come from? After all, my mother did feel the mango with some tenderness.

Ambua ki daari se boley Koelia (the Koel sings from the

branch of a mango tree) will remain the most popular 'bandish' or composition whenever Raag Bageshri is sung. Indian textiles, from Kashmir to Kanyakumari, will always be adorned by the motif of the mango which symbolizes fertility and regeneration. It was this eternal reality that my mother had seized upon. Right behind the Kalua tree, she had quietly planted a sapling of Langra, which had now begun to yield sufficient crop to enable my sister to turn up with a bagful of fruit.

As I think about the scenes of my youth, my remembering eye falls upon acres and acres of wheat and maize that make for a bright foreground against which the dark green mango groves bring the sort of relief that monsoon clouds bring. This is the picturesque scene from my village all the way to Allahabad, which falls outside the cultural boundaries of Awadh but is, nevertheless, good for mangoes. When Akbar Allahabadi sent a box of choice Langras to Allama Iqbal in Lahore, Iqbal sent him a couplet by way of receipt:

Asar hai teri aijaz e masihaee ka ae Akbar
Allahabad se Langra chale Lahore tak pahunche

(Akbar, this is a miracle: you have healing powers, like Jesus.
Langra—the lame—travelled from Allahabad and has reached Lahore!)

My story of the mangoes of Mustafabad is also a tale about how families and societies wish to preserve tradition and keep alive practices to which they are emotionally linked. Abbajan did not wish the mango eating spree every summer in our ancestral home to be discontinued, so he secretly procured the fruits from orchards that we once owned. My mother too wanted the family to remember the mango which symbolized so much—that was why she planted a Langra sapling. They are both gone now, but the mangoes of Mustafabad continue to bring back memories.

THREE

Partition's Long Shadow

OURS WAS A family steeped in politics. As I have pointed out in previous chapters, many of my ancestors were at the forefront of the First War of Independence in 1857. My great-grandfather in Rae Bareli had spent years in Naini Jail with leaders like Motilal Nehru. My father's elder brother, Sayyid Wasi, was a senior Congress leader from Rae Bareli. My great-uncle Syed Mohammad Sadiq, a brilliant lawyer in Kanpur, spent a lifetime in the Congress with leaders like Maulana Hasrat Mohani. My father's family were Congressmen, but my mother's family, with rather larger landholdings, were communists. Feudalism to communism was an interesting transition, but it came about after the family's fortunes went into precipitous decline.

Our family's immersion in the politics of the time greatly influenced how we responded to Partition. August 1947, therefore, registered with the family not as independence but as the partition of India. I do not recall any celebration of independence. True, I was only seven, too young to remember. But a bevy of senior relatives recall only suspense and uncertainty. Heart-rending stories of sudden death and penury were commonplace.

Women those days did not work and the professions favoured by men were law and teaching. Just as English literature was the 'snob' subject in Delhi University of the sixties, Urdu was the snob subject among genteel Awadhi elite in the fifties. This was ironical because after Partition, Urdu scholarship was giving diminishing returns. It was the sheer momentum of pre-Partition interests which carried Urdu scholarship forward after 1947. Most of these Urduwallahs had enhanced their unemployability by taking to communism as a creed. When the Party was banned in 1951, many of these relatives were in jail unless they were nimble enough to go underground.

Sayyid Mohammad Nasir Naqvi, a dear uncle, with a strong aquiline nose, light green eyes and a penchant for being caught, beaten up and tossed in jail, almost epitomized the tragedy of the times. With his past, it was difficult to find jobs.

CPI leader B. T. Ranadive's suggestion that some Indian leaders must take advantage of the open borders and cross over to Pakistan to stoke armed struggle a la Telangana inspired hotheads as well as the most effete of communists. Sayyid Sajjad Zaheer (Banne Bhai), country gentleman with a degree from Oxford, chose Pakistan as the laboratory for revolutionary field work. Along with poet Faiz Ahmad Faiz, Banne Bhai was arrested in what came to be known as the Rawalpindi Conspiracy Case.

The cover of communism gave Naseer a suitable excuse to find work as a lecturer in Pakistan, a country he was otherwise vehemently averse to.

Problems arose when his attempts to visit India, the land of his family and 'beloved' comrades, were repeatedly thwarted because of a confidential report which became a black mark against his name in the consular section of the Indian High Commission in Karachi, then the capital of Pakistan.

For seventeen years Naseer tried for his visa in vain. He overcame his homesickness by seeking out friends from Kanpur, the city of his college and communism. His closest friend became a former Kanpur policeman. They were in the same city at a time when Naseer was repeatedly on the wrong side of law for his revolutionary pranks. It was ironic that his friend, the 'plainclothes' cop who had recorded Naseer as the 'city's most dangerous and violent communist' when in India, was now an inseparable friend in Pakistan.

Naseer was one story. But there were other poor cousins who ran helter-skelter for jobs. In those days, not a single member of the family knew anything about passports. Remember Naseer had crossed over when borders were open. Some were adventurous enough to escape to Pakistan by an ingenious system called the 'gardaniya' passport. They reached Assam by train where touts on both sides of the border arranged for their crossing. The tout in India would hold the Pakistan-bound relative by the neck (gardan) and push him over the border. In this 'gardaniya' operation, timing was of the essence. The person had to be pushed exactly when the tout in East Pakistan was ready to receive him.

How this miserable state of affairs came about could not be discussed except behind closed doors, and never with outsiders. The suffocating, surly silences continued for years. We lived like hypocrites who had a massive grievance but felt it was dangerous to give vent to it publicly in any meaningful way. Say what you liked at home but be careful what you say to 'Mishraji' or 'Guptaji' who had accepted Partition as a happy outcome! When you talked of the problems Partition had created, they would shake their heads and exclaim, 'How sad'.

The hypocritical silence adopted in the early years of Partition began to putrefy over the years and turned into closet communalism. And yet the conspiracy of silence about who was really responsible for the partition of India continued. Our country's leadership, from Mahatma Gandhi, Jawaharlal Nehru, Sardar Patel and others, all the way up to the leadership of today, encouraged the chant: 'Jinnah partitioned India; he was the villain.' We had our doubts.

We have lived this fallacy from the day India was partitioned. The Congress leadership, and therefore the Congress party, which has ruled the country for most of the years since Partition, has never felt compelled to clarify its role in partitioning India.

∾

One has to rewind to events before the Partition to understand why, for a large percentage of India's Muslims, this writer included, Partition was a great betrayal. After the 1857 Uprising—which, as I mentioned, was the first pan-Indian revolt against colonial rule in India—any news that showed the Empire in poor light was officially blacked out by the British. One such example is the very high-profile murder of the Viceroy Lord Mayo on 8 February 1872 by Sher Ali Afridi, a cavalry trooper from Peshawar.

Sher Ali was a much-loved mounted soldier with certificates of appreciation from his superiors. At one point in his career he was imprisoned for reasons that were never really clear. The British were averse to give the Sher Ali episode any political colour. The story put out was that he killed a relative in a family feud. If this was indeed the case why was he transferred all the way from the North West Frontier Province to a penal colony beyond the southern tip of India? Lord Mayo was on an inspection tour in the Andaman islands when Sher Ali pounced on him with a knife, killing him on the spot. It was unclear if this was an act of political revenge because of British actions in the North West Frontier Province, where Sher Ali was born, or something else altogether. The murder of the Viceroy sent shock waves through London. A thick curtain was pulled over the incident. This was exactly the sort of event that would serve to demoralize Britain just as it was recovering from the 1857 Uprising.

The timing of the incident was awkward for the British for another reason. Queen Victoria had just about persuaded herself that the most loyal subjects of the Crown were Muslims, and now Sher Ali had gone and turned everything upside down by murdering the Viceroy. This was at a time when the Queen's fondness for her favourite servant, Abdul Karim—whom she adoringly called 'Munshi'—had become something of a scandal in the royal household.

After the shock of 1857, the British strategy was obvious: devise ways to keep Hindus and Muslims in conflict. The arrival of more British troops to boost the British component in the armed forces in India led to an unexpected complication. When numbers rose from 20,000 in 1857 to more than 60,000 in the next two decades, the provision of beef for British troops became a priority. This became a sensitive issue because of the rapid increase in gauraksha or cow protection organizations across north India which, in the early twentieth century, were patronized even by national leaders like Mahatma Gandhi.

The British establishment kept itself insulated from Hindu anger by allowing official underlings to point fingers at Muslim butchers who actually performed the physical act of slaughtering the cows. This led to numerous Hindu–Muslim riots. Exhaustive correspondence between British officials, quoted by senior Gandhian scholar Dharampal—who spent months in the India Office Library and the British Museum in London studying British records on the subject—shows the Raj deliberately provoked Hindus against Muslims, sowing the seeds of their divide and rule policy. In 2002, Dharampal and his colleague T. M. Mukundan published their research. The title of the book says it all: *The British Origin of Cow Slaughter in India*. The book is replete with instances of Muslim leaders, editors, social workers joining cow protection groups as a mark of solidarity with the Hindus. But the British persisted in hiring Muslim butchers, who were blamed whenever the administration was faced with an agitation.

Queen Victoria gave the game away in a note to Viceroy Lord Lansdowne on 8 December 1893: 'Though the Mohammedans' cow-killing is made the pretext of the agitation, it is in fact directed against us, who kill far more cows for our army than the Mohammedans.'

⌣

The partition of the country in August 1947 led to the birth of two distinct states—India and Pakistan—from the same colonial womb, one cloaking its Hindu aspirations in multiculturalism

(Nehru called it secular) and the other overtly committed to Muslim theocracy. The equation between the two was conflictual from the very start.

In March 1945, Lord Wavell, the then Viceroy of India, had returned after a long meeting with Prime Minister Winston Churchill, convinced that the division of India was Churchill's preferred scenario. This, because the northwest of India, which was to be the core of Pakistan, had become strategically important for British interests in the Persian Gulf and West Asia. All the more so because with the end of the Second World War in 1945, the hostility for the Soviet Union that the West had kept in abeyance during the war in order to jointly defeat Hitler was no longer concealed. A protracted Cold War would soon follow. In this scenario, the Islamic state of Pakistan would become an essential ally of the West for strategic reasons.

These global geo-political imperatives, along with local demands, had a very strong bearing on the decision to partition India and create Pakistan. As I have explained in the Introduction, and as the reader will discover throughout the book, I have dealt with momentous historical events in the post-Independence era that have had an impact on the way Muslims have fared in this country in a somewhat unconventional manner. I have not provided detailed histories of the events in question, as these can be found elsewhere, and are anyway beyond the scope of the book. With the exception of Partition, which I was too young to remember, I have analyzed these events in the light of my own experience of them. Often, I have chosen one or two aspects of the event to illuminate it as a whole. This is the approach I have followed for Partition as well, except that I have relied on the accounts of others.

Sir Cyril Radcliffe, chairman of the Border Commissions, was given the task of delineating the boundaries of 450,000 square kilometres of territory and dividing the population of about 400 million between India and the new state of Pakistan. He was told to complete his assignment in five weeks. Why was Jawaharlal Nehru in such a hurry to have Sir Cyril Radcliffe demarcate the Indo–Pak boundaries? We have Nehru's correspondence stating that the work of the Border Commission had to be done 'fairly rapidly'. That this complicated task was done in such a rush could be attributed to the fact that news had leaked that Jinnah was terminally ill. After Jinnah, no one knew with whom, and for how long, negotiations would have to be conducted. It is argued that Congress leaders like Nehru were getting on in years and were therefore impatient and accepted Partition in a hurry. But Nehru was only fifty-eight in 1947! A much more straightforward theory is that only in a partitioned India did Congress leaders see themselves coming to power, without having to share it with the Muslim League.

The principal excuse given for Partition is the two-nation theory credited to Muslim League supremo Mohammad Ali Jinnah. However, what is not widely known is that the theory about Hindus and Muslims being separate entities was actually first articulated by a colonial theorist James Mill who belonged to the Utilitarian School. In 1940, Jinnah gave a speech during a Muslim League session in Lahore in which he stated that Hindus and Muslims were two separate and irreconcilable monolithic religious communities. However, as is well known, Jinnah was anything but a devout Muslim; he rarely went to the mosque, drank whisky, was clean-shaven and favoured bespoke suits and ties—far from the Islamic-attire-wearing Father of Pakistan that he appears as on that country's currency. In fact, as senior Congress leader K. M. Munshi points out, 'it was [Jinnah] who warned Gandhiji not to encourage the fanaticism of Muslim religious leaders'. And it was Jinnah who, in 1916, succeeded in allaying the fears of Hindu domination among League members, which resulted in the famous Lucknow Pact—a list of demands for the establishment of self-government submitted to the British jointly by the Congress party and the Muslim League.

Note Nehru's tone in a letter he wrote to Jinnah on 6 April 1938, after refusing a coalition with the Muslim League:

...the Muslim League is an important communal organization and we [Congress] deal with it as such. But we have to deal with all organizations and individuals that come within our ken. We do not determine the measure of importance or distinction they possess.

Jinnah replied:

Your tone and language again display the same arrogance and militant spirit, as if the Congress is the sovereign power. I may add that, in my opinion, as I have publicly stated so often, that unless the Congress recognizes the Muslim League on a footing of complete equality and is prepared as such to negotiate for a Hindu–Muslim settlement...a settlement would not be possible.

The Nehru–Jinnah personality clash was not a negligible factor when it came to events that led to Partition.

⌢

Although there have been many versions of the various factors that led to the partition of India, the story is still incomplete. Much more new material has to be incorporated—like the Transfer of Power papers published in Britain in 1983—to get a complete picture of what actually transpired. The Transfer of Power papers constitute a comprehensive record of all that passed between Indian leaders and the British government during the crucial period between 1942 and 1947. Its unveiling should have excited subcontinental scholars. It did not. The truth is that the establishments in India and Pakistan had made their adjustments with the reality handed to them in 1947. Upsetting this status quo would expose leaders of the freedom struggle as men with feet of clay. *The Economist* of April 1990, reviewing H. M. Seervai's book based on the Transfer of Power documents, recommended that 'there must be a reappraisal of reputations'. This 'reappraisal' has never taken place.

Two years after the Transfer of Power papers were published, Pakistani historian Ayesha Jalal was able to establish in her Cambridge dissertation, *The Sole Spokesman*, that 'it was the Congress which insisted on Partition. It was Jinnah who was against Partition.' It has been widely accepted that the call for partition was a bargaining ploy whereby Jinnah hoped to strike a better deal for Muslims in a united India. But partnership with Muslims would have made it impossible for the Congress to achieve what Maulana Azad described as 'unadulterated Hindu Raj'. Partition, in a way, was the gift the Congress gave to the Hindu right, which in the fullness of time, is today's Hindutva.

Among the revelations made in the Transfer of Power documents was the fact that Lord Louis Mountbatten, who arrived in the country in March 1947 as Britain's last Viceroy, specifically tasked with overseeing the transfer of power, concealed from public view the Punjab award—the Punjab border delineated by Sir Cyril Radcliffe's Border Commission. It was expected that violence would most certainly follow the award—this would spoil the Independence Day festivities in which he was to star. The delay in publishing the report multiplied the scale of the holocaust. Timely publication of details of the award would have enabled the administration to take preventive measures. It could be said, therefore, that Mountbatten was largely responsible for the scale of the massacres. As an aside, but one which has a bearing on the events of the time, I should relate an incident which shows how enamoured Nehru was of Mountbatten. In 1957, he advised organizers to tone down the commemoration of the centenary of the 1857 Uprising. Mountbatten was still alive and Nehru was averse to the scab being lifted from an old colonial wound. The existence of this 'injunction' was disclosed to Kuldip Nayar in 2007 by a Congress minister after an all-party meeting in the prime minister's residence to chalk out plans to observe the 150th anniversary of the First War of Independence.

In his book, *India Wins Freedom*, Maulana Azad, one of the foremost leaders of the political establishment at the time of Independence and president of the Indian National Congress from 1939 to 1946, exposes the role his colleagues in the Congress Working Committee played in partitioning the country. He argues that, until the very end, Jinnah was merely using Pakistan as a 'bargaining counter'. The Maulana was vocal and vehement in his opposition to partition and tried to persuade Nehru and Patel to stop it. Sardar Vallabhbhai Patel, a barrister and statesman, was convinced that there were two separate nations within India and rather than be like brothers bickering every day, they should have 'one clean fight' instead. The Maulana was pained that Patel had now become an even greater supporter of the two-nation theory than Jinnah. 'Jinnah may have raised the flag of Partition but now the real flag bearer was Patel', he notes in his book.

But what about Mountbatten? In May 1947, he began to market partition. Why? That remains a subject for historians to enquire into, the evidence thus far is not entirely clear. What we do know is that he met with all the key leaders of the time to persuade them to accept partition. How willingly did they fall in line?

Ghalib's couplet comes to mind:

Dekhna taqreer ki lazzat ki jo usne kaha,
Maine yeh jana ki goya yeh bhi mere dil mein ha

(Just look at his persuasiveness,
Everything he says was in my heart too.)

Once Patel had agreed with his proposition, Mountbatten turned his attention to Nehru. This is the Maulana's testimony.

A multicultural India had been a passionate article of faith with Maulana Azad, of course, and he thought this was true of Nehru, too. The Maulana was understandably disappointed at seeing his friend Nehru, whom he considered a man of principle, abandon the idea of a united India. He notes in his book that one of the factors responsible for Nehru being won over was the personality of Lady Edwina Mountbatten who 'is not only extremely intelligent but has a most attractive and friendly temperament'. He adds that Lady Mountbatten admired her husband deeply and tried to 'interpret his thoughts to those who would not at first agree with him'. Whatever the case, by now it was clear that despite Nehru's initial repugnance and resistance to the idea of partition, he was growing used to the idea that there was no other alternative. The Maulana told historian K. M. Ashraf that Nehru was impatient and wanted to become prime minister while Mountbatten was still in India. For Nehru, one sequence of events was non-negotiable—British rule must be replaced by Congress rule in Delhi. If that entailed partition, so be it. And thus it was that the British Raj was replaced in this country by a Raj that was less than satisfactory—one that was billed as being secular was, in fact, what the Maulana described as, 'undiluted Hindu Raj'. Partition would cast a long shadow upon independent India.

The Maulana had left careful instructions regarding thirty-odd pages of *India Wins Freedom*—these were to be made public only after he and Nehru were dead. When Azad's brutally honest version exposing the duplicity of the Congress finally came to light in 1988, it invited some motivated criticism but it did not inspire the extended debate which it deserved.

History owes the Maulana gratitude for having recorded crucial facts which may have been erased by time. Where Azad disappoints is in his own role during this phase. The Congress volte face on partition was strong enough reason for him to resign from all posts in the party, even from the primary membership of the party. Why did he not resign? Had he resigned, the Congress would have been exposed for having partitioned the country into two entities—one led by Hindus and the other by Muslims.

By staying on, Azad provided the Congress with a fig leaf of secularism. It is instructive to note that the Frontier Gandhi, Khan Abdul Ghaffar Khan, one of the tallest Muslim leaders of the time, wept at the meeting where the partition decision was taken.

The Maulana writes about the time after Patel and Nehru had become supporters of partition and Gandhiji remained his only hope. When the Maulana met Gandhiji on 31 March 1947, he told him categorically, 'My only hope now is in you. If you stand against Partition, we may yet save the situation. If you however acquiesce, I am afraid India is lost.' Gandhiji replied passionately that if the Congress wished to accept Partition 'it will be over my dead body'. He added that as long as he was alive he would never agree to the partition of India nor allow the Congress to accept it.

But soon after, events took an astonishing turn.

Later that same day Gandhiji met Lord Mountbatten. He saw him the next day as well and again on 2 April. Sardar Patel came to Gandhiji after his first meeting with Lord Mountbatten and was closeted with him for over two hours. When the Maulana met Gandhiji again, he got 'the greatest shock of my life'. Gandhiji had changed: while he was not openly in favour of partition, 'he no longer spoke so vehemently against it'. What further surprised and shocked the Maulana was that Gandhiji had begun to repeat Sardar Patel's arguments. The Maulana proceeded to plead with Gandhiji for over two hours but failed to make an impression on him.

'In despondency I at last said, "If even you have now adopted these views, I see no hope of saving India from catastrophe."'

Gandhiji replied saying that he had already made the suggestion that they should ask Jinnah to form the government and choose the members of the Cabinet. He said that he had mentioned this to Lord Mountbatten and Lord Mountbatten was greatly impressed by the idea.

When the Maulana met Mountbatten the day after, he told him that if the Congress accepted Gandhiji's suggestion, partition could still be averted. Lord Mountbatten agreed that such an offer on the part of the Congress would convince the Muslim League and perhaps win the confidence of Jinnah. Unfortunately, this move made no headway as both Jawaharlal and Sardar Patel opposed it vehemently. In fact, they forced Gandhiji to withdraw the suggestion.

Eventually, Gandhiji conceded to the Maulana that partition appeared inevitable. All that was left to decide was what form it would take. This was the question which was now being debated day and night in Gandhiji's camp.

As we have seen, the Maulana was convinced that Sardar Patel had had a big hand to play in Gandhiji changing his opinion. Another probable consideration could have been Lord Mountbatten arguing that the Congress had agreed to a weak centre in order to meet the objections of the League. Provinces were therefore given full provincial autonomy, but in a country so divided by language, community and culture, a weak centre was bound to encourage fissiparous tendencies. Without the Muslim League, they could plan for a strong central government and frame a constitution desirable from the point of view of Indian unity. Lord Mountbatten advised that it would be better to give up a few small pieces in the northwest and the northeast to build up a strong and consolidated India. Sardar Patel was impressed by the argument that cooperation with the Muslim League would jeopardize Indian unity and strength. The Maulana was increasingly convinced that these arguments repeated by Sardar Patel and Lord Mountbatten had weakened Gandhiji's opposition to partition.

The distressing truth is that in all these exchanges between Mountbatten, Gandhiji, Nehru, Patel and Azad, there is no evidence that there was much thought given to Indian Muslims and their plight. Today's population of 180 million Muslims have to cope almost daily with a biased state. How could Nehru not have foreseen this state of affairs? Maulana Azad certainly had.

In his book *Guilty Men of India's Partition*, socialist leader
Ram Manohar Lohia wrote:

> [Congress leaders] paid no heed to Gandhiji's wish to let
> the Muslim League govern the country by itself, because
> they were far too eager to do the business of governing
> themselves. In fact, they were shamelessly eager. They could
> have been somewhat more patient, for their own personal
> advantage. They might not have needed to be patient for
> too long. Mr Jinnah would either have called them back to
> keep him company or they would have known how to make
> him go, if he acted too hurtfully. Congress leaders did not
> have at this time even that little patience, which is necessary
> for all selfish interest of a somewhat big size. Not only did
> they put their personal interest before the national interest,
> but they had also become incapable of striving for some
> big-size selfishness, if that meant sacrificing an immediate
> personal interest, however small it may be.

Such was the tearing hurry to accept partition that Congress
leaders had no time to consider precautionary measures that would
be required to maintain minimal law and order. What followed
Independence was no ordinary breakdown of order but rather
communal riots, carnage and arson on an unprecedented scale.
It resulted in more than 14 million people being uprooted and
between 1 and 2 million being killed. As Khushwant Singh writes
in *Train to Pakistan* about partition, 'Hundreds of thousands of
Hindus and Sikhs who had lived for centuries on the North West
Frontier abandoned their homes and fled towards the protection
of the predominantly Sikh and Hindu communities in the East—
they collided with panicky swarms of Muslims fleeing to safety
in the West... By the time the monsoon broke almost a million
of them were dead and all of northern India was carrying arms,

in terror or in hiding.'

A suggestion that a neutral army and police force be maintained for peace in the early days of Partition was overruled by a majority of Congress leaders. Nehru and Patel opposed it, of course, but not as vehemently as Dr Rajendra Prasad who emphatically opposed a unified army 'even for a day'. Why this extreme aversion to a joint army, 'even for a day'? Because Congress leaders were eager to seal Partition. They wished to leave no room for the issue to be re-opened. Leaders who otherwise stood on a platform of a united India were now adamant that the army must be instantly partitioned just in case a united army signalled the Congress's ambivalence on the question of Partition.

The undivided Indian army had remained untouched by the politics of religion. But once it was hurriedly divided on communal lines, a communal poison was injected into the army. When, after 15 August, the blood of innocent men and women flowed on both sides of the frontier, 'the army remained passive spectators'. Let us have the tragedy described in Maulana Azad's words:

> Lord Mountbatten said to me more in sorrow than in anger that Indian members of the army wanted to take part in [the] killing [of] Muslims in East Punjab, but the British officers restrained them with great difficulty. This, however, I know from personal knowledge that members of the former undivided Indian army killed Hindus and Sikhs in Pakistan and Muslims in India.

Not only were Congress leaders eager to wield power in Delhi, they very quickly lost interest in keeping up the pretence that partition had been imposed on them. They made it look like their first choice. Having brazenly embraced partition, the Congress Working Committee then watched the consequences of this decision from the sidelines. For decades thereafter, the blame for Partition was heaped on Indian Muslims.

Did Nehru not know that there was not a single member in

the senior echelons of the party (who later served in his Cabinet) who had any sympathy for the 90 million Muslims (at the time of Independence) who were to be left behind in India? Take the home minister, Vallabhbhai Patel, for instance. Lord Archibald Wavell made the following entry about him on 17 March 1947 in his book *The Viceroy's Journal*: 'He is entirely communal and has no sense of compromise or generosity towards Muslims, but he is more of a man than most of the Hindu politicians.'

Michael Brecher in his biography of Nehru is equally blunt: 'Patel was a staunch Hindu by upbringing and conviction. He never really trusted the Muslims and supported the extremist Hindu Mahasabha view of the 'natural right of the Hindus to rule India.' How did Nehru ever imagine that an India partitioned on Hindu–Muslim lines would, somehow, remain secular? Because that is what would make him feel good about himself? Such self delusion.

In the post-Partition mayhem, as Muslims were being massacred, Mahatma Gandhi and Nehru were unhappy with the inadequate police arrangements in Delhi. Patel thought otherwise. He said that the reports were 'grossly exaggerated'. When Gandhiji supported Nehru, Patel lost his temper. He said the situation in Delhi 'was being competently handled. He would not tolerate any further criticism'. He packed his bags and left for Bombay in a huff.

'What is the use of my staying?' he said when he realized Gandhiji was not prepared to listen. 'He [Gandhiji] seems determined to blacken the name of the Hindus before the whole world.' Patel was emphatic: he was concerned about the image of 'Hindus' not 'Indians'.

In fact, to explain police inaction to protect Muslims, Patel put out a story that 'deadly weapons' had been discovered in the Muslim quarters of Delhi. Azad describes this in his book. Patel's insinuation was that 'if the Hindus and the Sikhs had not taken the first offensive, the Muslims would have destroyed them.' Muslims were very well armed.

As proof, Sardar Patel ordered arms recovered by the police from Karol Bagh and Sabzi Mandi to be brought to the Government House and kept in the ante chamber of the cabinet room. This evidence was to be examined by Lord Mountbatten and the Union cabinet. Dozens of rusted kitchen knives, pocket knives, spikes and fences from old houses and cast iron water pipes were piled on a table. Mountbatten was amused at the exhibition. The Viceroy smiled and remarked that if they had really expected to take Delhi with pen knives then they had an incredible sense of military strategy.

Patel, it turns out, may well have established the pattern for the future. In all Hindu–Muslim conflicts, it would be put out that Muslims were well armed. Subsequently, in cases of communal violence, 'arms' would inevitably be found with the Muslims. These were the earliest signals given out to the police force of independent India. Today, this is usually the knee-jerk response of the country's police force towards the Indian Muslim. In cases of alleged terrorism and communal violence, ready-made evidence will be found heaped upon him.

So overwhelming was the trauma of Partition that reputations remained unscrutinized except at the personal level—as was the case among my elders in Mustafabad. Icons only began to be questioned after the publication of the Maulana's 'thirty pages'. Twelve volumes of the Transfer of Power papers (covering the period from 1942 to 1947), published in Britain under the editorship of the distinguished historian Professor Nicholas Mansergh, added to this. This was also when Professor Philip Ziegler's official biography of Mountbatten and Ayesha Jalal's *The Sole Spokesman* opened up the whole issue of the 'guilty men who partitioned India'.

After all this new scholarship saw the light of day, writers like Arun Shourie tried to pile all the guilt on Jinnah. Shourie wrote three articles in the October and November issues of the *Illustrated Weekly of India* on Jinnah 'the man who broke up India'.

He placed on Jinnah the entire burden of mixing 'religion with politics'. Distinguished jurist H. M. Seervai took Shourie to task in his masterly analysis *Partition of India: Legend and Reality*. It was Mahatma Gandhi who, admittedly, 'introduced religion into politics' against Jinnah's advice.

～

Maulana Azad's testimony about the reality of partition is valuable because few leaders command as much credibility. The premium Nehru placed on the Maulana's qualities of head and heart was enormous. Nehru's deep respect for the Maulana as a loyal friend and intellectual comes out clearly in the letters he wrote to Indira Gandhi from Ahmadnagar Jail, including his intention to learn Urdu and Persian poetry from the Maulana, 'an ideal teacher, except that he is too erudite'. But, as we have seen, the Maulana felt betrayed when Nehru lined up with Patel and others to accept the partition of India on 3 June 1947.

Dramatic irony attends Maulana Azad's role in the proceedings after the acceptance of the partition plan. In a letter to Nehru on 24 July 1947, Gandhiji suggested that Maulana Azad need not be accommodated in the Cabinet. My guess is that the suggestion had its roots in the fact that many leaders were uncomfortable with the Maulana's vocal discomfort with the enthusiasm with which the Congress had accepted partition.

Let me quote the letter from Gandhiji that his biographer Pyarelal records.

Dear Jawaharlal,

I did not say anything yesterday about the Maulana Saheb. But my objection stands. His retiring from the cabinet should not affect our connection with him. There are many positions which he can occupy in public life without any harm to any cause. Sardar is decidedly against his membership in the cabinet and so is Rajkumari. Your cabinet must be strong and effective at the present juncture. It should not be difficult to name another Muslim for the cabinet.

I have destroyed the two copies you sent me yesterday.

Blessings
from Bapu

This is a startling letter. Gandhiji had always shown considerable respect for the Maulana. Despite the austerities Gandhiji imposed on living conditions at the Sewagram Ashram, he made exceptions for Maulana Azad. To the surprise of many ashramites, Gandhiji allowed an ashtray—the Maulana was a chain smoker—in his cottage during Congress meetings. Even so, the devaluation of the Maulana in national affairs was sharp once partition had been achieved.

Note Gandhiji's tone in his letter to Nehru—'it should not be difficult to name another Muslim' for India's first cabinet. Gandhiji is quite clear. All that Nehru needs to keep up the secular pretence is to have a token Muslim in his cabinet. How different is this tokenism from the one in vogue all the years since 1947?

⤳

Gandhiji's introduction of religion into Indian public life was in stark contrast to the Ganga-Jamuni composite culture that we in Mustafabad found so attractive in Nehru. It was Nehru's endorsement of 'Bapu' that imparted to Gandhiji an aura in our eyes. We were vehemently opposed to Muslim religious leaders. How could the Mahatma's brand of politics have appealed to us?

We derived our pride from Mir Anis and Ghalib: the Mahatma was not conversant with their persona. Nehru befriended Urdu poets and scholars. He wrote to Indira Gandhi from jail that he intended to learn Urdu and Persian poetry from Maulana Azad. It was this aspect of Maulana Azad that elevated him in the eyes of the Urdu elite, not his mastery of the Quran. His writings in *Ghubar-e-Khatir* (Sallies of the Mind) were considered the most elevated form of Urdu, punctuated with choice Persian verses. His lyrical description of playing the sitar in front of the Taj Mahal during a full moon gave glimpses of the aesthete in him. How much of him could Gandhiji have appreciated? Nor was Gandhiji comfortable with the westernized cosmopolitan Muslim elite that Jinnah represented. He identified himself with the Muslim archetype who was the counterpart to the conservative Hindu archetype that he most identified with, the Hindu who was draped in a dhoti, drank goat's milk and revelled in bhajan and kirtan. I am not in any way suggesting that Gandhiji did not fight sectarianism whenever he found it, I am simply pointing to the belief system he was most comfortable with.

The Mahatma understood leaders like Mohammad Ali and Shaukat Ali, and their fight to preserve the institution of Khilafat (Caliphate) in Turkey. Gandhiji supported this movement. In *Young India* of 20 October 1921, Gandhiji explained his support for Khilafat:

> I claim that with us both the Khilafat is the central fact; with Maulana Mohammad Ali because it is his religion, with me because in laying down my life for Khilafat, I ensure the safety of the cow, that is my religion, from the Mussalman knife.

Was this not a rather obscurantist way to cement Hindu–Muslim unity?

Sunnis were the overwhelming majority among Indian Muslims. Shias—the intellectual and feudal aristocracy among Muslims—were totally indifferent to the call for Khilafat. In fact, the movement was lampooned:

> Boli amma Muhammad Ali ki
> Jaan beta khilafat pe de do.

> (Muhammad Ali's mother has given the call.
> Son, sacrifice your life for the cause of Khilafat.)

Abdulmecid II was both Ottoman Sultan and Caliph from 1922

to 1924. After the Ottomans lost World War I, the valiant Turkish military officer who led modern Turkey to victory, Mustafa Kemal Pasha Ataturk, would go down in history as the father of the Turkish nation. As part of his drive to build Turkey into a modern, secular nation, he disbanded the decaying institution of the Caliphate. Gandhiji and his friend Mohammad Ali Jauhar, the one who launched the Khilafat movement in India, were caught flat-footed. It was ironical that the Turks had disbanded an anachronistic system which Muslim religious leaders were still holding onto. Nothing of what I have said about the Mahatma's brand of politics is meant to diminish the enormous sacrifices he made in the course of the national struggle or his relentless fight for Hindu–Muslim unity. The only point I am trying to make is that his view of Islam was not the same as the Islam we lived.

He was not a creature of the Hindu–Muslim composite culture we were most comfortable with. No leader other than Nehru was. Our anguish has to do with the fact that Nehru must have known how Congress leaders felt about Muslims who would be in India after partition.

∽

A year after India gained independence one would have expected remorse to have set in among the Congress leadership. But, during and after 'police action' (in reality military action) in Hyderabad, a brazenly anti-Muslim attitude surfaced. The Nizam of Hyderabad had refused to surrender sovereignty to the new nation which outraged Congress leaders. These were the very same leaders who had talked of a secular state and were opposed to the two-nation theory. But in the immediate aftermath of Partition they were beginning to fear the idea of a 'Muslim State' of Hyderabad in 'Hindu India'. Patel called it a 'cancer' in the heart of India.

Nehru signalled for a division of the Indian Army, under Major General J. N. Choudhuri, to march in and take over Hyderabad in September 1948. The immediate pretext for military action

were the misdeeds of members of the powerful Razakar militia—
the armed wing of Hyderabad's most powerful separatist Muslim
political party aligned with the Nizam—who were terrorizing
Hindu villagers. The Indian troops defeated the Nizam's forces
within days. According to official estimates, the massacre of
Muslims that followed took the lives of more than 40,000. The
stories of atrocities committed are horrifying. This is the estimate
of the report of the fact-finding team under the chairmanship
of Pandit Sunderlal. A 2015 BBC documentary revealed that the
government (Nehru and Patel) tried to suppress the publication of
the report, a fact echoed by the jurist and writer A. G. Noorani
in his book *The Destruction of Hyderabad*. Once again, Nehru
demonstrated his helplessness, or was it acquiescence?

The military action took place at a time when the communist-
led secular Telangana movement against the Nizam's feudal
excesses was mobilizing Muslims and Hindus alike. The Nizam
was terrified of the 'peoples' armed struggle' and would not
have minded New Delhi's help to squash the armed agrarian
movement. But instead of selecting its targets carefully, the Indian
troops turned upon the left movement as well as supporters of
the Razakars resisting Indian forces. The troops may not have
had a hand in the massacre of Muslims that followed, but there
were instances where the army facilitated these massacres by
remaining neutral when Muslims were being killed and their
properties destroyed.

The veteran CPI(M) leader P. Sundarayya's book, *Telangana
People's Struggle and Its Lessons*, provides insights: 'It is to be
noted that the Union armies rescued the very Deshmukhs [sic]
and Razakar leader Kasim Razvi who were responsible for setting
fire to village after village and also for the killing of hundreds
of people. At the same time, the ordinary Muslims, who stood
against the atrocities of the Nizam, were pounced upon and untold
miseries inflicted on them. The Hindus in those villages rescued
such ordinary people to the extent possible, gave shelter to them

in their houses and rescued thousands of Muslim families from the campaign of rape and murder indulged in by the Union armies.' Obviously class conflict had got hopelessly mixed up with a massacre, mostly of Muslims, on New Delhi's instructions.

According to Sundarayya, 'the Telangana movement can take pride in this important achievement, namely, Hindu–Muslim unity in the villages. Just at a time when Hindu–Muslim riots could have been sparked off and could have spread like wild fire. In other parts of Hyderabad state, where the democratic movement was weak, hatred against Muslims and attacks on them were widespread.' It was in these areas that the massacre of Muslims took place on an unprecedented scale. RSS, Hindu Mahasabha and Arya Samaj groups from neighbouring states took advantage of the army's presence and fell upon the hapless Muslims in the rural areas.

Can Nehru be condoned for the killing of Muslims in Hyderabad (and Jammu) so soon after the Partition holocaust? I dwell on this later.

ᔕ

The irony is that my great-grandmother, an avid reader of Urdu newspapers, thought 'Nehru was more ours than even Maulana Azad'. My great-uncle, Saiyed Mohammad Taqi Naqvi, the Abbajan of my narrative, identified Nehru, not Maulana Azad, as the leader of Indian Muslims. He would sharply correct anyone less than respectful to the leader who eventually became India's first prime minister. Nehru's charisma kept millions of Indians in thrall. His proximity to Maulana Azad, Rafi Ahmad Kidwai, Dr Zakir Hussain, Mukhtar Ahmad Ansari, Dr Asaf Ali and others in the vanguard of the Indian renaissance, gave him considerable traction with the Muslim elite. Scions of the feudal order in decline were smitten by him quite as much as revolutionary Urdu poets. Even the revolutionary leader of the Telangana movement of the 1940s and 50s, Makhdoom Mohiuddin, was moved to write on

Nehru's death in 1964.

Woh shashjahat ka aseer
Nikal gaya hai bahut door, justjoo bun kar.

(Like an arrow, that prisoner of day and night,
Has shot into the distant spaces like aspiration.)

This was the esteem in which Nehru was held by Indian Muslims all these years. Imagine then the disillusionment that began to set in over time with the growing realization that even for Nehru, like all the other leaders, including the Mahatma, the secular project was negotiable.

FOUR

The Lessons of Meenakshipuram

IN FEBRUARY 1981, the obscure village of Meenakashipuram, about fifteen kilometres from Tenkasi, Tamil Nadu, shot into prominence because 558 of its Dalit inhabitants converted to Islam. I was with the *Indian Express* in Chennai at the time, and received instructions from the editor, Surendra Nihal Singh, to write on the mass conversions. Having been trained at my alma mater, *The Statesman*, to write balanced pieces, and not appear to be taking sides, I proceeded to do just that. My objectivity, on what was a sensitive issue, was understandably not appreciated by everyone.

The very next morning I found myself in the eye of a storm. Irathavan Mahadevan, executive director of the *Indian Express* and a brilliant scholar on the Indus Valley, came running down from his office upstairs, speechless with anger. I should have condemned the conversions, he stuttered; I should have chastised the Muslim groups responsible for it.

Meanwhile, in Express Estates, the publisher-proprietor of the paper, Ramnath Goenka, was bringing the plaster down from the ceiling. 'Hindu kahaan jaaye? Hindu kahaan jaaye? (Where should the Hindu go?)' He shook with rage: 'Tum to Makka chale jaao; Hindu kahaan jaaye? (You can go to Mecca, but where should the Hindu go?)'

K. Sambandam, the solitary non-Brahmin member of the editorial team, spread out Dravida newspapers on my desk to prove that the 'balance' in my editorial had been endorsed by the two Dravida parties. I had learnt the hard way that it is wiser to steer clear of these arguments. Many communal eruptions have intra-Hindu roots, an internal problem externalized.

I later came to understand that my editorial was used to build up a case against me by the then executive editor of the *Indian Express*, Arun Shourie. He even got a riposte written which however was not published. S. Nihal Singh, who was Shourie's boss at that time, shares this nugget in his memoirs, *Ink in my Veins*:

> My experience with Arun Shourie was not happy... To have to work with a hands-on editor who oversaw the news and editorial sections was an irksome burden for Shourie... My efforts were directed to making the *Express* a better paper, while he was basically a pamphleteer who was ideologically close to the Hindu right. Even while he oversaw a string of reporters' stories, which drew national attention (for which he claimed more credit than was his due), his aim was to spread the message [of Hindutva].

According to Nihal Singh,

> Goenka himself could be swayed by Hindu ideology. In one instance, he sent me a draft editorial from Madras full of all the clichés of the Hindu right. One of Goenka's men in the southern city was S. Gurumurthy, a sympathizer of the Rashtriya Swayamsevak Sangh (RSS), a pro-Hindu organization. The issue was the mass conversion of Harijans to Islam at Meenakshipuram (in Tamil Nadu)... I put two and two together and it added up to Gurumurthy's handiwork. I threw the editorial into the wastepaper basket. And I did not hear a word about it from Goenka.

⌣

The 1981 Meenakshipuram conversions happened when the communal cauldron was bubbling over on account of other factors—the insurgency in Punjab, Zia ul Haq's Nizam-e-Mustafa

(Islamic Rule) in Pakistan, the social imbalance caused by petro dollar remittances from the Gulf and the appearance of garish Dubai houses in Kerala. Conversions only served to ignite the fire.

Meenakshipuram was unique in the sense that no conversion to Islam in such large numbers had taken place in the past. Were the conversions financed by Dubai remittances? Were other incentives offered? Or was it organized to protest caste oppression?

Journalists took the issue to the converted groups in Meenakshipuram. 'Forcible conversion?' Madar Sahib, who changed his faith at Meenakshipuram when he was forty, would scream in anger. 'Yes, I was forced by the upper-caste Hindus to run away from a system that treated me like a street dog.' Madar Sahib 'defected' from an unfair system, it was not religious conversion. Madar Sahib was referring to the oppression of the Thevar community, which has been given the status of Most Backward Class in Tamil Nadu. Thevars consider themselves above the Dalits in the caste pyramid and so, when the latter made some economic progress, the Thevars retaliated by inflicting atrocities upon them.

The more oppressed a community, the greater its tendency to fall back on its larger myths. The more economically disadvantaged a Muslim, the greater his inclination to trace direct descent from Akbar the Great. This, in turn, invites an aggressive reaction from the majority community. Had Meenakshipuram happened in the heart of north India, the ramifications would have been different. The Muslim presence in north India has been portrayed as aggressive and dominant. The situation is different in the south. The Labbais, or Tamil-speaking Muslims, who settled on the east coast, mainly in districts like Kanyakumari, Tirunelveli and Ramanathapuram, are today among the most prosperous in the state, controlling, among other things, the leather industry, hotel chains and the dubious black market in Southeast Asia. Similarly, the Navayats who spread out from the Konkan and Kerala coasts are thriving businessmen. The per capita income of Muslims in Karnataka is much higher than that of their counterparts in the north.

Muslims in the south did not come as conquerors: they came as traders. It would hardly have been good business to go about proselytizing. They identified themselves totally with the language and culture of the area of their trade. They spoke the regional languages in which they have also produced great literature and music. The fruit of such cultural assimilation has promoted considerable social harmony.

The Meenakshipuram conversions received enormous media attention at the time. They became something of a watershed in the history of conversions. But there is no evidence that this remote Tamil village signalled a trend. While caste Hindus watched this battle from a distance, a Muslim group called the South Indian Islamic Society moved in stealthily with words of sympathy, perhaps not altogether altruistic. Proselytization was clearly the motive. After the Meenakshipuram conversions, some Arya Samaj groups screamed 'foreign money'. But the regional director of Scheduled Castes and Scheduled Tribes, after a visit to Meenakshipuram, cited 'untouchability' and the continued harassment of Dalits as the cause of the mass conversion.

The occurrence reveals a good many things about rural Tamil society. But the points pertinent to my narrative are very different: (a) it was astonishing that mass conversions could take place in India without riots. Imagine this happening around Varanasi, Patna or Bhopal. There would most certainly have been communal tension. (b) Dalits found Islam an attractive alternative because Muslims in the south are not perceived as an oppressed lot. On the contrary, they are a thriving community. Who would join the Muslims' battered ranks in the north?

That said, the Meenakshipuram conversions are a useful point of departure to examine the furore over conversions that erupts from time to time—largely as a result of canny and often cynical political manoueuvring. Hindu leaders excoriate the fact that conversions take place while conveniently side-stepping the reasons for these conversions. One of the greatest leaders of the right is of course Atal Bihari Vajpayee and, unsurprisingly, he was one of the few to acknowledge the ills that beset Hindu society. He had visited Meenakshipuram and Ramanathapuram districts in 1981. Vajpayee was candid in his speech at Meenakshipuram about the caste prejudices that exist in Hindu society. 'There is no doubt,' he said, 'that our Hindu society suffers from many ills. Distinctions on the basis of birth and caste practised for centuries have not been wiped off. Social ills continue to accumulate. The momentum of reform was not carried forward. But our religion does not approve of such discrimination. Untouchability has no place in our religion... The temples must be open to all; wells must be used by all our brothers and sisters.'

But such a stance was rare. The rhetoric from right-wing leaders over conversions would ratchet up periodically over the subsequent decades. Christian missionaries were often the target of such vitriol. Even a leader like Vajpayee said he was deeply worried about the rash of conversions to Christianity in the tribal areas of Odisha, Madhya Pradesh and Chhattisgarh. Vajpayee called for a national debate on conversions. K. N. Govindacharya of the RSS dedicated himself to reclaiming those who had 'strayed' from the Hindu fold. What was disconcerting about all this was that there wasn't enough soul-searching within the Hindu community on the real reasons that had led to conversions.

This was not the first time that conversions were discussed at the national level—the topic had surfaced in the first decade of independence. During a debate in the Lok Sabha in the 1950s on foreign Christian missionaries, Home Minister Kailash Nath Katju said: 'If missionaries come to India only for evangelical work, then I commend to them the thought that they stop coming here.' The statement created a furore among Christian missionaries. Nehru asked Maulana Azad to manage the situation.

The Maulana wrote a letter to Cardinal Valerian Gracias in Bombay.

> Let me assure you that we are fully aware of the outstanding work foreign missionaries have done over the past 150 years in education and other humanitarian fields. For years, the East India Company was opposed to imparting education to Indians. It was a missionary society, which opened the first school and college to impart modern education to Indians. After India's independence, many missionary societies asked us if they would be allowed to continue their work and we encouraged them to continue the good work.
>
> The acceptable way for religious conversion is simple: if an adult reflects on the faith he has been born into and feels intellectually compelled to adopt another faith, he has all the protection in the Constitution to exercise his free choice. This kind of conversion is a function of proper balance between the heart and the mind.
>
> But there is another method of conversion: for social reasons or for a common cause, a large group of people make up their minds to defect from one religion to another. If each individual of this group were asked to explain why he left the faith of his forebears, I am certain he will not be able to give a reasonable explanation on the question of religion and truth. Such groups are usually composed of people who have no education, people who are singularly incapable of making up their minds on matters as serious as religious belief.

Mass conversions, according to the Maulana, 'cannot be called religious conversions'. Instead of conversion, this sort of a shift should be called by some other name. The Constituent Assembly called it 'mass conversions'. The Maulana settled the debate two generations ago. As I will show throughout this chapter, if this sort of reasonable approach was followed by leaders of all our religious organizations and political parties, the communalizing of the country would be sharply reduced. But communalization does not take place unthinkingly. It is a deliberate means towards an end of saffronized nation building. Of course, incendiary material has been lying around for such exploitation since 1857. It became more commonplace after 1947.

ᵕ

The Hindu anxiety, according to people like Vajpayee, has been singular: his tribe can always be denuded, not augmented. This is because there is no conversion in Sanathan dharma. A Hindu will always belong to the caste into which he is born. This is a centuries old system not easily amenable to reform. The Muslim, in this circumstance, must demonstrate sensitivity to a people who do not convert but can be converted. Ill-advised conversions must become a thing of the past. Conscientious objection, dissent and defection from a faith are individual decisions. Nothing worries the Hindu more than conversions. All proselytizing systems will have to be sensitive to the fact that Hindus seek to convert nobody. Whether this is a strength or a weakness is not the question. The important fact is that Hindustan is the Hindu's home as it is the home of Indian Muslims, and there must be mutual respect between the two. That said, nobody disputes the fact that some aspects of Hinduism need reform. If these reforms do take place there will be even less cause for 'genuine' conversions. Any such reforms of Hinduism must necessarily come from within.

There have been different Hindu reform movements through Indian history that sought to eradicate oppressive and regressive practices of Hindu society, such as caste discrimination, the practice of Sati, child marriage, etc. Many of these movements began during the colonial period led by prominent reformers like Raja Ram Mohan Roy. Roy founded the Brahmo Samaj in 1828 and propagated ideas like the worshipping of one god, the education of women, and most importantly, the abolishment of

Sati, the practice of a wife immolating herself on her husband's pyre. Other influential and prominent movements included the Arya Samaj, started by Dayanand Saraswati, whose most important contribution to reform was the Shuddhi movement wherein low-caste Hindus who had converted to Islam and Christianity were readmitted into the Hindu fold.

Besides the Arya Samaj and the Brahmo Samaj, important reform movements were begun by organizations like the Manav Dharma Sabha, Paramahansa Mandali, Prarthana Samaj, etc. Most of these organizations were started during the British period and had a huge impact on Indian society of the time. Let me touch upon a few of them to illustrate how they focused on redressing social ills rather than politicizing the process and corrupting the whole idea of reform.

The Manav Dharma Sabha was started in Surat on 22 June 1844. Mehtaji Durgaram Manchharam was one of the prominent figures of this organization. The main reason behind the founding of the organization was the conversion of a Parsi student, Nasarwanji Manakji, to Hinduism. After a huge debate and controversy that continued for twenty days, Manakji recanted and was readmitted to the Parsi fold. However, the event encouraged Durgaram and a few of his friends to establish the Manav Dharma Sabha. The Manav Dharma Sabha rejected 'the existence of ghosts, their exorcism by means of incantations, the evils of early marriage and the bar against remarriage of high caste Hindu widows'. The Sabha also challenged magicians and the reciters of incantations to demonstrate their skills. Though the organization criticized the caste system, it did not take any direct action against this institution.

Another prominent reform-minded organization of the twentieth century was the Paramahansa Mandali which inveighed against the caste system and followed two major principles. The principles were that the Mandali would not attack any religion and would reject any religion which claimed that it had 'the infallible record of God's revelation to man'. The Mandali also rejected idols, orthodox rituals and Brahminical authority.

Established in 1867 to change the religious and social life of Maharashtra, the Prarthana Samaj drew its inspiration from the Paramahansa Mandali and was also influenced by Keshab Chandra Sen. Sen's visit to Bombay in 1867 generated considerable enthusiasm among the English-educated elite of Maharashtra. Many members of the Samaj were directly involved with the Paramahansa Mandali and they carried the ideology of the society with them. The Prarthana Samaj showed a syncretistic acceptance of all religions. It was committed to worship one God and to seek truth in all religions. It also campaigned against sectarian conflict. The Samaj believed that no created being or object that was worshipped by any sect should be ridiculed or condemned.

Another reformist Hindu organization that deserves mention is the Veda Samaj in south India founded in 1864 by Sridharalu Naidu and Keshab Chandra Sen in Madras. The Veda Samaj accepted the theistic ideals of the Brahmo Samaj. The Samaj considered marriage and funeral rituals as 'matters of routine, destitute of all religious significance'. It also strongly spoke for 'discarding all sectarian views, of gradually abandoning caste distinctions, of tolerating the view of strangers and never offending anyone's feelings'. Opposing polygamy and child marriage and campaigning for widow remarriage were some of the most important features of the Veda Samaj movement.

Most of the Hindu reform movements of the period were started to wipe out the conflict between Brahmins and non-Brahmins in the larger Hindu community as well as erase the inequalities and divisions created by the caste system. Eliminating retrograde practices like Sati, child marriage, dowry, polygamy, etc. were also some of the other prominent objectives of Hindu reform movements of the nineteenth and early twentieth century. Today, however, Hindu organizations seem more interested in re-converting those who have left the fold, and changing the very nature of Hinduism, rather than looking to any genuine reform of ills within the community. Many of the objectives of such organizations are overtly political and seem to have no interest in bettering the lot of Hindus.

⌐

The only way to put an end to the friction and divisions of this business of conversions and counter-conversions (the infamous 'ghar-wapsi' programmes) is to aggressively celebrate the syncretic culture that is endemic to this country of multiple, very old faiths. Let me illustrate this by sketching out an alternative scenario for a tendentious event that took place in the early nineties.

In December 1991, a decade after the Meenakshipuram conversions, Dr Murli Manohar Joshi, who was the president of the BJP at the time, embarked on a high profile Ekta Yatra (or National Unity March) across the country. When Dr Joshi's Ekta Yatra was announced, I teased him by coming up with an itinerary of my own. I said I would persuade friends to join his Ekta Yatra if he accepted alterations in his travel plan. I accepted his starting point—Kanyakumari, symbolically India's southern tip, which neighbours Kerala, the first state he was to travel through for any length of time. And, after all, it was in Kerala that Adi Shankaracharya began his epic journey, and there is nothing wrong with political leaders imitating great men.

I then suggested that Joshi should dwell a little longer in this marvellous stretch of land between the Western Ghats and the Arabian Sea because I cannot think of any place in the world which has accorded hospitality to more religions than Kerala. Christianity flourished here when our cousins in Europe were still rather behind by any measure. It was and continues to be Christianity in an Indian mould—marriages cannot be solemnized without the bride wearing the traditional thali. Why, even that new theology of our times—communism—was given entry into Kerala for the first time in the world through the ballot box, in 1957.

The rest of my suggested itinerary for Dr Joshi went something like this:

Once you have soaked in the Catholicism of this wonderful stretch, I would urge you, Dr Joshi, to make a short detour to the Cheraman Perumal mosque in Cranganore (Kodungallur), Trissur district. This mosque was built when Prophet Muhammad was still alive. Remember, there was no trace of Muslim rule in India then. Relations between us and the Arab world pre-dated Islam by thousands of years. After this detour, you should visit Calicut and find time for a Muslim guru in the classical Brahminical mould, C. N. Ahmad Mouli. He will show you copies of ancient newspapers published in Arabic and Malayalam. He will also furnish proof that the columns in Kaaba (Mecca) are made of teak from Kerala; the Kaaba, as one should know, predates Islam by thousands of years.

Since you are touching Kottayam, I thought that you, as BJP president, should make the pilgrimage to Lord Ayyappa's shrine in Sabarimala. (It is my belief that to discover the pure and secular soul of India one should go on these wonderful pilgrimages—to Sheikh Moinuddin Chishti's shrine in Ajmer, or Shravanbelagola, which is in Hassan district, Karnataka, and an important religious destination for Jains.) On the way to Sabarimala you will be required to obtain vibhuti from the shrine of the Muslim saint, Vavar Swamy, before you have Ayyappa's darshan. Incidentally, the best songs dedicated to Vavar Swamy have been sung by Yesudas—a Christian singer and an Ayyappa bhakt.

I see you are visiting Coimbatore as L. K. Advani did some years ago to address RSS volunteers. Advani's theme was: if Indonesian Muslims identify themselves with Ram, why do Indian Muslims identify themselves with Babur? This, to my mind, was a non sequitur. How can you compare Ram, a Hindu deity, with Babur, a king, a fleeting monarch? I suppose Advani was not familiar with verses like:

Hai Ram ke wajood pe Hindustan ko naaz;
Ehle nazar samajhte hain usko Imam-e-Hind.

(The very being of Ram, is the pride of Hindustan;
Men of vision respect him as the Imam of Hindustan.)

That was Iqbal on the son of King Dashrath. There are scores of others. All Indians can lay claim to Ram, how can he even be compared to a mere emperor?

Since your journey is being billed as the Ekta Yatra, I urge you, Dr Joshi, to pause at the point of confluence between coastal Andhra, Rayalaseema and the Telangana areas of Andhra Pradesh. Do visit Kuchipudi, known for its eponymous dance form. And, if you discover that the entire settlement owes its origin to Ibrahim Qutb Shah, do announce it to the nation. Such details are a casualty of contemporary amnesia which, admittedly, afflicts Muslims more than it does Hindus. Muslims, under the spell of the clergy, are embarrassed that Muslim rulers patronized dance, indeed all the arts. In fact, one of the contributions of Muslim rulers was to extend patronage to all art forms. Faith devoid of aesthetics is the drab contribution of Islamic reform schools.

By the time you traverse Maharashtra you will discover the mellow influence of poets inspired by Bhakti and Sufism. Do take in the shrine of Shah Sharif outside Aurangabad. One of Shivaji's ancestors was his devotee—in fact, he named his sons Shahji and Sharifji as an act of respect to the Haji Malang in Thana. Please pay a visit to a somewhat different genre, the Mother Mary Church in Mahim, at which all faiths worship. In Pirana, Gujarat, stands the shrine of Imam Shah Baba that was once looked after by the Hindu Patels. There are revivalist groups trying to tarnish the old piety but a tussle is still on between those trying to retain the composite culture of these shrines and those opposed to it.

In Kutch, you will see the very essence of our syncretic traditions in the lives of the Garasia and the Fakirani Jats—Muslims with faith in the Hindu Mother Goddess. In Rajasthan,

I would take you to the temple of Goga Merhi in Ganganagar, which has 'Praise be to Allah' inscribed in Arabic on its gate. For eleven generations the pujari of the temple has been a Muslim. In Jaisalmer, the Manganiars and the Langas, both Muslims, sing Meera Bai, Bulleh Shah and Shah Abdul Lateef with the same devotion as the Meos of Alwar and Bharatpur sing their version of the Mahabharata or ballads devoted to Hazrat Ali. Syncretism in all these places is being challenged because religious intolerance is increasing.

You will introduce great credibility into your Ekta Yatra if you could somehow skip Ayodhya. Let this issue be in cold storage. Dr Joshi, you should concentrate instead on places and things that bind us. Passing through Awadh and Braj, examine the literatures of these regions. Visit the ancient town of Jais, not far from my own village, and reflect on Malik Muhammad Jayasi's *Padmavat*. Look how the great poet compared Padmavati's eyebrows to the bows of Krishna and Arjun. Go to Vrindavan and let the entire congregation around your rath chant Raskhan's verses about the naughty boy from Gokul. The real name of this great Krishna bhakt was Sayyidd Ibrahim. And while many in Braj may have forgotten Raskhan, there are people in Orissa who to this day welcome Jagannath with songs written by Salbeg, a Muslim by birth.

Yes, do visit Kashmir, but not to hoist the national flag—not quite yet (Joshi's Ekta Yatra culminated in the hoisting of the national flag in Lal Chowk, Srinagar). Let us sincerely examine what has gone wrong with our handling of Kashmir, and when we dwell on terrorism let us not ignore state-sponsored terrorism. Don't forget that the Sufi order of the Kashmir Valley called itself the Rishis. It was founded by Nuruddin Wali, popularly known as Nund Rishi. His songs dedicated to the great yogini Lalleshwari or Lal Ded are at the very heart of Kashmir's composite culture. The Rishis were avowedly spiritual heirs of Hindu asceticism and Advaita Shaivism. Where has it fled, that visionary gleam? And yes, I have not even mentioned Adam Malik from Batkote village in Pahalgam who discovered the Amarnath shrine. To this day, one third of the proceeds from the shrine go to the descendants of Adam Malik.

If this syncretic India is your theme, and your itinerary, we shall be with you in what will then be a truly glorious mission for Bharat Ekta, now or at any time in the future.

FIVE

The Breaking of the Babri Masjid

THROUGHOUT HISTORY, PLACES of worship have been destroyed or constructed as a statement of assertion by the victorious. As has been said, times without number, the Babri Masjid in Ayodhya, Uttar Pradesh, was allegedly built circa 1528 by a nobleman, Mir Baqi, from the court of the first Mughal, Babur, as an act of conquest. That Babur never came this far is a separate story. There is evidence of it having been an explosive issue for a long time. As early as 1859, two years after the great uprising of 1857, the British colonial administration built a railing to separate the outer courtyard from the mosque. The status quo remained in place until 1949, when idols of Lord Ram were secretly placed in the mosque premises, allegedly by volunteers of the Hindu Mahasabha. This set in motion events that led to the demolition of the Babri Masjid on 6 December 1992 by a mob more than 100,000 strong, comprising mostly Hindu kar sevaks or volunteers, who literally swarmed up the structure with hammers, axes and grappling hooks, and brought down the dome of the mosque in a few hours. Police security, which had been set up in anticipation of religious violence, was vastly outnumbered by the crowds. The police could neither do very much nor did it make any effort.

The Babri Masjid demolition served as a shocking eye-opener for Indian Muslims. It destroyed whatever confidence the community had in the Indian political class and the political party which had governed the country for the greater part of the post-Independence era, namely the Congress. After the Babri

Masjid was brought down, Muslims began to reflect deeply on all the injustices that had been done to the community, beginning with Partition in 1947. They discussed promises that had been made and broken.

ᵔ

It all started as a brazen political project. In September 1990, in a bid to consolidate the Hindus, L. K. Advani embarked on a Rath Yatra from Somnath Temple in Gujarat to Ayodhya, demanding a Ram Mandir on the very spot where the Babri Masjid stood. The BJP claimed Lord Ram was born at the spot where the Babri Masjid was—a claim that was unsupported by verifiable historical fact. Those who believed that the Babri Masjid stood on the site of Ram's birth cited mythology to buttress their claims. All across the country, north of the Vindhyas, sectarian groups clashed. Saffron began to spread across the nation on a scale not seen before.

Unravelling the Ayodhya dispute was, for me, a personal pursuit. I realized there was much more history to it than sketchy newspaper reports conveyed. It was in 1855, during Wajid Ali Shah's rule, that a dispute arose in Ayodhya over Hanumangarhi—one of the most popular temples to Lord Hanuman in north India. Hindus believed that the ruins of a mosque was the site of an ancient Hanuman temple and started doing puja there. Aamir Ali, a nobleman of Bareilly, turned up in Ayodhya with a posse of soldiers to declare jihad on the Hindus. Aamir Ali's forces were overwhelmed by the larger Hindu congregation. The graves of Muslims who died in the clash still remain in the vicinity of the Babri Masjid. The Nawab's durbar in Lucknow remained strictly neutral in the dispute. This went down well with both Hindus and Muslims accustomed, during the reign of the Awadh nawabs, to peaceful co-existence. Nothing in the circumstances favoured self-appointed jihadis.

During this period, there was no live dispute at the Babri Masjid (Ram Janmabhoomi). But after the annexation of Awadh in

1856, and the exile of Wajid Ali Shah to Matia Burj that year, the new British administration placed a grill separating the built-up domes of the mosque and the forecourt or the chabutra where Lord Ram was supposed to have been born. Instead of conclusively settling a dispute, as the last king of Awadh had done in the case of Hanumangarhi, the British institutionalized the Mandir–Masjid issue by dividing the 1,500 square yard property almost exactly into half. It served the British purpose of 'divide and rule'. Remember Disraeli's speech in the British Parliament? Whenever riots were required to divide communities and consolidate British control that had been shaken after the joint Hindu–Muslim Revolt of 1857, they would revive the Mandir–Masjid dispute.

The Babri Masjid was neither an important enough mosque for the Muslim community nor even a remarkable architectural wonder to warrant the controversy surrounding it. When I first visited Ayodhya to cover the agitation, I was surprised that the mosque was there at all. The lanes of Ayodhya, lined with temples of all sizes, manned by saffron-robed sadhus, looked so patently Hindu. In that location a mosque—Babri Masjid—looked out of place. This was in contrast to Ayodhya's twin city, Faizabad, whose mosque was situated in what seemed to me a more appropriate context. This is nothing more than a personal observation and should be taken as such.

The communal picture changed after the demolition of the Babri Masjid. The insecurity of the Muslim grew with every passing year. The mosque was demolished on 6 December 1992, but the planning for the event had gone on for three years. It was a brilliant marketing strategy by Hindutva craftsmen who had outlined the project of casting bricks, some in silver and gold, to be consecrated in numerous temples of India, big and small, and eventually taken to Ayodhya in a procession for the construction of the Ram Temple. The project whipped up a furious awakening on the Ayodhya issue. The temple would have 108 pillars across two storeys sprawled over 270 feet, which would be its length, quite in harmony with its height of 125 feet.

The passage of the sanctified 275,000 shilas or bricks through towns and villages towards Ayodhya created strife en route. The Bhagalpur riot of 1989 was an exemplary consequence. I happened to be there when violence broke out on 24 October 1989. I heard of the Chanderi carnage and visited the place to see things for myself. The area was tense enough to warrant the appearance of Major G. P. S. Virk of the Jammu and Kashmir Light Infantry regiment. He took up position in Sabaur thana overseeing the contiguous settlements of Chanderi and Rajpur.

The two villages had a population of about 2,000 each. (Remember I am describing the scene as I saw it in 1989.) Rajpur had a ramshackle mosque which the Chanderi Muslims visited on Fridays. But because of the fear that a shila pujan procession would pass by, the Chanderi Muslims set up a small shack to serve as a mosque to avoid the risky journey across paddy fields to Rajpur for their Friday namaz.

The sight of the modest thatched mosque was resented by those high on the idea of sanctified bricks being carted to the site of the Ram Temple. The thatched mosque was not seen by the Hindu majority as a temporary structure for the security of Chanderi's hundred or so Muslims during the passage of the 'shilas'. It was seen as an act of defiance. Sensing danger, Major Virk shepherded the Muslims to the largest Muslim house in the village. To ensure security, he left a posse of policemen to keep watch.

Next morning when Virk returned, he was shocked. The policemen were missing. The safe house had been gutted. From Chanderi's hyacinth-covered central pond protruded human parts—hands, legs, heads. The people around the pond denied they had seen anything. When I walked towards them to ask they turned the other way.

Three years later came the Babri Masjid demolition. The first person to inform me that the mosque was being razed was the

Raja of Mehmoodabad, whom we address as Suleiman Mian. He sounded totally bewildered. I had had an inkling earlier that evening that something disastrous might happen when Arjun Singh, Union Minister for Human Resource Development, invited me to his Race Course Road residence on 4 December, two days before the demolition, and expressed his grave fears of what he thought would take place. 'The mosque is inadequately protected,' he warned. 'It can be pulled down because there are no arrangements to hold back the mob.'

I thought he was being alarmist. There had been an ongoing battle in the Congress party between Arjun Singh, the leader from the north, and Prime Minister P. V. Narasimha Rao, who was from the south. Since the majority of Congress MPs at the time were from the south, Rao saw north Indian Congressmen like Arjun Singh and Narayan Dutt Tiwari as adversaries. Here was a Congress prime minister for whom a Congress revival in the north was a threat to his political future.

Rao was also paranoid about the Brahmins' declining power nationally and within the Congress. This was another reason for him to instinctively checkmate Arjun Singh, a Thakur, from playing a larger role in north Indian politics. He was more comfortable playing the politics of accommodation with Atal Bihari Vajpayee, a Brahmin, even on the issue of Babri Masjid–Ram Janmabhoomi. When the demolition began, he and Home Minister Shankarrao Chavan did what they were best at—indulging in deep thought. When Chavan described Vajpayee as Rao's 'Guru', Vajpayee, with warm familiarity, called him 'Guru Ghantal' (Guru of Gurus). Lal Krishna Advani declared Rao the best prime minister since Lal Bahadur Shastri. As it turned out, these leaders of the BJP were the main beneficiaries of Rao's handling of the situation.

Vajpayee expressed anguish at the demolition but an intelligence video of his speech in Lucknow, given a day before the demolition (which surfaced in 2005 and was accessed by *Outlook* magazine), seems to suggest he was aware that it might happen. Speaking to kar sevaks, Vajpayee, in his trademark style, without any reference to the masjid, said, 'The Supreme Court has allowed bhajan–kirtan. One man cannot perform bhajan alone. And kirtan cannot be performed standing up. How long can we stand? Sharp stones are emerging from the ground. No one can sit on them. The ground has to be levelled (Zameen ko barabar karna padega).' The irony in his tone was unmistakable.

Vajpayee continued with his speech even as the crowd applauded: 'If yagya begins tomorrow there will be some construction...It is winter. There are those who have come from the south who are not used to this weather. For them, a shamiana will have to be put up...I do not know what will happen tomorrow...I wanted to go to Ayodhya but I was told to go to Delhi.'

This footage of Vajpayee's speech, recorded by intelligence, was surely available to Narasimha Rao. But the footage never saw the light of day for over twelve years. According to sources, it remained under wraps because someone at the highest level in the central government did not want it to be made public. Had the video been released, it would have been embarrassing for Vajpayee.

The destruction of the mosque sparked outrage among Muslims throughout the country, resulting in several months of communal rioting in which Hindus and Muslims attacked one another, burning and looting homes, shops and places of worship. Several BJP leaders were taken into custody, and the Vishwa Hindu Parishad (VHP) was briefly banned by the government. Despite this, the ensuing riots spread to cities like Bombay, Surat, Ahmedabad, Kanpur, Delhi and several other places, resulting in over 2,000 deaths, mainly of Muslims. The Bombay riots alone, which occurred in December 1992 and January 1993 in the aftermath of the demolition, and in which the Shiv Sena played a major role, caused the death of around 900 people, and property damage of around ₹9,000 crore.

For Indian Muslims, their place in Indian society changed radically after the Babri Masjid demolition. Imagine the pain Kaifi Azmi, the well-known poet, must have felt as he groped his way up the unlit staircase leading to the apartment of his mentor and friend, Ali Sardar Jafri, during the 1993 Bombay masscares. Jafri's Kemp's Corner apartment block was threatened by arsonists. Or take my friend Jawed Laiq's story. His father, Professor Nayyer Laiq Ahmad, had been principal of Bombay's Elphinstone College in the fifties, a historian with a catholic vision. His mother was a Congress MLA and among the earliest delegates to the Human Rights Commission in Geneva. During the Bombay riots, Jawed found himself in the entrance hall of his Churchgate apartment building, candle in one hand, a screwdriver in another, diligently pulling out the nameplate 'Prof N. L. Ahmad' so that arsonists and murderers would not find their way to his mother on the floor upstairs.

After the demolition and subsequent riots, covert dislike of Muslims in this country has become a lot more open and frequent. My daughter, Farah, returned after eight years of education in the US, with a much prized immigrant visa, the stepping stone to a green card, which she surrendered upon her return to India, saying that she was 'now home'. She would have a US visa stamped on her Indian passport if she needed to travel to the US. US Ambassador Frank Wisher had never seen anything like this—an Indian surrendering her right for permanent residence in the US. Many 'Bharat Mata ki jai' enthusiasts have their wards parked in the US. The ironic twist to the story came later. Farah began to work for Nirantar, an NGO dedicated to working among rural women. Returning from Banda in UP by train in the summer of 1993 she had her first encounter with the altered reality in the country. At one railway station, everyone around her in the train unanimously resisted the entry of a family which was quite obviously Muslim. Farah thought they had not been allowed to enter because the compartment was full until an anti-Muslim tirade picked up as soon as the train left the station. A kindly looking elderly man, noticing Farah's silence, offered her an apple which she gently refused. 'Lay lo bitiya, hum bhi to tumhare tarah Hindu hain, koi Mussalman to nahin hain (Take the apple, daughter. After all I am also a Hindu like you, not a Muslim.)'

The destruction of the Babri Masjid was responsible for several riots in the 1990s and after. After the Bombay bomb blasts of 12 March 1993, I was invited by senior editor Russi Karanjia and his friend Olga Tellis for dinner at the United Services Club in Cuffe Parade. On the way I tried to engage the taxi driver in conversation but he did not respond. I could sense that he was from UP—Pratapgarh or Allahabad. Many taxi drivers in Bombay are. I tried to allay his insecurity by saying that I was a Muslim. But he remained silent. As a last resort, I recited the Kalma to prove that I was indeed a Muslim. All I wanted to know from him was the Muslim response to the Bombay blasts. He parked his taxi near the kerb, looked at me with piercing eyes. He then smiled and introduced himself as Hanif (name changed) and shared with me a truth as he would with a long lost-friend. 'It had to be done,' he said. Slowly, this calm man began to explode. 'They pulled down the mosque—they began to beat Muslims, burnt their houses in Jhansi, Pratapgarh, Bhopal, Kanpur. As if that was not enough—they started it in Mumbai. Sharad Pawar was defence minister. Why didn't he send in the troops? Because he wished to score points over Chief Minister Sudhakar Naik.'

I was astonished. A diminutive taxi driver was now a political commentator. I asked him to continue. I was late for my appointment. 'Come with me in the suburban train,' he said 'and say "Assalam alaikum". They will all move back two steps. You will have your right of way.' When I narrated this story to

Russi Karanjia, he became beetroot red with rage. 'You should have delivered this man to the police,' he shouted. I told Russi that if injustice becomes law, people like Hanif would be part of the resistance.

All this and more came to pass because the Congress failed to read the signals building up to the demolition. Instead of gearing up the law and order machinery, the Congress got into a state of funk when the Ram Mandir movement gathered momentum in the late eighties. In 1989, it instructed Chief Minister Narayan Dutt Tiwari to arrange for the 'shilanyas' or stone laying ceremony of the Ram Mandir's outer walls at the disputed spot as demanded by the VHP. How could the Congress allow the laying of the foundation on a legally disputed spot? Publicly, the Congress denied permission because the courts had banned construction on this land. So the Congress government in UP cheated—it allowed the ceremony exactly where the VHP wanted it but asked officials to put out a story that it had not violated court orders and that the bricks had been laid on land which was not disputed. I was present on the spot to see this almighty fudge.

Those who blamed Prime Minister P. V. Narasimha Rao for having donned soft saffron during the Masjid demolition forget that the pro-Hindu strategy, inaugurated by Indira Gandhi during the Jammu elections in 1983, was patented by the Congress. Her son, Rajiv Gandhi, was no exception. During the Bhagalpur riots in 1989, Bihar's chief minister, Satyendra Narayan Singh, had removed the superintendent of police in Bhagalpur, Krishna Swaroop Dwivedi, because he had not been able to stop direct police involvement in the carnage that followed. When Rajiv Gandhi visited Bhagalpur he promptly reinstated Dwivedi.

Since 1984 his cousin Arun Nehru had taught him a mantra: we must not allow our Hindu support to drift away. Even before the shilanyas, Rajiv Gandhi had done something equally damaging. He kicked off the party's general election campaign in 1989 from Ayodhya promising 'Ram Rajya' in India. Rajiv Gandhi had actually promised to establish a 'government based on the principles of Lord Ram'. He thought he was stealing the Sangh Parivar's platform. It was within this framework that he allowed the temple's bricklaying ceremony to take place. This encouraged Hindu organizations to raise the bar a little higher. 'This is not the foundation of a temple; this is the foundation of Hindu Rashtra,' said Ashok Singhal of the VHP.

ʃ

On 9 November 1989, one of the wisest Congressmen I have known, Saiyid Nasir Hussain, sat in his office in the Faizabad mosque, contiguous with Ayodhya, holding his head in his hands and weeping: 'They have cheated the Muslims.' He then blurted out: 'The deal with the VHP was struck at the very top.' He knew what he was talking about. 'In UP the Congress is finished,' he declared. His words would prove prophetic.

In a move to pre-empt Hindu mobilization to liberate Ram's birthplace in Ayodhya, Prime Minister Rajiv Gandhi had ordered the locks of the Babri Masjid to be opened in 1986. This would allow Hindus to have 'darshan' or be able to see the Ram idols which were placed under the central dome of the mosque. Rajiv Gandhi was advised that by opening the locks of the Babri Masjid, he would kill two birds with one stone—he would defuse Hindutva mobilization and, at the same time, silence mounting criticism that he was appeasing Muslims on the Shah Bano issue.

The Shah Bano case was a landmark judgement in April 1985, in which the Supreme Court ruled that Muslim Personal Law could not stand in the way of Section 125 of the Criminal Procedure Code, which applied uniformly to all Indians, including Muslims. The issue was the case of Shah Bano, a sixty-two-year-old divorcee claiming maintenance, which Muslim Personal Law denied her. Conservative Muslim opinion was incensed at the court interfering in their Personal Law. Rajiv Gandhi decided to placate the Muslim vote bank. He put into force the Muslim

Women's Act of 1986. In defiance of the Supreme Court verdict, the new act restored the supremacy of Muslim Personal Law. There was uproar among Hindu and Muslim liberal groups.

With this retrogressive act, Rajiv ended up achieving exactly the opposite of what he had intended. He opened himself to the charge of appeasing Muslims. It was not just a charge but a fact: he was appeasing the clerics without having done the community a jot of good. Yes, the Muslim clerics could claim credit for confining Muslim women to their Personal Law. For this Rajiv Gandhi earned some brownie points among the mullahs, but liberal Muslims like Congressman Arif Mohammad Khan were isolated. To make matters worse, Rajiv tried to build bridges with Hindu hardliners on the Ram Temple issue.

Let us take a longer view. The mistakes perpetrated by the Congress had begun much earlier. The growth of the RSS in north India was not without Congress support. In the 1950s, Pandit Govind Ballabh Pant was not just the chief minister of the United Provinces but also a man close to Nehru. The genesis of the temple–mosque controversy in Ayodhya is owed to Pandit Govind Ballabh Pant who, in 1949, did not take action when the idols of Lord Ram 'mysteriously' appeared beneath the central dome of the Babri Masjid. Prime Minister Jawaharlal Nehru directed Pant to have the idols removed but the chief minister expressed his helplessness. The district magistrate of Ayodhya, K. K. Nair, refused to remove the idols and resigned from the Indian Civil Service. Now how does one explain Pant's sympathetic attitude towards the most important RSS leader to date—Guru Golwalkar? The first Home Secretary of UP, Rajeshwar Dayal, ICS, has in his book *A Life of Our Times* exposed the Congress-RSS collaboration.

Pandit G. B. Pant was chief minister from 1950–1954 when the RSS drew up a plan to cleanse Muslims from the areas around Muzaffarnagar in Western UP. By focusing on Muzaffarnagar as the point of ignition for communal polarization on the eve of the 2014 elections which brought Narendra Modi to power, Amit

Shah was only following an old script. According to Rajeshwar Dayal, RSS chief Golwalkar was directly involved in a 'diabolical plan to destroy Muslim economic power'.

Dayal records an episode of a very 'grave nature' about the UP Cabinet's indecision which resulted in dire consequences. When communal tension was at fever pitch, Dayal records, 'the Deputy Inspector General of Police of the Western Range, a very seasoned and capable officer, B. B. L. Jaitley, arrived at my house in great secrecy.' He was accompanied by two of his officers. They brought with them two large steel trunks, securely locked. When the trunks were opened, 'they revealed incontrovertible evidence of a dastardly conspiracy to create a communal holocaust throughout the Western districts of the province.' The trunks were 'crammed with blueprints of great accuracy and professionalism, of every town and village in that vast area'. Worse, they prominently marked out Muslim localities and habitations. There were detailed 'instructions regarding access to the various locations'. It all pointed to a heinous conspiracy. Alarmed by those revelations, Dayal immediately took the police party to the chief minister's house. There, in a closed room, Jaitley gave a full report of his discovery, backed by all the evidence contained in the steel trunks. Dayal notes that timely raids conducted on the 'premises of the RSS' had brought the massive conspiracy to light. 'The whole plot had been designed under the direction and supervision of the supremo of the organization himself. Both Jaitley and I pressed for the immediate arrest of the prime accused, Shri Golwalkar, who was still in the area.'

'Pantji' [the chief minister] could not doubt this evidence. But even so, instead of agreeing to the immediate arrest of the 'ringleader as we had hoped', he asked for the matter to be placed for consideration before the Cabinet at its next meeting. Dayal was under no illusion about what was going on. He wrote: 'There were also other political compulsions, as RSS sympathizers...were to be found in the Congress Party itself and even in the Cabinet.

It was no secret that the presiding officer of the Upper House, Atma Govind Kher, was himself an adherent and his sons were openly members of the RSS.'

At the Cabinet meeting which Pant had called to consider the evidence against Golwalkar, 'there was the usual procrastination and much irrelevant talk'. The fact that 'the police had unearthed a conspiracy which would have set the whole province in flames and that the officers concerned deserved warm commendation hardly seemed to figure in the discussion'. And what was the outcome of the deep deliberations of these worthies? A letter was to be written to Golwalkar 'pointing out the contents and nature of the evidence which had been gathered and demanding an explanation'.

In fact, Pantji asked Dayal to prepare a draft. He records with some irony: 'the letter was to be delivered forthwith and two police officers were assigned for the purpose.' But in the meantime Golwalkar had been tipped off. He escaped and was nowhere to be found. 'He was tracked down southwards but he managed to elude the couriers in pursuit.' This 'infructuous' chase continued from place to place and weeks passed.

Pant later became Union Home Minister in Nehru's Cabinet. Was Nehru complicit? Or are we to continue to grant him the benefit of the doubt?

In the style of Congress dynasties, Pant's son, K.C. Pant, rose to become Union Defence Minister. But, not inconsistently, he and his wife eventually joined the BJP. Of such stuff was the Congress aversion to 'communalism' made!

After the mayhem of the 1992 demolition and its aftermath, the Congress went back to its old drama of trying to convince Indian Muslims that it would protect them and care for them. Once again they were to be accorded the most favoured citizen status by the so-called secular state. This, it was felt, would take care of all the police excesses against them during the post-demolition disturbances—forty Muslims were shot dead by the police in Bombay and seventeen in Jaipur in the first days after the demolition on 6 December 1992. And there were similar such incidents across the country.

That these killings and violence were not prominently mentioned by secular newspapers of the secular state was said to be only in the interest of the Indian Muslim. It saved him the pain of knowing what was actually happening to him. Moreover, it was felt that front page displays of such excesses would only incite Muslims and the police forces to resort to more violence.

One of the most disturbing things about the actual demolition itself was something that you can see even today on a VHS tape of the incident made by *India Today*'s Newstrack divison. The tape opens with a shot of a group of frenzied kar sevaks threatening to drop a bomb on Pakistan and Bangladesh. Cut to a group of young ladies clapping themselves silly to a song: 'Ab yeh jhanda lehrayega saarey Pakistan pe (The saffron flag will flutter over the whole of Pakistan).' Then a swamiji with flowing hair makes a powerful speech: 'We must now go to Mathura, then Kashi, Lahore and Rawalpindi.' The camera then cuts to Bal Thackeray in Bombay. He is cool and unflappable as he speaks to the camera: 'I am the happiest man on earth with the fall of the Babri Masjid. Muslims can go to Pakistan if they like.'

Shockingly, none of the bhakts or their leaders make any mention of Ram, Ayodhya or a Hindu Rashtra; instead, there is a compulsive obsession with Pakistan. Here's why. The incantations about Pakistan were designed to taunt Indian Muslims who were identified as the Other—the hate objects and against whom the general frenzy of the Ayodhya mob was directed.

⁓

It is important to stay a little longer with the post Babri Masjid chaos to understand how the hard Hindutva–soft Hindutva dynamics which had afflicted the Congress from Independence onwards surfaced yet again. Parliament had been stalled and a bandh called in various parts of the country to protest the arrest of L. K. Advani and other BJP leaders for their alleged hand in the demolition of the masjid. The BJP protest seemed to imply that its leaders did not have a hand in the demolition. In other words, the demolition was the work of others at whose door the blame must lie. But there was an unmistakable impression that the BJP was rejoicing in the publicity that had been generated by the fall of the mosque and the subsequent arrest of its leaders. This was the political profit from the demolition. What the BJP was implying was this: we did not demolish the structure but we rather like the fact that it was demolished. We dissociate ourselves from the act of demolition but we would like to rejoice in this event in Indian history.

Let's examine the sequence of events.

On 7 December, a day after the demolition, the CBI charge sheets were brought before Vijay Verma, the special magistrate dealing with the Ayodhya case. Kalyan Singh, former chief minister of UP, appeared before the magistrate for the first time, as did one Pawan Pandey of the Shiv Sena. Pandey claimed he had helped destroy the mosque. From the debris of the mosque he had picked up the stone on which was engraved the name of Mir Baqi, Babur's general, who had allegedly built the Babri Masjid. Two days after the vandalism at Ayodhya, on 8 December, Advani and others were arrested and detained at Mata Tila, in Jhansi. The Lalitpur court unconditionally released them on 10 January 1993. The arrested leaders had not applied for bail.

The difference between Pawan Pandey and the BJP leaders was that he admitted to having participated in the vandalism at Ayodhya on 6 December. Oddly, there was no mention of Pawan Pandey or the party he belonged to (Shiv Sena) in any of the publicity generated by the demolition. He had admitted guilt but he was not given any publicity. In whose interest was it to provide the publicity only to the BJP leaders, and deny this little 'hero' his fair share?

When the charges against Advani and six others were brought before Special Magistrate Vijay Verma, the defence counsel for the BJP, K. K. Sood, argued that the BJP leaders had been released by the Lalitpur magistrate unconditionally on 10 January. They had not been released on bail as the prosecution was trying to make out. The special magistrate said that he would not alter the Lalitpur court's ruling. Kalyan Singh was not among the six BJP leaders freed by the Lalitpur court. Therefore, the special magistrate asked Kalyan Singh to furnish a personal bond of ₹1,000. Singh refused to furnish the bond. At this stage, Kalyan Singh stood a very good chance of being the sole martyr from among the BJP ranks. He would go to jail, and benefit from all the publicity!

The defence counsel for the BJP asked how Kalyan Singh could be sent to jail and the remaining six set free when the initial charges against the chief minister was the cause of their earlier detention. In other words, the defence was arguing that the ruling which set the six free was politically motivated—to deny them publicity—and they would, therefore, not accept it. Congress not sending them to jail was an act of malice. Advani and company had asked to be jailed so that they could get some publicity. The consequence of this turn of events was huge drama in Parliament.

Let me explain the competition between the Congress and the BJP which began on 4 October 1993 when the election campaign in UP was in full swing. On that day, when the courts in Lucknow were on strike, the CBI (P. V. Narasimha Rao was prime minister at the time) managed to get the special magistrate to file charges against the BJP leaders. But no challans were served on them. The idea was that publicity about the filing of charges would please the Muslims. This was sufficient for them. Challans not being served would give comfort to the BJP. Here was the typical

Congress sleight of hand: Sheikh bhi khush rahay, shaitan bhi naraz na ho (Please God and the Devil at the same time).

While the BJP was basking in all the attention in Parliament, one primary fact in the whole case deserved notice. The case filed in Special Magistrate Vijay Verma's court was not against the BJP at all. The case was listed as *State vs Bal Thackeray and Others*. Ironically, the redoubtable leader of the Shiv Sena was getting no publicity. Nor was poor Pawan Pandey who was screaming from rooftops that he actually helped bring down the Babri Masjid!

What was the outcome? The BJP got all the publicity whereas the case in the magistrate's court was against Bal Thackeray. You scratch my back, I scratch yours. This sort of coordination between the Congress and the BJP dates back to at least 1989. Remember the courts had ruled that the spot on which the VHP planned to lay the foundation stone of the Ram Temple was 'disputed land'. The government produced an order which said that the bricklaying ceremony was being permitted on land which was 'not disputed'. The truth was some BJP leaders had been taken into confidence: they would be allowed to perform the shilanyas on the spot in dispute, but the public posture would be that the government had persuaded the VHP to shift the venue for the shilanyas to an undisputed location. But Ashok Singhal called the bluff that very evening. 'The shilanyas had taken place exactly at the spot previously marked out by the Samiti.'

One final impression of the lamentable incident of 6 December 1992. Not only was the incident itself condemnable but the manner in which it took place was reprehensible. Let me be clear: the demolition of the Babri Masjid was not a pious, solemn act of faith; it was an assault by a frenzied mob in a black mood. At home, my wife's reaction was numbed horror. My mother hurriedly called a family meeting. There was a touch of déjà vu about this. I have gone through several such meetings in recent years: Ayodhya, after all, was the culmination of an extended process. But there was a major difference: this was no outpouring of religious fervour, it was a calculated political act.

ᔕ

In 1990, the Babri Masjid–Ram Janmabhoomi agitation was at its peak. The RSS was extremely angry with Prime Minister V. P. Singh for 'dividing Hindu society' by adopting the Mandal Commission report which promoted Other Backward Castes (OBCs), thereby promoting caste politics. The RSS's knee-jerk reaction was to seek the consolidation of the Hindu community by accelerating Hindu–Muslim polarization. For clarity I turned to the most important ideologue of the RSS at the time, Bhaurao Deoras. I owed this meeting to the former editor of the RSS mouthpiece *Organiser*, K. R. Malkani, a warm-hearted human being and a friend.

To get to Keshav Kunj, the four-storeyed office of the RSS in New Delhi, one has to go past the most congested streets of Karol Bagh facing the Jhandewalan Temple. Having negotiated the heavy mass of traffic and pedestrians that impeded our progress I entered the rather impressive building and met the then seventy-five-year-old Deoras in a first floor living room.

Deoras joined the RSS soon after it was founded in 1925. Though K. B. Hedgewar was the spirit behind the founding of the organization, it was M. S. Golwalkar who built the RSS into a nationwide organization of lathi-wielding aggressive Hindus. His book, *Bunch of Thoughts*, drew inspiration from Hitler's *Mein Kampf*. At the time of the interview, Balasaheb Deoras, the elder brother of Bhaurao Deoras, was the Sarsanghchalak or the Supremo of the organization.

Since Balasaheb Deoras had been ailing for the past few months, Bhaurao had emerged as the most important leader within the organization—his primary responsibility was coordinating the RSS's relations with the BJP and other political parties. The two-hour-long interview was conducted in English and Hindi. There were three of us in the room, including

K. R. Malkani. The transcript has been edited for the book, but what follows is a verbatim account of the conversation with Bhaurao Deoras.

Naqvi: Communal riots on an unprecedented scale have broken out in various parts of the country. What role can the RSS play to control the situation? Is the situation out of control?

Deoras: Who are the people behind these communal riots? I am afraid that some political parties are playing a role.

Naqvi: What is your plan—regarding the Babri Masjid?

Deoras: No Muslim goes to say his namaz there. All things around the mosque are connected with Hindu sentiments.

Naqvi: Do you believe that because of communal tension the Hindu mass is getting consolidated on the Ayodhya platform and in favour of the BJP?

Deoras: That is an important factor.

Naqvi: In other words, the benefits of the communal tension are going to the BJP? And he who benefits must have a hand in communal tension...

Deoras: I think Advaniji, by his Rath Yatra and the speeches he has given throughout the country [mobilised Hindu sentiments]. But not a word in his lectures...is anti-Muslim.

Naqvi: But look at the slogans going on in Aligarh, in Hyderabad. You are aware of the poison of Ms Uma Bharati's tapes [audio recordings of her speeches]. You know the kind of poison that is being spread is dividing the hearts and minds of the people. Are you going to sit back or avert another Partition in the minds of the people?

Deoras: What about the speech Mr Mulayam Singh Yadav gave? I do not know about the Muslim leaders. The Babri Masjid Action Committee must have their tapes. They may be speaking. I do not know what is going on in their minds.

Naqvi: Do the slogans contained in Ms Uma Bharati's tapes offend you?

Deoras: I do not like it.

Naqvi: Therefore you should stand up and condemn the provocative slogans.

Deoras: I do not like the meanings behind the slogans. At present, just as no Muslim will like to make a statement, I will also not like to do so.

Naqvi: Are you willing to issue a statement condemning the communal riots and condemn provocative slogans?

Deoras: Both Hindus and Muslims should condemn them together. Muslims had come here. It was I who arranged the meeting of Mr Javed Habib and some other people with the VHP. And the first meeting took place and they decided to meet again so that there should be an understanding.

Naqvi: To change the subject, do you endorse the two-nation theory on the basis of which Pakistan was found?

Deoras: We never accepted it.

Naqvi: So it follows that you will not accept Hindus and Muslims as two separate nations.

Deoras: We do not accept. It is one nation. From Kanyakumari to the Himalayas it is one nation.

Naqvi: You have not given up the agenda of Akhand Bharat?

Deoras: We have not given up. If the time comes we shall do it. We shall ask the Muslims in Pakistan—what have you gained? Muslims who went there from Bihar and UP—are they happy?

Naqvi: If you do not accept the two-nation theory then it follows that you accept the proposition that Hindus, Muslims, Sikhs and Christians in India should all live together and prosper together. Since you are allergic to the term secular let us find another term—India's composite culture.

Deoras: One culture—why do you say composite culture.

Naqvi: If you do not like the word 'composite' also then as an adjustment I am willing to delete it. I said composite because various streams have contributed to Indian culture.

Deoras: Say Bharatiya culture.

Naqvi: Okay, Bhartiya culture, Indian culture. There is a contradiction between your Akhand Bharat perspective and the Hindu Rashtra. Is there not a contradiction? Akhand Bharat is all-embracing from Kanyakumari to the Himalayas, but Hindu Rashtra further subdivides. What are we left with?

Deoras: Nation and state are two different concepts. States have equal rights, equal citizenship—that is the concept of state. This nation is not created by the British or anything. It is there from a long time, from Ram, from Krishna—thousands of years ago. The whole country had that concept of Ram, the concept of Krishna, the concept of Mahabharata, etc. Anywhere you go you will find the same thing. That is the binding thing. Culture was the binding factor throughout the country. There may be different kings, different rulers in the last 1,000 years or something like that...then the foreigners came and all that.

Naqvi: You have glided past a very important detail. Did we become independent after 200 years of British rule or have we become free after 1,000 years of foreign rule?

Deoras: I do not think that in many parts in our country Muslims really think that they were the rulers. There have been some Afghans, Turks and all those who came and invaded the country. They came and ruled the country.

Naqvi: They came and settled here.

Deoras: But they came and ruled and changed many of our people. Those who were Hindus—you may say downtrodden or something like that—changed their faith and they became Muslims. If they go back seven generations...probably they may say that they belong to this caste, they were Rajputs, they were this and that. So, they themselves know that they are Hindus and only in the last two or three generations have they become Muslims. But somehow, maybe Britishers fortified this feeling, Muslims living in this country at present feel that they were the rulers of this land. Why should they have any connection with Babur? He came from Central Asia.

Naqvi: Even your forefathers came from Central Asia—Aryans came from Central Asia?

Deoras: There is some controversy in this. That is now being contradicted. There are so many books contradicting this.

Naqvi: You mean Aryans did not come from anywhere?

Deoras: No, we have not.

Naqvi: So they just happened here, they simply sprouted here?

Deoras: Yes. The term Aryans and Adivasis, what is all this? Britishers have created this (looks irritable). Arya means not a caste, Arya means noble. There are enough books with documents that we are the original people who have been living here. Aryan theory, Dravidian theory, are all devised to break the Hindus.

Naqvi: Sir, if all the communities live and prosper together in India, then we constitute a threat to the basis of Pakistan. The success of Indian secularism is a threat to Pakistan which came into being on the assumption that we can't live together. Do you agree?

Deoras: I think Pakistan will go.

Naqvi: Let us go step by step (question is repeated).

Deoras: Bharat is all right. But as things are going in Pakistan, they have defeated Ms Benazir Bhutto, they are helping Khalistan elements in Punjab, the JKLF or whatever elements in Kashmir and all that. Unless this sort of government at the top goes in Pakistan, I think no change is possible at present. This will have to be changed.

Naqvi: How do we change that?

Deoras: The Hindu leadership should come [take control]. I do not know what will happen in Bangladesh. Leaderships may change but that may not help. I think during this Ershad regime, I have got the latest report that 1,100 temples have been destroyed.

I do not know when the elections are going to be held. Some Hindus in Bangladesh may fight elections. Very few of them will win. But suppose change comes in Bangladesh, tension will not be there and I think they can live in harmony. Then there is poverty and other problems, and they may say that there is no use of remaining separate let us join together. And if that happens then I think the atmosphere may change. Sindhi people in Pakistan, and those who have gone from UP and Bihar—what have they gained? They are not liked there. So, if these movements gather strength let us once again work for one Bharat.

Naqvi: Sir, that is only possible if you and I live in harmony. But if we clash in Aligarh, Ahmedabad, Ayodhya, the example we set is not attractive enough for others to emulate us. We are not setting the right example. On the contrary...

Deoras: Foreign powers are trying to create divisions and Muslims in major parts [of the country] are playing into their hands. There has to be reform in Muslim society in India.

Naqvi: What about Hindu society?

Deoras: There are regular movements of social reform going on in Hindu society. But in the Muslim community I do not find any movement. If somebody starts [one] they are not liked by the community. They are being controlled by mullahs.

Naqvi: Indian Muslims have a minority complex. Therefore, reform is even more difficult. The most backward Muslims in the world reside in India and by keeping them under pressure you are contributing to their backwardness.

Deoras: Who is keeping them backward?

Naqvi: We have got them involved in non-issues. You and I have all got them involved in Babri Masjid; they are involved in the Shah Bano case; they are supposed to be objecting to our relations with Israel. They are agitating about Rushdie's book. None of these are bread-and-butter issues. And you say they have been pampered. What have they got with all this so-called pampering?

Deoras: Due to their minority complex should we allow them to do anything?

Naqvi: What is the advantage Muslims have derived since Independence? Look at their economic conditions, look at the job quotas. Okay, they got the Muslim Women's Bill, but has one Muslim woman gained in real terms?

Deoras: They get minority rights; special rights in the Constitution.

Naqvi: Please answer my question. What have the Muslims gained?

Deoras: To appease Muslims they have got a Minority Commission.

Naqvi: This is precisely what I am saying. These are hollow, insubstantial gifts. An impression has been created by all governments that there is something special going for the Muslims. But in essence they have got nothing, no jobs, no education, no businesses.

Deoras: There is no difference between Hindus and Muslims as regards poverty. As for the question of jobs, if you are capable for that post you will get it. There should be no distinction. Now the government comes out with Mandal Commission and it has created so many divisions in the country itself.

Naqvi: Do you think the whole Ayodhya agitation has been able to cement some of the divisions in the Hindu society that have been created by the Mandal Commission.

Deoras: A little bit definitely. Ram is not the god only for forward castes. He is the god for the entire community.

Naqvi: We have not spoken of Kashmir. How can we hope to keep Kashmir if a perception is created all over the world that we treat our Muslims shabbily?

Deoras: Do you think the Kashmiri Hindus who have become migrants in Jammu can go back to the Kashmir Valley?

Naqvi: Maybe not at this point. Again, the Pakistan factor comes into play, Pakistani support for those elements which are creating the trouble in Kashmir. We have to handle the Pakistani factor by love and respect for each other in this country. The Germanys were united because East Germans saw that life on the other side was better. Similarly, people in Bangladesh and Pakistan should say that life on the other side is better. Many Pakistanis used to say this privately a few years ago. Now I feel embarrassed. I used to show off to my Pakistani relatives and friends—look at our composite culture, our freedom, our democracy. But look at the mess now. And you must take your share of the blame, sir.

Deoras: There is no difference between Hindus and Muslims as regards poverty. Communalism is not the only factor. There are a lot of tensions among the Hindus also. We can work together to see that everybody, whether Muslim or Hindu, gets bread twice a day.

Naqvi: By your logic you are coming around to my view. Bring down the communal temperature, generate love and caring, not hatred. They are making bombs in every mohalla. This is what we are reducing our country to—a cottage industry of illicit arms...

Deoras: They are selling it. This is business.

Naqvi: Unless you give a call, this will only go on.

Deoras: Let us, you and I together, give the call to the country.

Naqvi: It is fine with me. Let's shake hands on that. But please convince your rank and file that it is in Pakistan's interest that Hindus and Muslims fight each other in this country. This is my entire thesis. During my visit to Aligarh I saw two bombs were dropped in a mosque and two similar bombs were dropped in a Hindu locality.

Deoras: Some Muslims must have dropped it.

Naqvi: I like the abruptness with which you have come to this conclusion. Okay, but who are these Muslims?

Deoras: When something happens in Pakistan why should there be a reaction here? When Bhutto was hanged it had nothing to do with us. But there were demonstrations in Kashmir and trouble in all other places.

Naqvi: What has that got to do with Babur? You yourself agree that Pakistan was unnatural. Then you expect Indian Muslims and for that matter even Hindus to have an unnatural hatred towards Pakistanis.

Deoras: We need a great national reconciliation on the basis of understanding and good humour. All the Muslims who are getting elected to Parliament and the assemblies belong to the fundamentalist variety. This is the problem.

Naqvi: Not all leaders, but, yes, we need good leadership in the Muslim community. There is no doubt about it.

Deoras: Why don't you try and create that leadership? Just like you. Why don't you become a leader?

Naqvi: Zahid e tang nazar ne mujhe kafir jaana/Aur kafir yeh samajhta hai Mussalman hoon main (The kafir thinks I am a Muslim and the mullah thinks I am a kafir).

Deoras: (Laughs heartily) I have close contacts with the BJP. I do not know the exact figure but for kar seva a number of Muslims have joined us. What I am trying to say is we are ready to take Muslims with us. They can join the BJP.

Naqvi: You have also persisted with the same old attitude, the same complaint. Indian Muslims identify with Babur and Indonesian Muslims identify with Ram.

Deoras: It is important that Muslims identify with Ram as an Indian symbol.

Naqvi: I will challenge you about this Ram and Babur comparison.

I will recite numerous couplets written by Muslim poets in praise of Ram and in praise of Krishna. You show me one line in praise of Babur written by a Muslim poet. If you show me one couplet I will change my faith. This Babur business is a canard. There are any number of Muslim rulers, poets, philosophers who looked at Hinduism with great admiration, its philosophy, its aesthetic range. Someone like Dara Shikoh. Now Hindus must accept him as a hero. I am asking you: is Dara Shikoh acceptable to you?

Deoras: He is a hero. But the Muslim community did not permit him to live.

Naqvi: I am taking you on record that Dara Shikoh is your model for a good Muslim and a model Indian.

Deoras: I have not read his whole life. But it is true. He was a fine gentleman. He translated the Upanishads. But remember he was not allowed to rule this land. The establishment was against him.

Naqvi: What is your last word for national reconciliation?

Deoras: At present, Ram Mandir should be allowed to be built. We accept Dara Shikoh as an Indian hero; you accept Ram as part of our common cultural heritage.

Naqvi: Who can dispute that Ram is part of our cultural heritage. Our poets have written about him.

Deoras: Let the temple be built first. I will be the first person who will say let us forget the past.

Naqvi: Sir, if I get you right, what you are saying is that if the Ram Mandir is allowed to be built then you will come out openly and say let bygones be bygones. All the structures, monuments will remain intact exactly as they were in 1947 or 1950.

Deoras: I am ready to say once the construction of the Ram Temple takes place, it will take a long time...it will be one of the biggest temples. I know the demand of VHP is three sites— Mathura and Kashi Vishwanath.

Naqvi: You will prevail upon them to give up their claim to the other two?

Deoras: I cannot say they will accept. But I will try. Let this Ram Temple be built first and start national reconciliation. Let us not go to the government. Let us sit together and solve the problem.

Naqvi: For that you have to issue a whip to your cadres. Let there be peace.

Deoras: I promise you, we do not like what is going on.

Naqvi: You condemn the violence?

Deoras: Yes, of course. These riots create a bad image throughout the world. I do not like it. I want every Muslim to live here in peace. He has got equal rights. But just because he is a Muslim he should not demand something separate from others. Civil rights and other things, everything is common. They should mentally prepare for this. No special status. No minority preferences. They do not have one language. Urdu is not a Muslim language. It is a common language for so many people.

Naqvi: Do you think Urdu should be taught at school and encouraged in every way?

Deoras: Of course. If people want they should be able to learn it. We are not saying all these cultural things should be thrown out.

Naqvi: Do you share the vision of a confederation covering Pakistan, Bangladesh, Nepal, Sri Lanka—without prejudice to their sovereignty?

Deoras: This is an excellent political concept. Just like Europe. Have something in common, build common bridges, common bridges with Pakistan, Sri Lanka and Nepal.

Naqvi: This can happen only when there is peace in our country.

Deoras: Unless there is peace nothing can happen. Peace is the fundamental condition for solving all the problems of the country.

Naqvi: So you will use your influence asking your cadres to

maintain peace?

Deoras: Yes, but you have to speak to Muslim society also.

Naqvi: Sir, you are also using Ram Janmabhoomi for political purposes.

Deoras: Everything will be all right. Let this temple be built. Let Muslims help us build it.

Naqvi: But the condition is peaceful settlement so that this temple to Ram is also a temple to peace.

Deoras: Peace should be there. It is important for Muslims to maintain peace. They rush to the government and political leaders. They have to live with Hindus, particularly the younger generation. They have to make some sentimental adjustment.

I have reproduced almost my entire interview with Deoras because I think it is important to know that even a hardcore RSS leader was willing to accept that the Othering of India's Muslims couldn't go on indefinitely without turning the country into a war zone where no one, not the majority nor the minorities, especially the Muslims, would prosper. Unfortunately, two years after the interview took place, the Babri Masjid was demolished leaving a permanent scar on the nation's psyche. Things would never be the same again.

SIX

Unholy Riots

DURING THE 1947 post-Partition pogroms in Jammu and Hyderabad, a pattern was established: the police and the armed forces would side with Hindus (or remain neutral) in Hindu–Muslim conflicts. I was not around for those mass murders. But I did cover various riots over nearly five decades. These include the Gujarat riots (1969), Moradabad (1982), Bhagalpur (1989), Aligarh (1990–1991), Bombay (1992–1993), Gujarat (2002), Gopalgarh (2011), Ghaziabad (2012), Faizabad (2012), Dhule (2013) and Muzaffarnagar (2013). In this chapter, I will attempt to arrive at some insights into how and why communal riots happen and what needs to be done to eradicate them.

This is a phenomenon that needs to be studied in great detail so we know just how much damage communal conflict has caused to the country and the Muslim community in particular. In 2012, *Outlook* magazine reported that there had been fifty-eight major communal riots in forty-seven places since 1967: ten in the south, twelve in the east, sixteen in the west and twenty in the north, with a death toll of nearly 13,000. How much more of these pogroms must we suffer before cynical politicians, godmen, bullies and thugs finally cry halt? What I touch upon in this chapter, and elsewhere in the book, is not a comprehensive list of post-Partition riots. The number of big and small riots would be at least fifty times more. But the ones I covered will serve to give the reader a fair idea of the causes and effects of communal riots.

In September–October 1969, Ahmedabad in Gujarat became the epicentre of terrible Hindu–Muslim riots which saw widespread arson, looting and killings. According to the Justice Jaganmohan Reddy Commission report, the riots claimed 512 lives, mostly Muslim. The state was then ruled by the Congress and on the watch of Chief Minister Hitendra Desai whose handling of the riots came in for severe criticism. It would be another two years before the government appointed the Reddy Commission, which submitted its report in 1971. It blamed 'Hindu nationalist groups' for the carnage which targeted Muslims. It also questioned the role of the police and cited six examples where Muslim places of worship were attacked without the police trying to protect them. According to official records, eighty-seven mosques, dargahs and three temples were destroyed.

It was virtually on the day violence erupted in Ahmedabad that I accompanied Pashtun leader Badshah Khan, as Khan Abdul Ghaffar Khan was fondly known, to Gujarat as his press secretary. I am in Kuldip Nayar's debt for many things in my life. When the political leader and activist Jayaprakash Narayan requested Kuldip for a reporter from *The Statesman* to be loaned to him for a year, he named me. JP in turn asked me to function as Badshah Khan's press secretary.

On his return from the US in 1929, Jayaprakash Narayan was invited by Nehru to, first, join the Indian National Congress and later lead the Congress Socialist Party within the Congress. He played a key role during the 1942 Quit India Movement. Later on, JP grew close to Acharya Vinoba Bhave and joined his Bhoodan (land gift) movement. He then renounced politics. Ramnath Goenka, the publisher of the *Indian Express*, and his RSS friend, Nanaji Deshmukh, decided that JP would be the perfect person to be pitted against Indira Gandhi who, in the early seventies, seemed invincible after winning the Bangladesh

War in 1971. She had achieved this victory with the help of the Soviet Union. This factor, plus her growing dependence on the Indian Left, alarmed the Indian Right.

RNG fell back on the theory that Indians revere renunciation. JP had renounced political power and he, therefore, would be the right person around whom a movement could be launched. The idea had started germinating ever since Indira Gandhi split the Congress in 1969. The Navnirman Youth Movement in Gujarat gave further impetus to the idea of a Bihar Movement under JP's leadership. This framework was already in some minds when Badshah Khan, the Frontier Gandhi, was invited to India. A year-long Bharat Darshan would keep JP in steady focus by association.

Khan Abdul Ghaffar Khan was born in the Peshawar Valley in British India, and over the years gained much respect as a man of peace. He was strongly opposed to the partition of India, as we have noted in an earlier chapter. Despite a close friendship with Gandhiji, after Partition he felt an acute sense of betrayal.

Badshah Khan arrived in New Delhi in 1969. Given his VIP status as a special guest of the Indian government, the Intelligence Bureau appointed B. K. Chaudhari, a deputy director level officer, to look after the visitor for the entire year that he would be in the country. A uniformed policeman could not have been planted 24x7 on the Frontier Gandhi. Therefore, Chaudhari had to pretend he was Badshah Khan's 'helper'.

The initiative to invite Khan Abdul Ghaffar Khan was taken by the Gandhi Peace Foundation, run under the leadership of JP, twenty-two years after Partition. This was also the centenary year of Gandhiji's birth. I must make clear that the riots had not drawn Badshah Khan to Ahmedabad; he was there as part of his 'Bharat Darshan' programme.

At the time of the Frontier Gandhi's visit, the Congress was forking out on two ideological paths. One wing of the party was acceptable to professional Gandhians. This club included socialists and even the RSS from the days of Sardar Patel. This wing was ignored by Indira Gandhi when she split the Congress in 1969. By doing so, she freed herself of the growing stranglehold of regional party bosses, named the 'Syndicate', who were considered close to big business houses and to Gandhian institutions where leaders like JP were prominent.

Members of this conservative wing of the Congress were ideological descendants of that powerful faction of the Congress Working Committee which took the lead in dividing India in 1947. Distancing herself from this Syndicate, Indira Gandhi fell back on left-leaning intellectuals in the party like Mohan Kumaramangalam and P. N. Haksar. She also roped in the secretary general of the Communist Party of India, Shripad Amrit Dange. This new grouping spelt out a theory of Unite and Struggle which in simple language meant: Unite with the Congress on its progressive line but 'struggle' against its anti-people policies. The CPI attached itself as an ideological motor to the Congress. Unmoored from Indira Gandhi, the Syndicate became a project of the right wing that could be used to obstruct communists and fellow travellers around Indira Gandhi. They all found JP's ideals were closest to Mahatma Gandhi's. Since Badshah Khan held the same ideals dear, the Syndicate sought to appropriate him too.

Badshah Khan's relative, Mohammad Yunus, was a friend of the Nehru family, a sort of in-house entertainer whose company Panditji enjoyed greatly. Yunus became a great friend of Indira and her husband, Feroze Gandhi. In 1969, Yunus was India's ambassador to Algeria where he had become a friend of President Houari Boumediene and other revolutionaries of the Algerian War.

Indira Gandhi had a brainwave. She invited Yunus to look after Badshah Khan. There was no one she could have thought of who was closer to the Frontier Gandhi. This trumped JP's arrangements. As Badshah Khan's press secretary, even though I was an inexperienced journalist, I suddenly became someone that two of the most powerful politicians in this charged political atmosphere had begun to woo. Both Indira and JP expected me to coax statements out of Badshah Khan—supporting each of them respectively. This, at a time, when he was in a mood to chastise both.

From my vantage position I observed all those who visited the Frontier Gandhi. They were all escorted by JP's courtiers. Key figures in this group were Ramnath Goenka and Nanaji Deshmukh, who was at that stage the tallest figure in the RSS. In supporting roles were Congress socialist leader Chandra Shekhar, Minoo Masani, George Fernandes, C. R. Irani of *The Statesman*, Shyam Nandan Mishra, Dinesh Singh (both Congressmen), socialist leader Karpoori Thakur and numerous youth leaders in the making—Lalu Prasad Yadav, Nitish Kumar and Ravi Shankar Prasad. All these leaders were to emerge in important roles during JP's Bihar Movement which ultimately challenged Indira Gandhi.

What did I make of the Frontier Gandhi from my stay with him during his Bharat Darshan? On the whole, he came across as a wise and measured leader. But at times I also assessed him as someone with human frailties and idiosyncrasies. Before he retired for the night he would count the shawls gifted to him to see if some had not been stolen by his personal staff (read the IB official turned 'orderly' Chaudhari). And when ordinary folk called on him in the night he would send them away with disdain. But he would be only too willing to meet VIPs and royalty. The feudal upbringing had not left him. He placed great premium on 'achcha khandan' or 'good family'.

After one of his chicken lunches in Bhopal he left instructions not to be disturbed. 'Send them away,' he waved his hand in irritation when some trade union workers sought an audience. Just then, Chaudhari walked in saying, 'The Begum of Bhopal is here to see you!' He got up like lightning, quickly donned a new shalwar-kameez and eagerly settled down to receive the Begum.

Thirty-three years after my first visit to the state as the Frontier Gandhi's press adviser, I was back in Gujarat in 2002 and heading for Godhra—the nondescript town that was suddenly in the news because a mysterious fire in a train compartment at its railway station had triggered one of the worst communal pogroms in recent history. Given the situation, I knew that as a Muslim it would be dangerous to travel alone to Godhra. So I invited Rajiv Vohra of the Gandhi Peace Foundation and Brooke Unger of *The Economist* to accompany me. It was a carefully crafted coalition. Vohra was a Gujarati Brahmin and Unger, a skullcap-wearing Jew, a much valued entity among extreme Hindu groups. At the Bhalka Tirth Krishna Temple, just outside Godhra, two men identified me as a Muslim and lunged at me. Vohra told them sternly: 'I am a Gujarati Brahmin and he is with me.' The two thugs slunk away.

Godhra, 120 kilometres from Ahmedabad, is the district headquarters for Panchmahals district, which has a population of 20 lakh, of whom 20 per cent are Muslims. Godhra itself has a population of two lakh, approximately half of them Muslim—an invisible line divides the city into two communal zones. Tauntingly, some members from the more prosperous side of the dividing line describe the others as 'Pakistanis'.

On the morning of 27 February 2002, angry kar sevaks were returning from Ayodhya on the Ahmedabad-bound Sabarmati Express. The reason for their anger: the loss of the BJP–RSS combine in the UP elections that had taken place days earlier, on 24 February. Despite their carefully choreographed revival of the Ayodhya–Ram Janmabhoomi issue, the BJP, led by Rajnath Singh, had lost the elections. The Sangh Parivar was shocked.

The kar sevaks, as well as other passengers, were trapped when a fire began in Coach S-6 of the train between 7.45 a.m. and 8 a.m. Fifty-eight died. Allegations that the train was attacked by local Muslims stoked Hindu anger. The pogrom that followed targeted the minority community across the state and left an estimated 2,000 dead and thousands homeless and orphaned. It also broke the back of any residual faith in governments and political parties that the Muslim community might have retained after the twin shocks of the Babri Masjid demolition and the 1992–1993 Bombay riots that followed.

Contrary to my expectations, in the context of the 2002 chaos, we met some very helpful people in Godhra. Jayanti Ravi, the elegant IAS officer and Collector of Godhra, was one of them. The three of us who drove from Ahmedabad were seated in a narrow, neglected sitting room adjacent to her office, decorated with a '60-million-year-old dinosaur egg'. After an hour's wait, a peon escorted us to her room. She said she could not talk about the inquiry into the train incident as it was being handled by Vijay Vipul, DIG, anti-terrorism squad. 'But why the anti-terrorism squad?' I asked. She smiled cryptically without offering any answer. There had been no preliminary inquiry. Here was an opportunity to clamber onto the rolling bandwagon of the global war on terror. With this end in mind, presumably, Gujarat Chief Minister Narendra Modi (as he was at the time) instantly declared Godhra an act of terror.

Where was the routine police bandobast on the train? After all, the demoralized, angry kar sevaks had been travelling between Ayodhya and Ahmedabad by the Sabarmati Express for the past few days. Well, I was told, there was bandobast when they travelled to Ayodhya. However, their return was only expected around 10-15 March. This assessment was based on inputs from the Ayodhya police; they felt that the kar sevaks would celebrate the BJP victory in the UP assembly elections before returning home. Of course, the BJP's loss in the polls prompted the kar sevaks to return early and in great frustration and anger.

Since 24 February, the returning kar sevaks had been misbehaving with passengers and hawkers, and teasing women in burqas. This behaviour continued throughout the journey, at various stations including Dhanol, one stop before Godhra. On 27 February, as the train pulled out of Godhra, a Muslim hawker chased kar sevaks, who hadn't paid him, into Coach S-6. The hawker's daughter pleaded with the sevaks. She was dragged into the train. Her father's beard was pulled. He was abused and asked to say 'Jai Sri Ram'. As the train began to leave the station it was pelted with stones by a mob that had gathered and passengers pulled down the windows to protect themselves. Someone pulled the chain.

Remarkably, the mob pelting stones at S-6 and S-5 consisted mainly of Muslim women. By the time Jai Singh Katija, Godhra Station Superintendent, reached the bogey along with police help it was 8.30 am. They saw smoke coming out of S-6. 'We banged on the windows, shouted from outside. There was no reply. Nothing moved. It appeared someone had used the vestibule linking S-5 and S-6 to move in and set fire to something in the compartment.' How could someone from a group of rioting women (and some men) calmly walk into S-5 amid hostile passengers, then enter S-6 through the vestibule and set fire to the bogey from within?

By the time Collector Ravi reached the spot, Coach S-6 was gutted. Inside, she saw a horrible scene: 'There was nobody at the two ends of the compartment, the spaces closest to the door. In the middle, in one big gory pile, were bodies of the dead.' Were they trying to escape some kind of gas or smoke from the burning rexine?

The majority of Muslims in Godhra are a group called ghachis—low in education, high on crime. Power-cable theft in the district was once the highest in the country. The women do not veil themselves and are in every sense as tough as the men, adept at felling trees and removing railway tracks for profit. The official description—Scheduled Tribe—makes them sound like the denotified criminal tribes of yore.

A dozen years after the tragedy, and despite numerous committees and inquiries, there are several unanswered questions including a key one: who set fire to S-6? There are passengers who escaped from S-5 and even from S-6 whose names were on the railway reservation list. They were all easily accessible eyewitnesses. If they were ever interrogated their testimonies were given no play in the media.

The NDA government led by Prime Minister Atal Bihari Vajpayee, which came to power in 1999, had nearly completed half its term in February 2002. The state government hurriedly circulated the theory that the Gujarat riots were a reaction to Godhra, a line that was repeated by Prime Minister Vajpayee. Sonia Gandhi said nothing. This was an inexplicable omission.

Moreover, victory in the UP elections, which the kar sevaks had taken for granted and for which they had assembled in Ayodhya, coincided with the outcome of three assembly by-elections in Gujarat. It was felt that once the BJP won these elections, the movement for the Ram Temple would move into top gear.

Having lost the elections in UP, and the by-election in Gujarat, Narendra Modi and Rajnath Singh were shocked by the reversal in the BJP's fortunes. Modi had been made chief minister because the previous BJP government of Keshubhai Patel had collapsed under the weight of the Bhuj earthquake in January 2001. Modi was on test. The by-election from Rajkot would give him a seat in the assembly, but only by a margin of 14,728 votes. For a long innings in Gujarat he would have to do something on a bigger scale. Perhaps it was only a coincidence that this was the state of play when Coach S-6 of the Sabarmati Express was set alight.

Modi's defenders point to the fact that none of the charges made against him have stuck and he has been cleared by the courts and commissions of inquiry. But he cannot deny the fact that he was the man in charge when hundreds of Muslims were killed across Gujarat in the anti-Muslim tumult that gripped the state for three days following the Godhra incident. Reports would later come in of numerous horrific and spine-chilling incidents of men and women being dragged out of their homes and being cut to pieces in front of their children, women being brutally raped, foetuses ripped out of wombs and burnt, and widespread looting and arson. It must be said to the credit of the mainstream media that it kept its head; its coverage was balanced and truthful. Among the one lakh Muslims who were moved to relief camps across the state were 42,000 children, many of whom were now orphans who had witnessed the murder of their parents and were severely traumatized. Will they ever be able to come to terms with the trauma?

There is little left to be said about the Gujarat riots that has not already been said. But the scars left by the tragedy on the Muslim community are permanent.

During the riots, the mobs destroyed the grave of Wali Gujarati, Urdu's first great poet, the Chaucer of Urdu. Wali was born in Aurangabad but lived all his life in Ahmedabad and Surat, showering adoration on both. He wrote: 'Koocha e yaar, ain Kashi hai/Jogia dil wahan ka basi hai (My beloved's neighbourhood is like the holy city of Kashi where the yogi of my heart has taken residence.)' In Vadodra, rioters tried to desecrate the grave of the greatest singer of the Agra gharana, Ustad Faiyyaz Khan. 'Man Mohan Braj ke rasiya (The heart-winning way of Krishna from Braj.)' Never was this passage sung better in Raag Paraj. Among more gruesome atrocities, it was also this heritage that was laid to waste in Gujarat during those desperate times.

◡

GOPALGARH RIOTS—SEPTEMBER 2011

When the National Advisory Council appointed by Sonia Gandhi proposed an anti-communal violence bill in 2011, which would make the local administration accountable for communal clashes, Congressmen were more vociferous than the BJP in opposing it.

Of the riots I covered, Golpalgarh in Rajasthan was unique. This was the first time in India that police had entered a mosque and shot dead six Muslims. At the core of the violence was a set of three properties—a mosque, a two-acre enclosure for special Eid prayers, and a disputed parcel of land which the Muslims used as their graveyard. Some Gujjars had encroached on this. It is at this point that communal politics got mixed up with a land dispute. On 13 September 2011, Gujjars beat up the maulvi of the mosque. Gopalgarh—which is just a two-hour drive into Rajasthan from New Delhi—became tense. On 14 September, RSS, VHP and Gujjar leaders mobbed the superintendent of police (SP) and the collector and forcibly obtained orders for the police to fire on Meos (a Muslim community from northwest India) seeking shelter in the mosque. Here was the RSS colluding with the local police years before Narendra Modi ever became prime minister. Congress was in power in New Delhi and in Jaipur. This is what I was told at Meel ka Madrasa, situated about three kilometres from Gopalgarh and the police station. When I turned up, everybody was aching to tell a story. Each one was the other's proxy. Except for the *Indian Express*, I saw no other media in the area.

Meos are a fascinating community. They are descended from the Meenas, a powerful tribal group politically opposed to the Gujjars. Here comes a sociological twist. A Meena may belong to the BJP but he can still claim support in Muslim Meo pockets by virtue of his 'gotra' (tribal) or sub-caste links.

Of the nineteen policemen at Gopalgarh police station, nine were Gujjars. In the entire Meo belt, beginning from Nuh on the Delhi–Alwar highway, and spreading across Rajasthan, Haryana and UP, there is an overwhelming preponderance of Gujjars in the police force. Even though the Meos are much the largest population in the area, Gujjars are more self-assured after their much publicized agitation for reservations in 2008, 2010, and 2015. They also feel stronger because of the support they get from the police. Indeed, as I have mentioned, they are often the police.

The great historian and author of *Life and Conditions of the People of Hindustan*, the late Dr K. M. Ashraf, was a Meo. The Meo community was, until a few years ago, a unique blend of

Islamic faith and Hindu culture—rather like in Indonesia, where the practice of Islam has no conflictual equation with the local culture which derives from the Mahabharata and the Ramayana. Ramzan Chaudhry, a lawyer, remembers his grandmother wearing the Hindu 'lehnga' and organizing Govardhan Puja. This did not come in the way of her daily namaz.

The Meos were part of an exquisite pattern in India's cultural tapestry which should have been preserved. Instead successive administrations treated Meos with neglect. This gave an opening to Islamic groups like the Jamaat-e-Islami and the Tableeghi Jamaat to step in, 'refine' the faith and dilute Meo syncretism. Islamism in India, indeed South Asia, has grown, as I point out repeatedly in this book and elsewhere in my writings, because our leaders have never really fostered syncretism even where it existed naturally.

✧

Rajasthan's Congress Chief Minister Ashok Gehlot had 96 seats in the state assembly of 200. He made up the deficit with the help of BSP MLAs from the Meena tribe with whom Meos have 'ties of blood' and whom Gujjars are traditionally opposed to. (As we know, Meos and Meenas have the same sub-castes and gotras.) After the killings, Gehlot suspended the collector and SP and removed all the Gujjars from Gopalgarh police station but only after months of agitation. He announced a judicial and CBI enquiry and ₹5 lakh compensation for the relatives of those killed. The dead were quietly buried after relatives accepted the cheques.

But Kirodi Lal Meena of the BJP, who had emerged as the leader of the Meos, asked for the compensation to be raised to ₹25 lakh and a plot of land for a memorial to the dead. He also sought the resignation of Rajasthan Home Minister Shanti Dhariwal who had not acted strongly and swiftly on the Gopalgarh tragedy. Kirodi Lal knew Gehlot could not afford to annoy the Meenas. His survival in state politics and office depended on them.

He was also helpless about Dhariwal, whom he could not sack, as his hold on the 'Hindu' vote was priceless. So the Rajasthan chief minister found himself in a bind—which votes to keep, which ones to lose?

Zahida Begum, the Congress MLA from Kama in Rajasthan, was under pressure from Gehlot to use her influence and end the Gopalgarh impasse before New Delhi tweaked the chief minister's ears. If she succeeded, she was promised the reward of a ministership. Bhupinder Singh Hooda, chief minister of Haryana, pressed his Meo MLA, Aftab Ahmad, to stop Muslim anger from spilling over into his state. Aftab and Zahida were political enemies but came together to limit the 'Gopalgarh effect' for their own reasons. Zahida's brother, Fazal, would be given an assembly ticket in Haryana if she joined forces with her political enemy Aftab Ahmad to help Hooda.

Despite these attempts to cobble together a solution to limit the damage, everything was being neutralized by Kirodi Lal Meena, the most influential leader of the Meos. Delegations met Rahul Gandhi and Home Minister P. Chidambaram. Their efforts were in vain. No Congress leader found it worth his while to take a twenty-minute helicopter ride to visit an entire community of frightened and isolated Meo Muslims, a people once proud of their 'Hindu' culture and now desperate, even though the Congress was in power. They were once the Congress vote bank too. The mishandling of the Gopalgarh killings is yet another example of the dismal Othering of the Muslim community in India.

∫

GHAZIABAD RIOTS—SEPTEMBER 2012

Exactly a year after the Gopalgarh atrocity, I found myself in Ghaziabad. Here, an international event had found an echo in the nearby village of Dasna, where on the evening of 14 September

2012, a nervous police shot dead six Muslim youth.

The adage about the world being a global village was never truer than in this instance. The trouble started when a fourteen-minute long anti-Islamic video, *Real Life of Mohammad*, was uploaded on YouTube. This amateurish video set the Muslim world ablaze. In Egypt and Libya hundreds were injured and at least fifty were killed in violent protests. Fatwas were issued against Basseley Nakoula, the filmmaker. A Pakistani minister offered a bounty for killing Nakoula who, it was made out, was part of a global conspiracy to desecrate and demean Islam. So Muslims all over the world were charged up. To boost Indian Muslim anger, pages of the Quran were found strewn on the ground in Ghaziabad.

Behind the Masoori police station, which serves thirty-three villages, a village fair is held every Friday. The Friday of 14 September was no different. By evening, say about 5 p.m., when shoppers were returning home, a whisper went around that someone had thrown torn pages of the Quran from a moving train, covering the entire stretch from Ghaziabad to Moradabad, a nearby town. Most of this turned out to be an exaggeration. I met nobody who had actually seen these pages.

The chairman of Dasna Municipality, Sajid Hussain, a lanky, 6'4" tall man who looks like a retired fast bowler, narrated the nightmare he had lived through. He spoke almost in a daze and said that he had seen 'the desecrated page very briefly at the police station'. Behind Sajid Hussain's office was the mosque of the adjacent village of Rafiqabad. Someone brought the pages of the Quran to Abdul Qadir, the muezzin of the mosque. Accompanied by a group of disturbed devotees, Qadir turned up at the Masoori police station, shaking with rage. He announced that he had come to file an official complaint. The crowd meanwhile rapidly transformed itself into a mob. The mob grew exponentially in size, because 'calls were being given at all the village mosques asking the congregations to rush to the Masoori (Dasna) police station', says Sajid Hussain.

When the station house officer (SHO) of Dasna asked Qadir to let him have the pages of the Quran so he could attach it or make a copy of it for the FIR, Qadir refused. The Quran would become 'unclean' if the SHO handled it. Was not that particular page from the Quran already 'desecrated'? After all, that, specifically, was Qadir's complaint. Moreover, anyone can buy a copy of the Quran from a bookshop. Do Qurans thus sold become unclean? I tried looking for Qadir to get his side of the story but he remained elusive.

By 6.30 p.m. the district magistrate (DM), additional district magistrate (ADM), along with every acronym in the administrative and police catalogue were crammed into one small 'Complaints' room from where they all crawled into the 'Khazana' or the strong room to protect themselves. 'Reinforcements please,' shouted the SP repeatedly into the telephone, 'or we will be killed.' The mob had held up traffic on NH24, blocking reinforcements, Sajid Hussain was told. As the mob, by now in the thousands, surged towards the room, setting fire to vehicles on the way, the ADM ordered the constable with his finger on the trigger to 'fire in the air'. The constable followed his instruction. Nothing happened. He shouted, 'Bandook kharab hai (The gun doesn't work)'. Where was the armoury? There was no armoury, just one .303 rifle. Encouraged by the absence of fire from the virtually unarmed police station, the mob broke open the door.

The ADM ordered the police to fire the solitary gun in their possession. This time it worked. Some members of the mob were shot in the head and died immediately. A deep angry silence settled on Ghaziabad as curfew was announced later the same day. Neither the chief minister of UP, Akhilesh Yadav, nor the BJP president and MP from Ghaziabad, Rajnath Singh (now union home minister), showed up in the area that week. Some mysteries remain: who threw pages from the Quran along the railway tracks covering thirty-three villages? And why was a police station, tasked with law enforcement across thirty-three villages in a communally charged district, equipped with only one .303 rifle?

Every riot, every communal incident, leaves several unanswered questions which are never probed. The truth somehow remains hidden and allegations of guilt are often directed at the victims. The perpetrators, almost always, get away.

In an atmosphere charged with communalism any mischief-maker can create conditions of a riot to benefit any of the political parties looking for votes. In this instance, the BJP, Samajwadi Party (SP) and Bahujan Samaj Party (BSP) were all in the fray. No one was eventually found guilty of the deaths of the six Muslim youth who were felled by police bullets that day. Just one more tragedy in the unending chain that has increased the insecurity of India's Muslims.

FAIZABAD (UP)—NOVEMBER 2012

Until 2012, the riots I covered in Ayodhya–Faizabad were linked with the Babri Masjid–Ram Temple controversy. But the conflagration that took place on the eve of Muharram in 2012 happened because the Samajwadi Party (SP) and the BJP decided to take political advantage of existing communal tensions.

I was talking to Shahjehan Bibi, a woman of about fifty. She had covered her shoulders with a yellow dupatta so as not to expose the grimy, torn kurta underneath. Fatigue was written all over her face. Tears flowed without pause from her eyes. The torn sleeve in her right hand was held like a handkerchief to wipe her face. She whispered, with gentle deliberation, the floral names of her three daughters—Gulshan Bano, twenty-six, Gulistan Bano, twenty-four, and Gulfishan Bano, twenty-two. They were hiding in a distant village. 'I was beginning to collect jewellery for their marriage,' she said hesitantly. What kind of jewellery? 'Three silver earrings.'

Her house bears evidence of the mob attacks. Around Shahjehan Bibi's house are a dozen others that have been likewise gutted. Phoolpur Takia is a colony of Muslims called Faqirs. It would be derogatory to describe them as beggars but they have traditionally survived on alms. Here, they live in rows of thatched huts and their primary occupation is seasonal: the making of small tazias (papier mache replicas of Imam Hussain's tomb in Karbala) for the observance of Muharram. To burn their huts on the eve of Muharram is to destroy them financially. But there is always that indestructible will to survive. I was quite amazed to see some of them sitting on their haunches making bamboo frames for tazias in their roofless, charred homes.

In a sense, the tensions in Faizabad were a continuation of a dozen or so incidents of communal violence across the state that began soon after the SP's Akhilesh Yadav ascended the chief minister's gaddi in Lucknow in March 2012. One is not suggesting that the chief minister or his party are responsible for the violence. However, there is incontrovertible proof that his grip on the administration in his early years in power was very weak. Violent incidents kept recurring. And the chief minister never considered it worth his while to visit the places where these incidents took place.

Such neglect of Muslims in a state where the community has, in the phase of their total disenchantment with the Congress, repeatedly voted for the ruling Samajwadi Party, is shocking. But the riots actually work in the SP's favour. The party leaders would not even have to move a finger and the Muslim, his life shattered, would blame the BJP. In a state of perpetual fear, the community vote would remain glued to the SP just as it had been to the Congress for fifty years.

The SP's calculation is based on simple arithmetic: Yadavs plus Muslims equals a majority. The Savarnas, or the upper castes, were not physically involved in the riots. The lower castes, the Dalits, were. In recent decades, the Dalits in the state have acquired a degree of self-assurance because of the rise in the political firmament of Mayawati, a leader from their fold. Dalits—Valmikis,

Khatiks, Nais, Mochis, Kumhars, etc.—were all mobilized as foot soldiers in these riots. For them, it was a new sense of power. For generations they had never been on the same side as the police. This time, police officers actually gave them protection and support during the riots. According to some observers, they were gradually beginning to see themselves as the Hindu infantry. The arrival of Amit Shah as the BJP's election chief for UP, and later as party president, pitched the party into a mode of perpetual conflict with Muslims.

What happened in Phoolpur Takia on 25 October 2012 followed a set pattern: a series of hamlets or villages around Bhadrasa town, within a stone's throw of Faizabad, were surrounded by rioters and all the huts belonging to Muslims, without exception, were gutted. Diligent care was taken to ensure that the fire did not spread to a single Hindu hut. Dalits were later allowed to acquire some of the gutted plots. Henceforth, a riot would ensure for the Dalits security and upward mobility.

The arsonists, brandishing trishuls and lathis, chanted 'Jai Shri Ram'. They ran from the predominately Hindu village of Phulwaria, across the pond, towards Phoolpur Takia. Petrified women heaved a sigh of relief when three police vehicles drove towards Phulwaria. But after a conversation with the torch-carrying mob, the police vehicles drove away. The mob descended on Phoolpur Takia and burnt everything—even the bamboo skeletons for the tazias. What was that conversation between the police and arsonists about?

Tension in Faizabad was palpable nearly a month earlier when the idols of Kali, Lakshmi and Saraswati at the famous Devi Kali temple nearby were found missing from their pedestals on 22 September. BJP leader and MP Yogi Adityanath and his cohorts turned up, flaring their nostrils and threatening to shake heaven and earth if the idols were not restored. Assuming that the culprits were Muslims, the police searched for the idols in Muslim homes in Azamgarh. They were disappointed. The idols were recovered from the possession of four Hindus from Kanpur.

Dussehra and Eid fell on 24 and 27 October respectively that year. The communal game plan searched for another booster. Stories were floated of a Muslim boy having teased or molested (take your pick) a Hindu girl. These dominated the front pages of Hindi newspapers published on Dussehra, 24 October.

It is a simple plot but how neatly implemented! On Dussehra day, the Muslim boy–Hindu girl story appears. There is tension. Inquiries reveal the story has been concocted to promote a communal divide. But, because of Dussehra, there will be no newspaper the following day to publish the correction. So the rumours multiply. Two days later would be Eid ul Adha; more rumours of cow slaughter are spread so as to agitate the Hindus on one side and Muslims on the other.

Loot, arson, anti-Muslim violence gripped Faizabad on 24 October when a large procession carrying Durga idols went through the main market past the historic eighteenth-century mosque, which is considered a model of communal harmony. In earlier years, Hindu women in their hundreds would climb the mosque for a darshan of the Durga procession. The mosque would arrange for the flowers to be showered on the idols. That year, the organizers of the procession had asked the women to stay home. Could there have been more telling proof of advance planning for the violence? And yet the police did nothing. At least fifty shops were looted and burnt.

The next day, the arsonists reached Shahjehan Bibi's village. Mitrasen Yadav, an SP MLA, told me that 'Hindus and Muslims had both voted for the SP in the recent elections. The effort now is to separate them'. Just who was to gain from this separation became clear in the May 2014 elections when the BJP won 73 out of 80 seats. Also, there was careful social engineering involved in the pattern of conflict. As I've said earlier, it was no longer Hindu vs Muslim. This time Pasis, Lohars, Mallahs and a series of sub-castes from among the Dalits were being individually pitted against the Muslims—a consolidation of Dalit sub-castes, if you will, with the Muslim as the common object of hate.

Many of the most ominous slogans in Faizabad gave a clue to the working of the minds of people like Yogi Adityanath who, while a Thakur, is the mahanth or chief priest of the Gorakh Nath Temple in Gorakhpur. He has been a BJP Member of Parliament since 1998, known for his Hindutva extremism in and out of Parliament. As the firebrand Hindutva leader during the Faizabad riots, he coined the slogan:

UP ab Gujarat banega
Faizabad shurruaat karega.

(UP will follow the Gujarat model.
Faizabad is the start.)

Social engineering of this kind has gone on for years. The contagion is now widespread.

DHULE RIOTS—JANUARY 2013

On the fateful day of 6 January 2013, the city of Dhule in northwest Maharashtra was preparing to watch an India–Pakistan cricket match. This is how it all began: A Muslim auto driver had an argument with Kishore Wagh, the owner of a restaurant in Madhavpur near Machchi Bazaar in the heart of Dhule. The issue: non-payment of a ₹30 bill. Wagh hit the driver in the face with a ladle. Bleeding profusely, the auto driver reached a police chowki a hundred yards away, where the constable refused to register his injuries.

So the driver returned to the scene with his own reinforcements—a dozen or so youth. The crowd near the restaurant had also swelled. Stone pelting began from both sides. The police chowki, like a kiosk, is situated in the middle. Missiles from both sides were flung with increasing intensity. Instead of intervening, the constables simply ran away. The Muslim mob pulled out the furniture and papers from the chowki vacated by the policemen, and set fire to the items in the middle of the road. The mobs on both sides had multiplied by now.

By setting fire to the chowki, Muslims had expressed their lack of confidence in the police. This is not surprising. In earlier riots that had taken place in 2008, the police had shot dead eleven Muslims. Police behaviour on this occasion followed the same pattern. Armed police arrived and opened fire. Six young men were killed. Barely a stone's throw from the police formation, shops and houses were looted and gutted virtually under police supervision. Smartphones with cameras came into operation. All of this is available on videos in popular circulation. No one can dissemble. The videos reached Mumbai too but the Congress chief minister, Prithviraj Chavan, remained silent.

Sensible citizens began to ask questions. Dhule has a State Reserve Police camp, so why the delay in asking for reinforcements? Moreover, in a town with such a large Muslim population, would it not have helped if there were some Muslims in the police force?

Supposing the local SP, Deepak Deshpande, wanted to reach out to the youth—he had no means of doing so. Strangely, he had no direct access to Muslim youth. The youth were quite literally 'alienated'. They kept to themselves in surly groups. Meanwhile, social media facilitated the wide circulation of a hard-hitting speech by Hyderabad's Akbaruddin Owaisi, of the All India Majlis-e-Ittehadul Muslimeen party. The speech, though condemned as communal by the mainstream media, had groups of youth riveted to it. On my drive from Dhule to Aurangabad, I saw groups at nearly every intersection or tea stall listening to Owaisi with the reverence reserved for icons. The spell the Owaisi brothers have cast on Indian Muslim youth is a phenomenon that has not yet been fully fathomed. And they have done it through the clever use of social media. 'The government, police, electronic media are against us; for them we are "ghair hazir" (not there),' a young man with a trimmed beard told me. 'We have the Urdu press and the social media.' He said the electronic media and the English press 'are with them'. He sketched a frightening image of two communal, tectonic plates moving parallel to each other. 'One day they will crash.'

Muslim youth in riot-hit areas, or districts where they have been held by the police for years on suspicion of terror and later found innocent, will understandably be alienated from the authorities. This is obvious. But what is not so obvious to the government is that youth in their anger will begin to coalesce around an icon, a hero, a declamatory Rambo on a pulpit. So, from district to district, city to city, video images of none other than Akbaruddin Owaisi ranting to thunderous applause were being shared and viewed on mobile phones.

Earlier, among a group in Dhule, I had protested the playing of video footage of Owasi's speech. 'Please stop this…this is a dangerous, inflammatory speech. It can create riots'. A dark man with leathery skin regarded me sternly. 'Where were you or the government when Bal Thackeray was spewing venom, without a break, for decades? They didn't have the guts to arrest him.' There was a pause. 'And they arrested Akbaruddin because he is a Muslim, a soft target?'

MUZAFFARNAGAR RIOTS—AUGUST–SEPTEMBER 2013

Muzzafarnagar in Uttar Pradesh has been a target of the RSS and the Congress for communal polarization since the forties. In pre-Partition days, western UP, with Muzaffarnagar as the centre, was the economic power base of Indian Muslims. Acres upon acres of sugarcane plantation, brought into focus during television coverage of the Muzaffarnagar riots, bear witness to that although Muslim power is now a thing of the past.

The 'trigger' of the Muzaffarnagar riots bears an uncanny resemblance to the rumours introduced at Faizabad: Shahnawaz Qureshi of Kawal village had apparently teased a Hindu girl in the neighbouring village. This allegation was never proved. A group of young Hindu men turned up at Qureshi's village. Their anger seemed palpable. 'Seemed' is an essential qualifier because the Muzaffarnagar riots, in retrospect, turned out to be a planned affair. The plan was to fill the air with blinding saffron in preparation for the elections that would bring Modi to power nine months later.

It was easy to whip up frenzy among Jats—the only rumour that needed to be broadcast was that a Jat woman had been seduced by a circumcized Muslim. Over the decades, circumcision has been built up as a challenge to Hindu virility. Acharya Giriraj Kishore warned women journalists to steer clear of Muslim men 'who get themselves circumcised to give our girls greater pleasure as part of their love jihad'. This is demoralizing stuff, inducing great psychological anxieties. As it is Jat women are in short supply. Poaching by outsiders would lead to further depletion.

But there are more reasons for the shortage of women in this part of the country. The phenomenon of doing away with the girl child is the desperate desire on the part of many families to have more sons. For this, there is a simple reason. Here, in their perception the economics of holding on to land militate against having too many women in the family—small landholdings would be divided and subdivided if each one of the brothers in a family brought in a wife. In a few generations there would be nothing left to divide and share. Naturally, none of this was openly stated, but the fact remains that for decades now there have been fewer women than is normal in Jat society. Another consequence of this attachment to land was that most of the men in a Jat family were perforce tied in perpetuity to pastoral pursuits, peasant lives. By contrast, Muslims, against whom much ire is directed, are seen on TV screens as stars; they are young men like Shahnawaz Qureshi, who wear designer jeans, T-shirts, dark glasses and ride motorcycles.

It does not come as a surprise, then, that it was a Qureshi

who triggered the Muzaffarnagar pogrom. He is the rare Muslim who represents upward mobility. In north India or Hyderabad or Maharashtra, they are the visible faces of Muslim prosperity. They have a near monopoly in the meat export industry. Thousands of crores of rupees worth of meat is exported annually, most of it mutton.

In large measure, the purpose of the riots was electoral. The riots were sparked with the aim of intimidating a handful of the more prosperous but mostly to isolate the economically downtrodden Muslims and consolidate the Hindu vote. That would benefit the BJP electorally in the elections which were scheduled for May 2014. It was made out that Jat sugarcane owners had turned upon the Muslims. This was blatantly untrue.

There were, in other words, layers upon layers of combustible ingredients available in Muzaffarnagar when BJP leader Amit Shah was given charge of elections in Uttar Pradesh after the riots. He set to work immediately, summoning up images of medieval hordes setting upon the chaste land, despoiling temples and violating Hindu womanhood. He was remarkably brazen on TV. 'Yeh badley ka election hai (This is an election of revenge),' he said. This speech went viral on social media.

'Bahu-Beti ko bachao (protect daughters and wives)' from rapacious Muslims was the battle cry in every mahapanchayat or congregation in Muzaffarnagar. The one held on 7 September was the biggest and most threatening of all. If the BJP had won forty out of eighty seats in UP, it would have been a grand success. The BJP won a record seventy-three seats. Modi's triumphant journey to New Delhi would not have been possible without this pro-BJP tsunami in UP. Were the results a consequence of the specific circumstances that obtained that season or has the BJP hit upon a formula? Time will tell.

In August-September 2013, the rural areas and towns of Muzaffarnagar and Shamli districts witnessed the worst communal violence since Gujarat in 2002. Muslims fled their villages and were accommodated in 'camps'. Many refused to return to their villages even three months later because incidents of attacks against the community continued.

The overwhelming evidence points to the fact that Muslims were disproportionately at the receiving end of the communal violence that swept Muzaffarnagar. According to information available from the office of the superintendent of police, sixty people died in the communal disturbances of which forty-three were Muslims and seventeen were Hindus. There are strong reasons to believe that many more died. While Hindus died in one pitched battle outside a Muslim-dominated village after the Jat Mahapanchayat at Nangla Mandaur on 8 September, the Muslim deaths took place in different villages over a period of time. These were planned attacks. Muzaffarnagar erupted at a time when Akhilesh Yadav, the forty-year-old son of Mulayam Singh Yadav, had been chief minister of Uttar Pradesh for a little over a year. During this period, fifty or more instances of Hindu–Muslim conflict were reported in the area. As we have noted, the theory was as follows—Muslims were believed to be the Samajwadi Party's vote bank, continuous communal riots would keep Muslims in the Samajwadi paddock for fear of the BSP. The BJP projected the logic differently: SP was keeping tensions high to scare the Muslims so that they would, in a state of funk, stay with the SP. In reality, excessive communalization would cause Hindu consolidation. The Hindu vote would come to the BJP.

∿

The Muslim boy–Hindu girl element was inserted into the Muzzafarnagar narrative of August-September 2013 in which Shahnawaz Qureshi was killed by two men who alleged that the Muslim boy had teased or stalked the sister of one of them. This story turned out to be totally untrue. Supporters of Shahnawaz retaliated by murdering the two Hindu boys.

Various versions of what actually happened were available

in the aftermath: one was that two motorcycles collided, leading to a scuffle, and the girl angle was an afterthought. The second version was that a Muslim and some Hindu boys claimed the same girl's favours, leading to a fight. The third was that a girl had supposedly complained to her family that Muslim boys teased her whenever she passed their village on her way from school. It was custom-made for what the Hindu right describe as 'love jihad'.

VHP leader Chandra Mohan Sharma's interview to *The Hindu* in September 2013 was in character: 'First, good-looking Muslim men are identified. They are given neutral names Sonu and Raju,' he told the paper. '[They] are then given jeans, T-shirts and bikes and taught to behave.' This he said was called 'love jihad' and was a practice that had allegedly spread across the country. The truth, as far as Muzzafarnagar is concerned, is elusive because such allegations are common in a traditional, rural society coping with rapid change. Jat leader Naresh Tikait was frothing in the mouth over the Supreme Court's ban on khap panchayats—the traditional way of meting out social justice in Jat society. Seated on a charpoy in the compound of his house in his village near Shamli, Tikait was a bundle of grievances, from 'society had lost control over "our bahu-betis"' to 'our traditional ways of managing our affairs was taken away from us.'

Such statements are usually accompanied by more generic comments aimed at Muslims—for instance, that they do not follow family planning and have large families and their loyalties to the country are suspect. Now the lament was loud and clear: 'They want to reduce us to minorities in our own country.' It was remarkable that these comments were repeated in almost the same words by all the Jats we met irrespective of the distance that separated their villages. This is probably indicative of a well-organized campaign over a period of time to communalize the atmosphere in the entire area.

During key by-elections in UP in September 2014, the leader of the BJP campaign, Yogi Adityanath, raised the love jihad slogan to fever pitch. The Yogi's overkill boomeranged electorally. Of the 11 seats in which by-elections were held, the BJP won only 3; the remaining 8 were captured by the SP. This was shocking because, just four months ago, in the 2014 general elections, the BJP had won 73 out of 80 parliamentary seats. The moral communal souffle, sometimes, rises only once. This reversal notwithstanding, love jihad was firmly a part of the Hindutva armoury. The subject has attracted academic enquiry. Professor Mohan Rao of Jawaharlal Nehru University has researched the subject. According to him, 'One of the most remarkable campaigns by right-wing forces over the last few years in India goes under the startling name of love jihad. Love jihad crudely but effectively argues that Muslim men are waging jihad in India through so-called love marriages.' Given credence by the courts and police in some states, it is argued that the proponents of love jihad see this as a strategy by Muslim fundamentalists to lure Hindu and Christian girls into their fold, thus swelling the numbers of the Muslim community in an ongoing demographic war.

The Hindu Janajagriti Samiti (Hindu People's Awakening Organization) in Dakshina Karnataka district of Karnataka claimed that 30,000 young women had been duped by 'Love Romeos' (or those waging love jihad) in the state. The Kerala High Court ordered an enquiry in 2010 into this so-called phenomenon, while the Karnataka High Court, in the same year, stated that a case involving a twenty-three-year-old woman who had converted to Islam to marry a Muslim man had 'national ramifications concerning security, besides the question of unlawful trafficking of women.' Indeed, the Karnataka High Court went further, ordering the woman be 'restored' to her parents while the police investigated the case.

On its part, the Kerala police found no evidence to support the allegation. The Karnataka police clarified that out of the 404 girls missing during the period, they had been able to trace 332. The majority of them were Hindu girls who had eloped to marry

Hindu men. One of the girls who was said to have been a victim of love jihad had in fact been murdered by her Hindu lover.

Yet the media and various sections of Hindu fundamentalist groups such as the Bajrang Dal, VHP, RSS and Akhil Bharati Vidyarthi Parishad mounted a sustained campaign against imaginary love jihad. The student wing of the BJP in New Delhi's Jawaharlal Nehru University distributed pamphlets against this 'grand Muslim conspiracy'. All the campaigns focused on how 'they', Muslims, seek to outbreed 'us' in our own country.

As early as 1909, U. N. Mukherji had written a book called *Hindus: A Dying Race*, which went on to influence the content in many tracts and publications put out by the Hindu Mahasabha, the parent organization of the RSS. This book seemed to meet a widespread demand, it went into many reprints. It had a special appeal for those Hindus who were anxious to create a monolithic Hindu community in the face of demands for separate representation from Muslims and lower castes. Whipping up anxiety about the 'Muslim threat' would be one way to weld together hugely diverse, and often antagonistic, castes into one community, erasing the structural divisions in a caste-ridden society. This was before Partition—jockeying had begun to weld Hindu society into a unified India. Caste politics in post-Partition India made Hindu consolidation an imperative: targeting Muslims became an electoral expedient.

Mukherji's book is deeply riddled with inaccurate predictions. Nevertheless, the book provided 'demographic common sense functioning as a trope for extinction'. Also, fundamentally, it spoke to the conviction of communal Hindus who believed— and continue to believe—that this nation is defined 'culturally' as a Hindu nation, just as Muslim communalists define Islamic Pakistan.

⁓

In recent times, especially in the aftermath of riots, I have been intrigued by a relatively new phenomenon—Hindu fundamentalist groups opposed to family planning. They are waging, they say, a 'demographic war'. A leader of the VHP recently enjoined Hindus not to accept family planning because their numbers were going down, and those of Muslims were increasing. At a public meeting attended by thousands, and in the presence of the chief minister of Madhya Pradesh, Shivraj Singh Chauhan, leaders of the Madhya Pradesh unit of the RSS claimed that the Muslim population was increasing at a rapid pace, and that this, combined with infiltration of Muslims from Bangladesh, would portend 'doom for India'.

The same groups have also opposed access to abortion, arguing that a disproportionate number of Hindu women utilize abortion facilities. Controversy erupted when the Census Commissioner announced the religion-wise data from the 2001 census. He could not compare these figures to previous years because the 1991 census had not been conducted in Kashmir, a Muslim majority state. The Hindu right created an uproar about 'them' out-numbering 'us' in our own country. Expressions of anxiety were amplified by the national media. This was despite clarifications issued by the Census Commissioner: the figures showed that the rate of decline of the Muslim growth rate was substantial and indeed sharper than among Hindus.

Martha Nussbaum, noted US commentator and thinker, has pointed out that 'the creation of virulent masculinities is perhaps a part of the project of nationalisms of the European variety'. Emulating this project other communities, are also creating masculinities of the European sort. She notes that Israel and India are both seats of construction of this notion of virulent masculinities, both directed at Muslims, classified in colonial discourse as 'martial races'.

Historian and scholar Tanika Sarkar notes that 'there is a dark sexual obsession about the ultra-virile Muslim male bodies and over-fertile Muslim female ones'. Recounting the unspeakable horrors perpetrated on Muslim women and children in the

Gujarat carnage, she offers the following explanation:

'In readings of community violence, rape is taken to be a sign of collective dishonouring of a community. The same patriarchal order that designates the female body as the symbol of lineage and community purity, would designate the entire collectivity as impure and polluted, once their woman is raped by an outsider.' Sarkar goes on to describe the environment at shakhas where boys are fed legends of the rape of Hindu women during Partition and the abduction of Hindu women all through history by Muslim men, creating a perpetual fear of virile Muslim men luring away Hindu girls, 'a kind of penis envy and anxiety about emasculation that can only be overcome by doing violent deeds'. And finally, there are the anxieties whipped up over generations about 'Muslim fertility rates', of their uncontrolled breeding and 'the drying up of future [Hindu] progeny'.

These attacks engender fear and anxiety about the future. Such attempts to saffronize the minds and outlook of Indians make common people, you and me, complicit in morally offensive steps, which of course is their purpose.

SEVEN

A Procession of Prime Ministers

PRIME MINISTER ATAL Bihari Vajpayee (his tenure ran from May 1996–June 1996 and March 1998–May 2004) once said to me, tongue firmly in cheek, 'Partition was good for Hindus because we now have fewer Muslims to manage.' Despite Vajpayee's RSS lineage, he never came across to me in grim, communal light—in fact, I found him much less divisive than Congress prime ministers like P V. Narasimha Rao, for instance. I base this observation on years of reporting and interacting with a procession of Indian prime ministers. No one can lay blame at Vajpayee's door for patently anti-Muslim policies.

I say this even though it has always been believed that the Congress is comparatively more sympathetic to Muslims and despite the fact that Jawaharlal Nehru (who was prime minister from August 1947 to May 1964) was revered by the Muslim community. Vajpayee belonged to a party which regarded Indian Muslims as the Other. But he recognized that if the country was to come together and move forward, the Muslims would have to be reassured and integrated into the idea of India and Bharat. Like every prime minister of independent India, he made mistakes, had to compromise with Hindu fundamentalists and cope with the exigencies of electoral politics, but he set in motion promising initiatives such as his overtures to Pakistan, and other confidence building measures that displayed statesmanship. I will appraise Vajpayee in greater detail later on in this chapter.

With the exception of Nehru (I was very young when he was

prime minister) and Modi (I had given up day to day political reporting by then) I've had the privilege of reporting on or observing all the country's leaders. This is not an exhaustive account of their terms, rather it is an impressionistic recounting of their tenures, interspersed with personal anecdotes.

Let's start at the beginning with Pandit Jawaharlal Nehru. As I have said in the first two chapters, until his death, the first prime minister remained the darling of Indian Muslims. I have vivid memories of all of us seven brothers and sisters, and our parents, leaning over the windows of our Kutchery Road residence in the Lucknow of the late fifties, waiting in pin-drop silence for Pandit Nehru, wearing his trademark cap, a rose in the buttonhole of his sherwani, to drive past in an open Chevrolet towards Aminuddaulah Park for a public meeting. Along the entire route, people stood outside their houses in double and triple file or craned their necks from the windows of the upper floors of their homes for a glimpse of him. Never was a prime minister more adored.

He remained the undisputed leader of Indian Muslims to the very end despite the many ways in which he let them down. The trauma of Partition, the disappointment over the abolition of zamindari, the pogroms against Muslims in Hyderabad and Kashmir, all of which took place on Nehru's watch, were enough to shake the faith of Muslims in 'Pandit Nehru', as we affectionately addressed him. But the community did not desert him.

This apparently inexhaustible affection for Panditji had a reason: there was no one else the Indian Muslim could turn to. Maulana Azad, the minister for education and culture, was powerless and a recluse; Hafiz Mohammad Ibrahim, who was made deputy chief minister of UP as a sop to conservative Muslims, did not have national prestige.

So, Nehru was the only messiah. His foreign policy, for example, issued from a very eclectic appreciation of foreign affairs. It seemed to grow out of India's multicultural reality. As a leader of the non-aligned nations, along with Gamal Abdel Nasser of Egypt and Josip Broz Tito of Yugoslavia, Jawaharlal Nehru was more equal than others in the entire socialist Afro-Asian bloc. This grouping also included fifty-two Muslim countries. In each one of them Nehru was respected as a global statesman a little ahead of even Nasser, who, being Muslim, was seen as being ideologically divisive within the family of Muslim nations. At that stage Pakistan had no profile, only Western sponsorship. Nehru's Hindu background did not stand in the way of non-aligned Muslim nations embracing him as their own. Raees Amrohvi, a Pakistani poet of Awadh origin, wrote in spontaneous admiration:

Jap raha hai aaj maala ek Hindu ki Arab.
Baraham-zaadey mein shaan-e-dilbari aisi to ho!

(The Arab world is chanting the name of a Hindu!
A Brahmin with such an incredible ability to win hearts and minds!)

Hikmat-e-Pandit Jawaharlal Nehru ki qasam!
Mar mitey Islam jis pe, kaafiri aisi to ho!

(Look at the vision of Pandit Nehru!
A non-believer and yet the world of Islam lies at his feet!)

Nehru remained the undisputed leader of the Afro-Asian bloc until his death on 27 May 1964. Special links with Muslim nations in this grouping was a matter of comfort to Indian Muslims. With the Islamic Republic of Pakistan breathing down our necks, Nehru's non-alignment had given India a huge asset. It was a sort of straw the Muslim could hold on to. The ritual links with the Muslim world were retained even after Nehru because India was still part of the non-aligned bloc, that is, until non-alignment itself collapsed with the fall of the Soviet Union in 1991.

'Jana Gana Mana', India's national anthem, was composed by

Tagore for the Congress session in Calcutta on the occasion of King George V's visit to the city in 1911. There has, therefore, been a question mark on India's national anthem. Why did the song of independence have to derive from an event so patently a part of our colonial past? It was, it turns out, largely at Jawaharlal Nehru's behest that it was adopted by the Constituent Assembly as the national anthem on 24 January 1950. Indeed, even the martial rendering of the anthem, so familiar to everyone, was composed by the British musician, Herbert Murrill, and approved by Nehru. This was consistent with Nehru's high comfort level with English friends, officials from Oxford and Cambridge, clothes tailored in Savile Row, a great desire to be like the British aristocracy. The Anglaise in his makeup explains his pandering to the Mountbattens. This affected the course of Indian history.

His choice of Sir Girija Shankar Bajpai as the first secretary general of the Indian Foreign Office was in character. Nehru chose to overlook the fact that during the great man-made famine of 1943, Sir Girija, as British India's agent in Washington, coordinated policy with Lord Halifax, the British ambassador in the US, against Indian national interests, arguing for Winston Churchill's policy of diverting food stocks to the war theatre. Nehru overlooked Sir Girija's political past. He gave more weightage to his brilliance, courtly manners, expensive British habits, and an ability to club with the British aristocracy.

In a sense, two sets of Indians were orphaned after Nehru: Indian Muslims and Macaulay's children—creatures of Western enlightenment—who looked upon Nehru as a model. Nehru was never a traditionalist but he could abide by traditions to protect his political interests.

The establishment placed him on such a high pedestal that a great deal about Nehru was never openly discussed. Take the saga of his sister Vijaya Lakshmi's love affair with Syud Hossain, the brilliant editor whom Motilal Nehru had invited to Allahabad in 1919 to edit his newspaper, *The Independent*. Dr Asaf Ali, who spent years with Hossain at the Inns of Court in London, talks of his 'brilliant' intellect. Sarojini Naidu once described him as the 'last of the great gentlemen'.

Syud Hossain, thirty-one, was a few months older than Jawaharlal. Vijaya Lakshmi was nineteen. By 1921-22, quite mysteriously, Hossain had left Allahabad. It was rumoured that Vijaya Lakshmi and he had secretly married in Lucknow's Butler Palace.

According to my uncle, Wasi Naqvi, who was an MLA from Rae Bareli, and Chandra Bhan Gupta, UP chief minister in the fifties, Gandhiji was opposed to the marriage. A Hindu–Muslim marriage, involving the premier family of the Congress, would disrupt the national movement.

Nehru posted Hossain as India's first ambassador to Cairo. He clearly made a great impression on Cairo's ruling class. A street there is named after him.

Syud Hossain left an imprint in campus after campus in Britain for his oratory, analytical faculties, mastery of facts, erudition, and brilliant writing. He must have had a mesmeric hold on Vijaya Lakshmi because even after the scandal she accompanied him on these trips, particularly after the death of Ranjit Sitaram Pandit whom she had been quietly married off to. In more settled circumstances, the Nehrus would have settled for a Kashmiri Pandit. But for reasons known to them, her marriage was arranged to a barrister from Maharashtra. Ranjit Pandit died in 1944. In 1945, the UN League of Nations conference in San Francisco was attended by Hossain and Vijaya Lakshmi. Dr Harry A. Garfield, grandson of US President James Garfield, and president of the Institute of Politics, Williamstown, Massachusetts said, 'Mr Hossain's was the most balanced and brilliant presentation of the Indian case I have ever heard.' Professor George Fellowes, the head of the History and Political Science department at the University of Utah, said Hossain's 'was the most eloquent lecture I have heard in forty years'. Kingsley Martin invited Hossain to write for the *New Statesman*. Nehru had probably underestimated Hossain's charisma and the impact he would make on the world.

Hossain's family in Dhaka has documents which reveal a great deal more. 'He was too much of a gentleman to ever talk,' says Naila Khan, his grandniece.

In 1949, during a halt in Cairo, Nehru visited his grave. 'He was a great friend,' Nehru said. The Syud Hossain saga sheds some light on how Hindu–Muslim relations were viewed by Gandhiji. It says a great deal about Nehru too.

It is part of the Nehru magic that after having criticized him to my heart's content, an inner voice, possibly from the labyrinths of Mustafabad, pulls me back. French philosopher and political scientist Raymond Aron judged Andre Malraux as 'one third genius, one third false, one third incomprehensible'. It is unfair to compare apples and oranges but those proportions may quite accurately apply to Nehru.

⌣

When Lal Bahadur Shastri (June 1964–January 1966) succeeded Nehru as prime minister, it was generally believed that his proximity to Panditji swung the job for him. There was an expectation that there would be something of Nehru in him, despite the obvious differences between the two. *The Statesman* wrote an editorial focusing on the distinct cultures they represented. When Shastri took over the prime ministers' residence, modern art gave way to the plaster heads of gods and garish calendar art. Nehru counted Yehudi Menuhin and Harold Laski among his friends; Shastri's family was more in tune with kirtan singers and recitations of Ramcharitmanas. Nehru was an integrated intellectual carrying within his persona both Urdu and English cultures. Shastri was homespun. He had had to swim a river to go to school. He was the quintessential mofussil Hindu searching for pride in a Hindu past. In social and cultural terms, Shastri was more in the Gandhian mould. Gandhiji, as I've discussed, was uncomfortable with the

Western cosmopolitanism of Jinnah. He was equally unfamiliar with the liberal, irreverent sophistication of, say, Mirza Ghalib, indeed of Urdu culture. He was only comfortable with the Muslim as framed in religious terms. This is a little surprising because his twenty-one years in South Africa were spent with Muslim merchants who invited the young Gujarati barrister from London to represent them as their lawyer. Most of their children studied in the West, as indeed had Gandhiji himself. Shastri demonstrated his high comfort level with votaries of political Hinduism early in his innings. In 1965, India went to war with Pakistan. Shastri requested RSS supremo Guru Golwalkar to post RSS volunteers at city squares in north Indian cities for civil defence duty. That Nehru's chosen successor should have leaned on the RSS for civil defence surprised Indian Muslims. But there wasn't much of a flutter in the Congress party.

Shastri died in the most unusual circumstances. After the declaration of a ceasefire with Pakistan, the Soviet leadership arranged for him to meet Pakistan's president Ayub Khan in Tashkent in January 1966 where the two leaders formally ended the war with the signing of the Tashkent Declaration. After the negotiations, the Indian prime minister returned to his room where, to everyone's utter shock, he died of a heart attack. For the first time in history, a Russian prime minister (Alexei Kosygin) and a Pakistani president (Ayub Khan) were an Indian prime minister's pall bearers.

Shastri's untimely death paved the way for the accession of Nehru's daughter, Indira Gandhi (January 1966–March 1977; January 1980–October 1984). She became the country's first female prime minister in January 1966. Inder Malhotra, the political correspondent of *The Statesman*, the keenest journalist in the capital those days, asked me to hop into his Fiat one cold January morning and we drove off to the Congress office to see Indira Gandhi win. At the time, I was too junior in the business to have access to the prime minister, except as a sidekick to senior colleagues like Inder.

Nehru projected the grandeur of India, its place in the world. Shastri's was an inward focus, his most famous slogan being: 'Jai Jawan, Jai Kisan (Hail the Soldier, Hail the Farmer)'. Indira Gandhi's vision, on the other hand, had to do with the power of India. Even opposition leaders like Atal Bihari Vajpayee were moved to describe her as Goddess Durga after her victory over Pakistan in 1971.

Throughout the struggle for independence and in the early years of free India, the only national party of consequence was the coalition called the Congress party. This coalition was held together by Nehru, the only truly charismatic national leader the party had. Cracks in the coalition began to surface even during the brief Shastri interlude. By the time Indira Gandhi came into her own, many elements in the Congress coalition had begun to assert themselves, including the right wing which had propped up Morarji Desai (March 1977–July 1979) in direct competition to Mrs Gandhi as a possible prime ministerial candidate. The Lohia socialists, with their allergy to the Nehru family and the Soviet Union, took the lead in causing upsets in so many states.

As we saw in the last chapter, Indira Gandhi split the Congress in 1969 to free herself of conservative party bosses. I have already discussed some of the aspects of Indira Gandhi's time as prime minister but I'd like to focus a bit on the latter half of her initial term, as also the Emergency. After the 1971 war, Mrs Gandhi grew exceptionally powerful. This was a matter of great concern to those who opposed her within and outside the party. Several of those who wanted to build up a leader to checkmate her decided to support the socialist leader Jayaprakash Narayan or JP, as he was called.

JP had retired from politics. He had become a seminarist, taken up some Gandhian causes and joined Acharya Vinoba Bhave's Bhoodan or Land Gift Movement. In 1974, there were a rash of student agitations against the Congress chief minister of

Gujarat, Chimanbhai Patel. He had been accused of corruption. Patel resigned and President's Rule was imposed on the state. On 11 February 1974, two days after President's Rule was imposed on Gujarat, JP visited Ahmedabad where students had come out onto the streets, demanding the dissolution of the state assembly as well.

Taking heart from this, JP plunged headlong into the Bihar Movement. He called it a movement for 'Total Revolution'. He was helped by senior RSS leader Nanaji Deshmukh and Ramnath Goenka. Allegations were made against the somewhat anaemic chief minister, Abdul Ghafoor. Ghafoor was a wreck of a man when I met him in the chief minister's bungalow, when the movement demanding his ouster was at its zenith. He didn't quite know what his guilt was. To dispel the blues, he would dig out a bottle of Old Smuggler whisky from behind a pile of unwashed linen and proceed to drink from it, grimacing with every sip.

More than on the hapless Ghafoor, the Bihar Movement mounted maximum pressure on Mrs Gandhi. In concert with this movement, the socialist leader George Fernandes triggered a nationwide railway strike in March 1974. Everything seemed to be building up to a great crescendo. To add to the rising decibel level came the Allahabad High Court judgment which, on 12 March 1975, unseated Indira Gandhi from Parliament for six years. Justice Jagmohanlal Sinha took an extraordinarily dim view of the fact that official machinery had been misused for her election to Parliament. Government officials had participated in campaign activities during her 1971 election campaign from Rae Bareli.

For her coterie, the earth had caved in. In her sanctum sanctorum, Sanjay Gandhi, her younger son, Siddhartha Shankar Ray, legal adviser and former chief minister of West Bengal, and Mohammad Yunus huddled together. Mrs Gandhi and her coterie decided that the only way out of the jam would be a state of internal Emergency in the country, which would justify the adoption of a set of repressive measures to tackle the situation.

Ray drafted the text for its promulgation. On 25 June 1975, a state of Emergency was declared in the country.

Indira Gandhi was Durga no longer. My lasting impression of her was shaped by a startling professional experience as a journalist. I was a mid-level journalist when Mrs Gandhi became prime minister but my association with Jayaprakash Narayan during the 1974 Bihar Movement, as a correspondent of *The Statesman*, caused her advisers to turn to me for insights on the movement which threatened her.

Earlier, as I've said, my term as press officer to Khan Abdul Ghaffar Khan had brought me close to many politicians, most notably JP and Mohammad Yunus. Once the Emergency was declared, Yunus Bhai became its premier salesman. H. Y. Sharada Prasad, the Brahminical, low-key press secretary to the prime minister, was asked to cool his heels in the PMO. Yunus took over his responsibilities. He gave himself the title 'Special Envoy'. Even as a puzzled secretariat groped for a power centre, decisions were handed down by Sanjay, Yunus, and Ray.

Even though Yunus had earlier been given sinecures such as a posting as Indian consul general in San Francisco and ambassador to Algeria, he was not intellectually equipped to play the role of press secretary and all-purpose adviser to a prime minister facing an existential crisis. He was no P. N. Haksar or Sharada Prasad.

Yunus's understanding of the media was simplistic. In his words, the 'jute press' was one of the reasons for Mrs Gandhi's troubles. The term referred to the Marwari ownership of Indian newspapers. At the turn of the twentieth century, Marwaris originating from districts in Rajasthan had made a fortune from the jute trade in Kolkata. Marwaris like Ghanshyam Das Birla, Shanti Prasad Jain and Ramnath Goenka owned the *Hindustan Times*, *Times of India* and *Indian Express* respectively. The jute press was therefore always in the left liberal firing line. Yunus had picked up this 'wisdom' from Mrs Gandhi's leftist coterie. This press, in cahoots with Western imperialism, was principally responsible for giving Indira Gandhi a hard time. The left alleged that the jute press was working for Western imperialism and its Indian agents. Since Mrs. Gandhi had veered towards the left after the Congress split of 1969 and was leaning on the Soviet Union, particularly after the 1971 Bangladesh liberation, the jute press was out to weaken her. Therefore, this press would have to be placed on a tight leash and a new media created to sing paeans to the Emergency regime. It was for this purpose that *India Today* magazine was launched. There was a long-term perspective on the Emergency. *India Today* would be a coffee table publication to promote the 'new India', Yunus declared.

One of Yunus's schemes to amplify the wonderful things the Emergency regime was doing was to interview Indira Gandhi for the *Sunday Times*, London. I would do the interview because I was the stringer for the paper in New Delhi. The offer was a godsend. An interview with the prime minister so soon after her declaration of the Emergency would be an international scoop and quite priceless. I had just been admitted as a fellow at Princeton University. The fee I would receive from the *Sunday Times* would come in very handy for my sojourn.

I prepared a lengthy questionnaire. Yunus's secretary received me at the gate to the prime minister's office. Yunus was grinning from ear to ear. 'Tayyar hain aap? (Are you ready?)' He asked me to leave my tape recorder in his office. 'She will freeze up with that machine.' This was the first time I learnt that even she could 'freeze up'.

Yunus ushered me into Mrs Gandhi's presence. 'Teleprinter message dikhayiye (Show her the teleprinter message [from *Sunday Times*]).' Then to her 'Yeh dekhiye; yeh dekhiye (Take a look).' The import of this cameo act was: *your staff has failed you but look at how I have managed to get Fleet Street to write about the reinvented Indira Gandhi on the global stage.*

All this while, Indira Gandhi said nothing. She glanced up from the teleprinter message Yunus had thrust at her. There was a sad resignation in her eyes.

What took my breath away was her response to my first question. She placed her chin on the palms of her hands like a yoga asana, and looked into the far distance. I repeated the question. 'Why did you declare a state of Emergency?' It was not rocket science to anticipate that, under the circumstances, this would have to be the first question. But Yunus cut in. 'Ask the next question.'

All that I had heard about Mrs Gandhi being the 'Iron Lady' and 'Durga' vanished in that instant. I have seldom seen anybody look more petrified. Yunus kept saying, 'Aap likhey jaayiye, aap likhe jaayiye (Keep writing; keep writing).' Exasperated, I said: 'What can I write, Yunus Bhai? The prime minister is not saying anything.' I suggested we abort the interview and come back later—when she was less tense.

Without any goodbyes, Yunus dragged me away to his room. With a virtual gun to my head, Yunus asked me to write out the questions and dictated answers which made no sense.

With four typed pages of questions and answers, we trooped back into the presence of the prime minister who still looked as lost as she had been when we left her.

No sooner had I filed the interview than I received a message from Nicholas Carroll, the deputy foreign editor of the *Sunday Times*. It was to be the main feature in the paper. 'A bag of gold follows', he wrote.

When I turned up in London to collect my 'bag of gold' on my way to Princeton, I learnt of Yunus's parallel initiative to give Indira Gandhi the biggest media exposure in her life—an initiative which effectively destroyed my association with the *Sunday Times*.

Armed with my Q and A, Yunus invited a former BBC hand, Gaurishankar Joshi, to his office. Joshi was asked to send excerpts of 'an' interview to the rival Sunday paper in London, *The Observer*. To this day, I can imagine the scene that must have taken place at the *Sunday Times*' office on Grey's Inn Road—the editor, Harry Evans, small as a sparrow, hopping from one end of the room to the other in anger when he learned that the Indira Gandhi interview that had been billed as an international scoop had found its way to the arch-rival. I lost face.

Yunus was not the only villain of the Emergency regime but he was possibly the least equipped to handle his sudden rise to power. Others whose infamy will long be remembered include Vidya Charan Shukla, Minister for Information and Broadcasting, who imposed the most comprehensive censorship the press anywhere had experienced. Kuldip Nayar and other journalists were arrested on the instructions of Shukla who, symbolically, kept a tiger cub in his Sunehri Bagh Road residence. The divisions within the media were exposed by the Emergency. Most of them caved in, but a few held out. I still remember Romesh Thapar, the editor of *Seminar*, grasping Arun Shourie by the hand and trooping into Ramnath Goenka's house. 'Please don't compromise with Mrs Gandhi,' Thapar pleaded. 'You and Arun are the only opposition we have.' Newspapers were being invited to abandon their classical adversarial role vis-à-vis the establishment.

Fortunately for the country, the pundits were woefully wrong about the longevity of Emergency rule. After it ended and Mrs Gandhi was toppled in the election of 1977, the pundits got it wrong again. The Janata Party alliance under Morarji Desai, which formed the government in 1977, didn't last long despite their optimism. It soon split under the weight of its own contradictions. Charan Singh became prime minister briefly before elections were called in 1980. On 6 January 1980, Mrs Gandhi returned to power with a thumping majority of 353 seats. The 1977 defeat chastised Mrs Gandhi. She also became a shade more religious. Even the colours of her saris reflected her outlook. Her wardrobe came under the control of her social secretary, Usha Bhagat, a lady of considerable culture and deep religious beliefs. Dhirendra Brahmachari who, along with Sanjay, was a flying enthusiast and a family retainer, was something of a mysterious presence in the prime minister's household.

Mrs Gandhi brought her newly discovered religiosity most openly into her politics during the 1983 Jammu and Kashmir elections. During the campaign she dwelt at length on the Muslim invasion in the Jammu region. The Resettlement Bill passed by the National Conference gave Muslims who had left for Pakistan between 1947 and 1954 the right to resettle permanently in Jammu and Kashmir. Mrs Gandhi opposed the move. President Zail Singh helped her thwart the bill by granting it a presidential reference. The electoral harvest from her pro-Hindu stance was rich. The Congress won twenty-six seats from Jammu and Ladakh.

In a sense it was her 'Hindu' card which caused her to build up Sant Jarnail Singh Bhindranwale as the Sikh Other. Bhindranwale's excesses caused her to send the army in to get him, although it would mean damaging the holiest shrine of the Sikhs, the Golden Temple in Amritsar. She wrote the script for her own end, however unwittingly. She died a horrible death, shot by her own Sikh bodyguards on 31 October 1984. Her assassination was, in a sense, a consequence of her political misjudgements, of which there were many.

The day Mrs Gandhi died, I caught the flight to New Delhi from Chennai where I was then serving the *Indian Express* as editor of its six southern editions. When I reached our house in Safdarjung Enclave, I found my wife's brother-in-law standing guard at the gate. With him was a posse of neighbours armed with hockey sticks. This had been the scene outside every cluster of houses throughout my journey from the airport. On the way I had seen the burned down ruins of the shops of Sikhs who had abandoned them only to be caught by frenzied mobs round the corner who hurled them on to piles of burning tyres. I felt safe for a shattering reason. The taxi was not being driven by a Sikh but a Hindu! I am ashamed.

The anti-Sikh riots that followed Mrs Gandhi's assassination resulted in over 3,000 deaths, and would plague her son, Rajiv

Gandhi (October 1984–December 1989), from the first day he assumed office as prime minister. It coloured the young prime minister's thinking or rather his coterie's thinking on the majority community's equation with the minorities. Rajiv had been sworn in within hours of Mrs Gandhi's assassination. Elections took place in November 1984. Not even in the days of Jawaharlal Nehru had the Congress swept the polls so impressively. It won 48 per cent of the popular vote and 77 per cent of the seats in the lower House of Parliament—414 of 541 seats.

The massive mandate was interpreted differently by Congressmen. That there was a huge sympathy wave after Mrs Gandhi's brutal killing was recognized. But many saw the victory as Hindu consolidation against a decade-old Sikh extremism. This dangerous appraisal gave birth to a more lasting one vis-à-vis the biggest minority in the country, namely Muslims. Arun Nehru's hand as midwife to this tragedy was discernible in both instances. Just as old schoolmates positioned themselves around Rajiv Gandhi when he became prime minister, so did some cousins crawl out of the woodwork. Of these, the most overbearing was Arun Nehru. He was a big hulk of a man from La Martiniere college, Lucknow, where he was a year my junior. As a day scholar, he lived with his aunt, Shyam Kumari Nehru, who had married police officer Abdul Jamil Khan and was now Shyam Kumari Khan. In unguarded remarks at school, his embarrassment that a Nehru had married a Muslim was obvious. What riled him more was the fact that his cousin Kabir Khan, who joined the Bihar cadre of the IAS, was brighter than he was. Shyam Kumari Nehru's liaison always reminds me of Vijaya Lakshmi Nehru and Syud Hossain's which I have mentioned elsewhere.

Arun Nehru abandoned his career as a boxwallah in Calcutta to join Rajiv's entourage as an all-purpose adviser and companion to the prime minister. Arun Nehru and others began devising anti-Muslim strategies because apparently the feeling was that Muslims were being appeased. Even a sensible leader like V. N. Gadgil, who had not given up his habit of reading the *New Statesman*, told me in 1986: 'The feeling is growing among Hindus that Muslims were being appeased.'

Obviously the 'appeasement' talk scared Congressmen. Subsequent steps taken by the party were based on this fear—the opening of the Ayodhya temple locks, for instance. Even after the Ranganath Mishra Commission spelt out unambiguously what needed to be done to redress the condition of Muslims, Congress leaders refused to act.

The Congress's entire approach to Muslims during this period should be seen through the prism of electoral politics. Any overture to help Muslims would, in this appraisal, lead to a haemorrhaging of the Hindu vote. As we have noted, Congress leaders like Sitaram Kesri felt that one of the reasons for Rajiv's massive victory in 1984 was Hindu appreciation for strong action against Sikh communalism. An extension of this argument was that no minority community should be 'appeased' because that would precipitate a Hindu backlash. Congress had not given up on the Muslims quite yet, but it became ambiguous in its position vis-à-vis them—one step forward, two steps back.

This was the thread Rajiv Gandhi picked up. Consider the actions he endorsed. As we have seen, it was under his leadership that, in 1985, the Supreme Court verdict granting alimony to Shah Bano—a sixty-two-year-old Muslim woman with five children whose husband divorced her—was reversed in order to please Muslim conservatives. Towards this end, his government also banned Salman Rushdie's *Satanic Verses* and delayed the improvement of relations with Israel. Muslim conservatives were mighty pleased. When I argued with Rajiv that none of these were key issues for Indian Muslims who needed education, jobs, entrepreneurial help, he asked me to write him a note. I did. Rajiv promptly moved the files towards upgrading relations with Israel. P. V. Narasimha Rao completed that process.

But this halcyon period did not last. The appearance of

Being the Other

V. P. Singh, Rajiv's finance minister, on a white charger waving the banner against corruption disrupted any long-term course of political action Rajiv might have had in mind. The Bofors case, alleging large-scale corruption by Rajiv's close circle in the purchase of howitzer guns from Sweden, resonated with the people. In the general elections of 1989 the Congress came down to 197 seats from the record 414 seats it had won in 1984. V. P. Singh (December 1989–November 1990) became prime minister as the consensus candidate of the National Front alliance which assumed power, but only for a short spell.

While the Congress under Rajiv wavered, the BJP had its eyes focused on Ayodhya and the Congress's growing ambivalence on its traditional secular platform. It gained exponentially. From 2 seats in 1984, the BJP won 85 seats in 1989. Of course, as we have seen, the BJP's nationwide campaign to build the Ram Temple in Ayodhya created an atmosphere that was heavily tinged with saffron, leading to communal riots in Rajasthan, Uttar Pradesh, Bihar, Madhya Pradesh, Gujarat, Maharashtra, Karnataka, taking a toll of hundreds of lives. The Congress tried to devise a strategy of 'soft Hindutva' to win the Hindu vote. Naturally, the real Hindutva of the BJP was preferred.

Nevertheless, as we have seen, Rajiv made a last-ditch effort to attract Hindu votes. In 1989, he turned up in the holy city of Ayodhya and inaugurated the election campaign by promising Ram Rajya. This was quite extraordinary because Rajiv was a very unlikely devotee of Lord Ram. He was not in the least religious, like the majority of Doon School boys. Also, as he had surrounded himself with a coterie of these boys, his promise of Ram Rajya was not convincing. It only served to advance the BJP's prospects.

Rajiv set about making himself attractive to voters. Take his Sri Lankan diplomacy at the time of the crucial Indo-Sri Lankan Peace Accord which facilitated the entry of the Indian Peace Keeping Force (IPKF) into the island. How unsuccessful these efforts were became clear during the 1991 election campaign. While campaigning at Sriperumbudur in Tamil Nadu on 21 May 1991, Rajiv was assassinated. LTTE chief Prabhakaran's handpicked volunteers detonated their suicide vests while reaching out to garland Rajiv, killing him on the spot.

Rajiv's death gave the country its first Congress prime minister who did not belong to the Gandhi-Nehru clan—P. V. Narasimha Rao (June 1991–May 1996). He was also the first prime minister from south India. He needed help from a coalition of parties to form a new government. On 21 June 1991, P. V. Narasimha Rao became the seventh prime minister of India. As I've pointed out, Rao saw the Congress revival in the north as inimical to his political interests. He considered Narayan Dutt Tiwari and Arjun Singh from UP and Madhya Pradesh respectively not as fellow Congressmen but as factional rivals. The latter he was particularly opposed to because of his caste—Arjun Singh was a Thakur.

During the parliamentary elections in 1991, the Congress did poorly in Uttar Pradesh, Bihar, Rajasthan and to a lesser extent, Madhya Pradesh. Worse still, the Congress was trounced in the state assemblies. The situation was custom-made for Rao's real political inclinations. He could now evolve a policy of live and let live with the BJP. This meant: do not disturb the Congress at the centre and the centre will extend a helping hand to the four BJP states.

RSS supremo Rajendra Singh (Rajju Bhaiyya) wrote a newspaper article describing Rao's meetings with RSS leaders. Other such meetings were planned, he wrote. Rao had his own access to the sadhus and priests involved in the Ram Temple movement. In a way, Rao was only picking up an old Congress thread. After all, the Bharat Sadhu Samaj, a body of Hindu priests, was founded by Congress stalwart Gulzarilal Nanda who was senior enough to stand in as interim prime minister twice (May 1964–June 1964; January 1966). So why single out Rao for his Hindu leanings?

The Special Provisions Bill of 1991 was designed to impose

the status quo on all places of worship as they existed in August 1947. Yet the government excluded the Babri Masjid/Ram Temple from its purview. The exception introduced in the bill could have been interpreted either way. A 'mili kushti' or fake wrestling match in which the combatants would not really bruise each other. The BJP abstained from a public agitation but when the bill was to be passed it showed its 'displeasure' by abstaining from the vote. The effect of this abstention was that the bill had exceptionally smooth passage.

As I have mentioned earlier in the book, Rao's role during the demolition of the Babri Masjid on 6 December 1992 was dubious. On 4 December, upon his return from Lucknow, Arjun Singh, Rao's bête noire and Union Minister for Human Resource Development, told me there was every chance of the Babri Masjid being demolished by the 200,000 kar sevaks who had assembled at Ayodhya for the temple agitation. The leader of the Communist Party of India (Marxist) and chief minister of West Bengal, Jyoti Basu, telephoned Rao and said that he should impose President's Rule on UP because the BJP chief minister, Kalyan Singh, could not be trusted to protect the Babri Masjid and maintain law and order. This was the 'field' information Basu had obtained. The Babri Masjid was demolished exactly two days after Jyoti Basu made this phone call alerting the prime minister. In my view, by not taking strong action to save the mosque, Rao remained on the right side of the BJP. With the destruction of the mosque, Muslims who stayed with the Congress despite serious misgivings since 1947 came face-to-face with the stark reality: the Congress had short-changed them from the very beginning.

The 1991 elections brought Rao to power. But the result carried in it ingredients which disturbed him. Except for a handful, all Brahmin candidates from the Congress (and some other parties) were rejected by the electorate. As an overreaction, Rao planted Brahmins all around him as advisers. Traditionally, the vice president was invited to become chairman of the Indian Council for Cultural Relations (ICCR). On this occasion, Rao blocked K. R. Narayanan, a Dalit vice president, from the chairmanship of the ICCR. Vasant Sathe, who had been defeated in Maharashtra, was accommodated in the slot instead.

In 1993, a year after the Babri Masjid demolition, when Rao decided to have an elected Congress Working Committee, the results shocked him. Arjun Singh, who was fiercely opposed to Rao, led the pack. Apart from his political secretary, Jitendra Prasad, the top six candidates were non-Brahmins. On a flimsy pretext, Rao had the results annulled.

Rao was going through a phase when his interests as a Brahmin superseded his interests as a Congressman. It can be said without fear of being contradicted that if Rao were given the power to choose between Arjun Singh and Atal Bihari Vajpayee as prime minister, he would have, without any hesitation, cast his vote for Vajpayee. He was politically the most 'Hindu' of all Congress prime ministers. Kamaluddin Ahmed, a Congress MP from Warangal in Telangana, who had observed Rao closely, said to me: 'His sharp anti-Muslim edges are derived from the complexes he developed in Hyderabad under the Nizam's rule.' Ironically, Rao was well versed in Urdu and Persian.

Having watched Rao closely as a journalist, I hurriedly put together a book entitled *The Last Brahmin Prime Minister* in 1996. My friend R. K. Mishra, who was a close adviser to Rao, telephoned me with some urgency. 'You must place a question mark at the end of that title,' he advised. 'You must keep the door open for Vajpayee.' How prescient of Mishra, considering he said this on the eve of the 1996 elections when Rao brought down the Congress tally to its lowest in all the years it had contested elections to that point—140 seats.

This led to an interlude with Deve Gowda (June 1996–April 1997) and Inder Gujral (April 1997–March 1998) becoming prime minister for short spells with Congress support from the outside. When Congress president Sitaram Kesri pulled down the Gowda government by withdrawing Congress support, fear gripped senior Congress leaders that the low-caste Kesri would throw his hat in the ring for the top job of Congress president. Overnight a coup was organized and Sonia Gandhi was made Congress president. Kesri had been Congress treasurer for eighteen years with never the hint of a scandal. His son rode a rickety bicycle in Patna. What law of nature would have been violated if he had become prime minister?

In the general election held under his leadership, the Congress had won 141 seats; under Sonia this dipped to 114 seats. The Congress was heading towards a disaster.

Before the NDA government, led by Atal Bihari Vajpayee, ascended the gaddi, a situation arose when Jyoti Basu, the CPM chief minister of West Bengal, was being considered as a possible candidate for prime minister.

US Ambassador Frank Wisner hurriedly invited me for lunch. 'What is this I hear about Jyoti Basu?' he asked. I replied that the CPM Central Committee was in session even as we spoke. The argument against Basu taking over as prime minister was simple: the party did not have the numbers to control the coalition. Party General Secretary Prakash Karat led this point of view. 'Others believe this is a historic opportunity,' I said. Wisner threw down his napkin, got up from his chair and began to pace up and down. 'No,' he proclaimed, 'Jaswant Singh will be the finance minister.' How did he know? Jaswant Singh did become finance minister in 1996 in the thirteen-day Vajpayee government. During those thirteen days, the Enron deal was signed.

Elections were held in rapid succession in 1996, 1998 and 1999. It was only the last one which yielded a stable NDA coalition under Vajpayee.

My association with Vajpayee was spread over his two spells in government. He was external affairs minister in the post-Emergency Janata Dal. That is when he revealed his admiration for Nehru. K. K. Katyal of *The Hindu* and I were in the external affairs minister's room in South Block waiting for a word with Vajpayee on his first day in office. 'I am overwhelmed with emotion,' he said. 'I remember with reverence that Pandit Nehru once sat on the chair I am about to occupy.' This was his first spell at South Block as Minister for External Affairs from March 1977 until July 1979.

Vajpayee was receptive to the Indo–Pak, Hindu–Muslim, New Delhi–Srinagar triangle when I first sketched it for him in the course of the conversations his helpful press secretary, Ashok Tandon, arranged for me. Even during the bus journey to Wagah (advertised as the 'Lahore bus journey'), he whispered to me, 'Do you think one line of your triangle will have been addressed on this visit?' The triangle, in my view, is a pithy metaphor for the mess left behind by Partition. India–Pakistan, New Delhi–Srinagar and Hindu–Muslim are essentially one set of issues. Not one line or an angle of this triangle can be tinkered with without affecting the other two.

'It is a law of triangles that if one line, or angle, is addressed, the other two will be correspondingly affected.' He relapsed into one of his lengthy, intimidating silences.

Vajpayee did make a real bid for improved ties with Pakistan. His visit to Minar-e-Pakistan in Lahore (which marks the site where the Lahore Resolution—the first call for the creation of Pakistan—was passed) put to rest any doubts the Pakistani establishment may have had about the long-term Indian perspective. Vajpayee was confirming the finality of Pakistan.

Vajpayee had a combination of assets which qualified him to take initiatives on Pakistan that no prime minister in post 1947 India could have taken. He had national stature. More important, he was the tallest leader of the Sangh Parivar—especially the RSS and the BJP. Being the senior-most leader of the Parivar, he could, with a wave of the hand, silence dissent. Prime Minister Modi is also from the RSS stable. But he would never transgress red lines on Pakistan, Kashmir or Hindu–Muslim issues drawn by the Parivar. Vajpayee could think out of the box because he had evolved. Above all, he was a Brahmin. Modi is not—he is a Ghanchi. This will continue to matter so long as caste remains a determinant in India's social and political life.

When Vajpayee lost the 2004 election, his greatest regret was that he could not complete his agenda on Pakistan. His principal secretary, Brajesh Mishra, was heartbroken. He said: 'We had very nearly placed our Pakistan policy on an irreversible track.'

Manmohan Singh (May 2004–May 2014), who succeeded Vajpayee as prime minister for ten years—the longest term after Indira Gandhi (nineteen years) and Nehru (seventeen years), never summoned up enough courage to visit Pakistan despite arrangements having been made for him to visit Gah in Punjab, the village where he first went to school. Vajpayee did not have to look over his shoulder, Manmohan Singh did.

In the first flush of victory in 2004, Manmohan Singh took the first step any prime minister had taken to assuage Muslim hurt. He invited Justice Rajinder Sachar to lead an enquiry committee into the socio-economic conditions of Indian Muslims. As we have seen, the energetic economist and statistician, Abusaleh Shariff, who led the fieldwork, produced a stunning report (Sachar Committee Report) in 2006. It showed that in the fifty-eight years since Independence (over fifty of which were under Congress rule) the socio-economic conditions of Indian Muslims had become worse than even the economically weakest Dalit communities. Shockingly, the 30 per cent Muslim population in West Bengal, which had been ruled by communists for the past thirty-five years, was in a condition worse than the national average.

In 2007, the National Commission for Religious and Linguistic Minorities, also known as the Ranganath Mishra Commission, spelt out how the problems listed by the Sachar Committee Report could be addressed. At this point the government's attention was quite undividedly focused on the Indo–US civil nuclear deal. It took interest in little else, least of all the upliftment of Indian Muslims. The report gathers dust to this day.

During Manmohan Singh's tenure, Congress president Sonia Gandhi established a National Advisory Council to oversee policy decisions and advise the prime minister. In 2011, the subject of communal riots came up for review. The council recommended that such riots could be minimized if the local administration were made accountable. The draft of a communal violence bill on these lines was shot down by Congress leaders for exactly the reasons that such a bill would have been frowned upon by all Congress home ministers beginning with Sardar Patel—it was seen as anti-majority. The party was not willing to take the risk of alienating a large section of the bureaucracy, from the central secretariat to the district magistrate in the smallest district of India. The belief is that a touch of saffron smears the Indian bureaucracy too.

The Congress was voted out of power after two terms under Manmohan Singh for a variety of reasons. Scams completely overshadowed his second term—2009 to 2014. Manmohan Singh looked indecisive and powerless. One incident, more than any other, underlined his helplessness. The prime minister proposed certain conditions under which tainted politicians could contest elections. Crown Prince Rahul Gandhi turned up at the party spokesman's press conference and said, 'my opinion on the ordinance is that it is complete nonsense and that it should be torn up and thrown out.' The incident underlined the fact that Singh could not move a step in any direction without the approval of Sonia or Rahul. He allegedly lamented to his press adviser, Sanjaya Baru: 'I have come to terms with this. There cannot be two centres of power.'

Manmohan Singh's successor Narendra Modi (May 2014–) had a landslide victory in the 2014 elections, with the NDA winning an absolute majority of 336 out of 543 seats in Parliament, brushing aside the puny challenge of the Congress which was reduced to 44 seats. The other parties did no better—the AIADMK won 37 seats, the Trinamool Congress won 34 seats while the CPI(M) won 9 seats. Modi is perhaps the first Indian prime minister to take advantage of the global mood, which post 9/11, turned angrily upon Muslims as the 'Other'. Modi's rise to power was a turning point in Indian politics. For the first time since the Hindu right made a bid for political power it now had a firm grip on Parliament, and the national imagination. Modi who had proved, over and over, as chief minister of Gujarat, that he had the measure of his opponents no matter what crimes and offences he was accused of, showed his detractors both within and outside his party just how elections should be won. APCO, one of the world's most powerful PR firms, was given the contract to market Gujarat and Narendra Modi for the 2014 general elections. Former US ambassador to India, Timothy Roemer, plunged into the business of brand-building for Modi with offices in Mumbai and New Delhi. The expensive media campaign enabled Modi to harvest the anti Sonia, Rahul, Manmohan Singh mood in the country. During the campaign, Modi remained very much the Hindutva icon, but also tried to expand his appeal by talking of development for all, and how he would usher in a golden age for the country. For all this effort, he won 31 per cent of the vote; some percentage of this came from those who did not like his hardcore Hindutva message but who nevertheless felt he would be good for the country in terms of development and boosting the economy. The world of business took heart that Modi's was the first non-coalition government in twenty years. But, in reality, the outcome reflected the public's absolute displeasure with the Congress.

A couple of years into his prime ministership, Modi had had a decidedly mixed record. Although there were signs (inflation was down, for example, from 8.3 per cent to 4.9 per cent) that the economy was doing better than before, there were no lasting gains that his government could claim. On the debit side, there were ominous signs that intolerance was rising; thuggish right-wing elements would not be held to account. With Amit Shah as BJP president, the Hindutva agenda would be the blueprint whenever convenient.

Some Hindutva excesses during this phase leave one numb. The lynching of fifty-two-year-old Mohammad Akhlaq on 28 September 2015 by a mob of Hindu fanatics in Bisara village near Dadri, fifty kilometres from Delhi, shocked the nation. Akhlaq's guilt? He was allegedly eating beef or at least keeping some of it in the refrigerator. Modi did not condemn the outrage immediately. There is a silver lining though. One of the reasons the BJP was trounced in the subsequent Bihar elections was because of the electorate's deep disgust with the atrocity. Here is a signal that heightened communalism is no longer a guarantee of positive election results.

What has been a consistent feature of Moditva is the sectarian abuse of a section of his party. Here is a sampling: Giriraj Singh, BJP MP from Bihar, said at a poll meeting on 18 April 2014 near the temple town of Deogarh: 'Those speaking against Modi should be sent to Pakistan.' Another BJP MP, Sadhvi Niranjan Jyoti, said to a crowd at a public meeting in Delhi on 1 December 2014: 'You have to decide whether you want a government of Ram-zadas (Ram's bhakts) or of haram-zadas (bastards).' The trophy for intemperate speech, however, goes to the RSS-trained Tripura governor, Tathagata Roy, who tweeted on 4 January 2016 about the Muslim terrorists killed in the Pathankot attack: 'Wrap them in pigskin, bury them face down in pig excreta.' A serving governor employs this kind of speech only when he has the state's support.

EIGHT

The Making of the Kashmir Problem

MY KASHMIR NARRATIVE begins with Ian Stephens, editor of
The Statesman from 1942 to 1951, the years of the Quit India
Movement, the end of World War II, Partition and the commotion
that followed everywhere, including in Kashmir. I have settled on
Stephens as my witness to avoid an Indian or Pakistani bias in the
story. After a double first at Cambridge, Stephens joined the British
government's Information Bureau and was soon handpicked as
the editor of *The Statesman*, the most powerful newspaper in the
Empire at the time after *The Times*, London.

Mountbatten, Nehru, Patel, Jinnah were all dramatis personae
in the mishandling of Partition and, later, Kashmir. Stephens knew
them all personally and yet he was professionally equidistant
from them. *The Statesman* was my alma mater; I remember how
journalistic principles like 'independence', 'fairness' and 'balance'
were dinned into us by the seniors in that once wonderful
newspaper. Stephens was an athletic, outdoorsy man who would
bicycle from the Swiss Hotel, Civil Lines, where he stayed when in
Delhi, to *The Statesman* office in Connaught Place. Otherwise his
residence was the Statesman House, Calcutta. He was passionate
about Pathans, particularly his orderly, Karim, his 'companion of
fourteen years'.

On 28 October 1947, when the Kashmir issue was heating up,
Stephens published an editorial which caused a sensation. Before
I get to that historic editorial, let me provide the background.
Earlier that month, Stephens had moved from Calcutta to Delhi

to have a ringside view of developments relating to Muslim-dominated Kashmir ruled by Maharaja Hari Singh. Tangentially, the kingdoms of Hyderabad and Junagadh (both Hindu majority states ruled by Muslim rulers) also came into focus.

The big question post-Independence was this: where would these states opt to go? Would they choose to join Pakistan or remain with India? The Nizam of Hyderabad wanted his state to be an independent entity but India sent in troops and annexed it. The Muslim ruler of Junagadh wanted to go with Pakistan but India had the decision reversed since it was a Hindu majority state. So what about Kashmir? The Maharaja of Kashmir, Hari Singh, did not wish to go with Pakistan; he wanted to accede Jammu to India and later hold a plebiscite in the region where Muslims were in a majority. Hari Singh allegedly hoped to alter the demography of his kingdom by ensuring that a chunk of the Muslim population would be eliminated or pushed out of Jammu to Pakistan, thus placing Hindus in the majority. But that left Kashmir in contention—Pakistan insisted it was theirs because it had Muslims in the majority. India, on the other hand, was not willing to part with Kashmir because it had now been incorporated into the Nehruvian secular argument.

Stephens knew Mountbatten well. He first met Mountbatten in 1943 soon after he reached India as 'supremo' of the newly created South East Asia Command (SEAC). In fact, Stephens had done Mountbatten a favour by publishing the SEAC newspaper under *The Statesman's* roof. Mountbatten became Governor General of the Indian Dominion on 15 August 1947.

So piqued was he with Jinnah for denying him a piece of history as Governor General of Pakistan, that he began to settle scores with Jinnah even on sensitive issues like Kashmir. In his insightful analysis of the last days of the Raj, H. M. Seervai takes Mountbatten severely to task. In fact, the title of his book, *Partition of India: Legend and Reality*, is a direct attack on Mountbatten. *The Economist* applauds Seervai for having convincingly laid the blame for the post-Partition mayhem, 'massacres and population exchanges' at Mountbatten's door. According to Seervai, Mountbatten was 'preoccupied with his own self image; he lacked qualities of insight which Lord Wavell possessed.'

Nehru, as history tells us, had made his 'Tryst with Destiny' speech at the stroke of the midnight hour on 14-15 August. Two nations had been created in too unseemly a hurry for a matter so important. The oppressive heat of August was giving way to September. Just at this moment, Stephens noticed the beginnings of what was about to go seriously wrong where Kashmir was concerned. Stephens deserves a hearing because he had predicted how Kashmir was going to spell 'big trouble' for all concerned.

Let me quote a passage by Stephens:

> When I read in September that Mr Gopalaswami Ayyangar, a very able and reputedly anti-Muslim Madrasi Brahmin who was the prime minister of Kashmir from 1937 to 1943, had been made Minister without Portfolio in the new Indian Cabinet, I said to our editorial conference in Calcutta: 'That really does look as if India's up to something at Srinagar', and our correspondents were told to watch for news.

In fact, Stephens had seen earlier pointers to 'something' happening in Kashmir. In the run-up to Partition, Acharya Kripalani, President of the Congress party, some princes from East Punjab, and Mahatma Gandhi had visited Kashmir. The editor of *The Statesman* attached much significance to the Mahatma's visit. He felt Gandhiji was a 'saintly man' but was also 'one of the world's most ingenious politicians; it was hard to think what could have drawn him, as a saint, to Srinagar at that moment.'

Meanwhile, rumours had been reaching Delhi since July 1947 that Maharaja Hari Singh was looking for an opportunity to accede to India although his subjects were overwhelmingly Muslim. Stephens refused to go by the unconfirmed reports that he was receiving but there were too many of them, he noted, 'to be ignored.'

Ved Bhasin, later editor of the *Kashmir Times*, who was a student leader in Jammu in 1947, recalls what transpired. It confirms Stephens's observations. Bhasin's is not a spur of the moment emotional outburst, but a carefully worded and objective account from someone who was once a member of the RSS. He committed his memories to a paper ('Experiences of Partition: Jammu 1947') presented at the Jammu University in 2003. Bhasin recalls that after the 3 June Plan there was pressure on Maharaja Hari Singh to accede to India or Pakistan from both the Congress and Muslim League Leaders.

> In this backdrop Gandhiji visited Srinagar on August 1 and met the Maharaja. Though Gandhi declared that his mission was not political and he was only fulfilling an old promise to the Maharaja to visit Kashmir, there were clear indications that he had advised him to join the India Union. Gandhiji returned to New Delhi via Jammu where he arrived on June 3.

As far as Stephens was concerned, rumours were soon replaced by 'authentic news' in September of a large-scale insurrection by Muslim peasants, many of them 'recently-demobilized soldiers', in the Poonch region. They were revolting against oppression by the Maharaja's officials. This was, according to Stephens, an 'oppression long known, which had at one time appeared to distress Congressmen much more than the British bureaucracy.' But Congressmen were not interested on this occasion.

The insurrection was an important development but was ignored by the media of the day. Reports about it were deliberately killed in the newsroom since it was feared that publishing such stories might renew bloodshed and promote communal discord. The other reasoning was that Poonch was anyway a remote, hilly, inaccessible region from where news hardly filtered out so the reports could be censored. As a result, news of the insurrection went to the dustbin on what Stephens called 'higher humanitarian' grounds. No one wanted to stoke the fire.

But trouble continued to brew and spread. By October, reports started coming in of trouble around Jammu. The Muslims there were said 'to be in flight, having been terrorized and in places cut up by Sikhs and Hindus, at the instigation of the Maharajah's officials.' The news could no longer be concealed. So Stephens moved to the Delhi office to get a better sense of what was going on.

Once in the capital, he met General Roy Bucher, Chief of Staff of the Indian Army, who told him that the 'Kashmir climax was upon us indeed—and for a startling new reason: Pathan tribesmen had burst into the western part of the State. The message had just come, and [the General] said everyone was in a flap.'

That same evening, 26 October, Stephens was asked to dinner with the Mountbattens who had invited a select few. He was shocked by what he saw. Here is what he recorded in a memorandum after the dinner:

> I was startled by their one-sided verdicts on affairs. They seemed to have become wholly pro-Hindu. The atmosphere at Government House that night was almost one of war. Pakistan, the Muslim League, and Mr Jinnah were the enemy. This tribal movement into Kashmir was criminal folly. And it must have been well organized. Mr Jinnah, Lord Mountbatten assured me, was waiting at Abbottabad, ready to drive in triumph to Srinagar if it succeeded. It was a thoroughly evil affair. By contrast, India's policy towards Kashmir, and the Princely States generally, had throughout been 'impeccable'.

The contrast was glaring when Mountbatten showered praise on Nehru for his restraint on Kashmir. He felt that it was 'high-minded' of Nehru to have promised a plebiscite after the Maharaja's accession.

The next day Stephens met Deputy Prime Minister Sardar Patel with whom he disagreed on various issues but whom he respected for being cordial and frank. 'Five minutes with him [Patel] was in my experience worth fifteen with Pandit Nehru.' *The Statesman* editor wrote in his notes after the meeting that 'undercurrents in his remarks seemed only to confirm my surmise that India's policies towards the princely states had not been wholly "impeccable", in aim or method.'

Stephens, as the editor of an important paper, was briefed by Mountbatten on the 'facts'. He was told that, because of the Pathan attack, Maharaja Hari Singh's formal accession to India was being finalized. 'Subject to a plebiscite, this great State, its inhabitants mainly Muslim, would now be legally lost to Jinnah. Indian troops were to be flown into Kashmir at once; arrangements had been made. This was the only way to save Srinagar from sack by ruffianly tribesmen.' Mountbatten told him that Kashmir had many Europeans and attacks on them had already been reported. Stephens recorded in his notes that the Governor General was 'persuasive, confident, charming, a successful commander on the eve of an important operation, who manifestly banked on hustling *The Statesman* into complete support.'

Stephens was 'flabbergasted' by what he was told. He felt Kashmir was too sensitive and important a state to be handled so arbitrarily. He put these thoughts on record:

> The whole concept of dividing the subcontinent into Hindu-majority and Muslim-majority areas, the basis of the June 3 Plan, seemed outraged. At a Hindu Maharajah's choice, but with a British Governor General's backing, three million Muslims, in a region always considered to be vital to Pakistan if she were created, were legally to be made Indian citizens.

When Mountbatten took Stephens aside it became an exercise in the former influencing the latter to see value in the way India was proceeding. An ailing Jinnah had been outfoxed by a formidable team—Mountbatten, Nehru, Patel, Gopalaswami Ayyangar and so on.

The interplay between Mountbatten and Jinnah is the stuff of high drama. The great-grandson of Queen Victoria, cousin of the King, last Viceroy of the Raj—Lord Louis Mountbatten—had upon India's independence, agreed to stay on as Governor General of India. This begged the question: who would be the Governor General of the other dominion, Pakistan? Well, who else but Muhammad Ali Jinnah? That, Jinnah thought, was the proper thing to do. Why should the representative of a departing power stay on in a supervisory position in both India and Pakistan? This, as I've pointed out earlier, peeved Mountbatten.

The Governor General was known for his vanity, his almost childish love of pomp and ceremony. Stephens was present when Mountbatten revealed to journalists in July 1947 that Jinnah had decided to be Governor General of Pakistan. Stephens and others at that meeting noted that 'his [Mountbatten's] pride had seemed hurt, though we thought needlessly: how could anyone, however able, function effectively as Governor General of both the new Dominions?' Stephens was convinced that Mountbatten's dislike for Jinnah dated from then.

Later historians may have characterized it as obsequiousness, but one cannot but admire the show Nehru put on to win over Mountbatten. He knew he was dealing with a man who was susceptible to pomp and grandeur. What better ploy to get him on his side than to invite him to stay on as the first Governor General of independent India? Mountbatten, Edwina and Nehru were by now a famous trio and the corridors of power were filled with stories of their great friendship. Jinnah was quite aloof from Mountbatten and their relationship grew even more strained when Jinnah decided to take on the office of Governor General of Pakistan. Mountbatten did not hide his displeasure. Among other things, he advised Stephens to abandon plans of publishing *The Statesman* from Pakistan.

Stephens felt that a British-owned newspaper like *The Statesman* should 'try to maintain an inter-dominion policy, in fairness'. Mountbatten came down sharply on the idea. 'He thought we would find things much simpler as they were.' He said 'we could drop our Pakistani or Muslim circulation and concern ourselves primarily with Indian affairs.' How much of it was impulse, how much strategy?

✧

Jinnah died in September 1948. The date for the transfer of power set by the government of Clement Attlee was June 1948. If the original date for the transfer of power had remained unchanged, Jinnah would have had just three months to live. By this time he, indeed the country, would have discovered the gravity of his illness. Was this detail a relevant fact in advancing the date of partition? The first rumours of Jinnah's imminent death began to circulate when Mir Laiq Ali, prime minister of Hyderabad, turned up in Quetta, capital of Balochistan, where Jinnah was convalescing. Laiq Ali wanted to know what help Pakistan would give if India invaded Hyderabad. He returned with no guarantees of help but with certain knowledge that Jinnah was dying. Jinnah would not be able to attend Pakistan's first anniversary celebrations. It was suspected Jinnah had a more serious affliction than pneumonia, which was the official story that was being put out.

The possibility of Jinnah not being around would have implied opening up the negotiation on Independence and Partition with a new Muslim League leadership. Things would never have been as perfect for the Congress as they were under the present circumstances with the Mountbattens and Nehru in perfect coordination. Mohammad Yunus, a Khan and a member of the Nehru household, shared with me a confidence. Nehru never credited Mountbatten with too much intelligence. This enabled Nehru to get around the Viceroy on key matters. In his impatience to become prime minister, Nehru would certainly have been interested in an early end to the Partition drama, but Mountbatten had his own reason for dramatically advancing the date from June 1948 to 15 August 1947.

Larry Collins and Dominique Lapierre, authors of *Freedom at Midnight*, have quoted Mountbatten on why he chose 15 August: 'The date I chose came out of the blue. I was determined to show I was master of the whole event. When they asked: had we set a date? I knew it had to be soon. I hadn't worked it out exactly then—I thought it had to be about August or September and I then went to August 15. Why? Because it was the second anniversary of Japan's surrender'. It was Mountbatten's hour of glory too. It is unsurprising that he chose a date that gilded his rule as the 'supremo' of the South East Asian Command which had emerged victorious in the war.

⌣

Stephens found himself in a dilemma after Independence. Should he report honestly about what was happening in Kashmir or should he exercise extra caution to accommodate Mountbatten's biases? Should he hold back when it came to looking at the nascent Indian government and its actions critically? He explains his dilemma:

> Here then, far too soon after Independence to be healthy, for *The Statesman* or me, was a major issue on which it seemed that the new India had decided wrongly, and deserved criticism. Should I criticize, and if so how? On so big a topic we must express some opinion. But for a British-owned paper to disagree with the new Indian Government, still so sensitive and raw, was another. Clashes with Authority are indeed at times an essential part of an editor's job. During my term of office we had, for instance, disagreed sharply with Lord Linlithgow, in the autumn of 1942, over the then important matter of Mr Rajagopalachari's request to see Mahatma Gandhi in jail, and with Lord Wavell, and indeed the whole Cabinet Mission in June 1946. But they

were British, we were British, and we felt strong enough to do this; how strong were we now?

Like a good journalist Stephens added up the pluses and minuses. He saw the Pathan incursion as an outrage; many of the tribesmen, in their rush towards Srinagar, had behaved shamefully, killing burning, looting. And if the Indian claim that the attack was arranged by Pakistan was true then it was a reprehensible act. But he felt Pakistan would have to be questioned properly before arriving at a conclusion.

He also felt that Pakistan's acceptance of accession by the Nawab of Junagadh was 'absurd' and the first affront to the general principles of the 3 June Plan. But India already had Junagadh under economic and military blockade.

> If, as seemed likely, she occupied it, her cause for grievance
> there collapsed—and with it also much of her legal claim
> to be in Kashmir.

Stephens also put under his scanner the doctrine of secularism or non-communalism, already being pressed as the justification for India entering Kashmir, a Muslim-majority area. Stephens felt:

> If it worked it was an admirable doctrine, and Sheikh
> Abdullah, who had been chosen to head the administration
> in India-held Kashmir, seemed from his reputation a good
> instrument for it. But it had notoriously failed to work,
> and had therefore been set aside under the June 3 Plan,
> throughout the Provinces of British India. Would it really
> work in Kashmir? Why should such an exception be tried?

The editor then looked at the minuses. He noted that the Pathan raid was not the only such incident in Kashmir. He also felt it may perhaps not have happened if there hadn't been bloodshed in Poonch. In effect, he seems to suggest that the Pathans had rushed to Srinagar in retaliation for the attacks on Muslims in

Poonch. Stephens goes on to note:

> Casualties among the innocent on both sides might be much
> bigger than in the Pathan raid; no one yet knew, owing to
> the bad communications. And now horrible rumours were
> arriving, too many to be baseless, of organized eviction and
> slaughter of Muslims around Jammu, with the Maharaja's
> alleged approval, an affair which perhaps had been in motion
> before the Pathan raid was launched.

After Stephens examined the pluses and minuses of the Kashmir
crisis he came to the conclusion that *The Statesman* could not
support the Indian government as Mountbatten had expected.
The result was the editorial 'Dangerous Moves' which irked
Mountbatten. Reproduced here is the 639-word piece dated 28
October 1947 that shook the Governor General.

Since the editorial was on an extremely sensitive matter,
I have refrained from paraphrasing it. To clash frontally with
Mountbatten required conviction. But was it not risky to take
on the new Indian establishment?

> Both the new Dominions have been behaving rashly about
> certain of the States to the probable detriment of the
> common people's peace and happiness. Pakistan began it. Her
> acceptance of Junagadh's accession, though justified legally,
> and perhaps by a long stretch of the term geographically—
> communication between them being practicable by sea—was
> ludicrous ethnologically, little Junagadh's population being
> (like Hyderabad's) predominantly Hindu. Such conduct
> seemed explicable only as a short-sighted, spiteful gesture to
> annoy India, or as a planned subtlety of much wider bearing.
> On either count it was unstatesmanlike, unworthy. India's
> reaction however, in our view, lacked balance, a shortcoming
> manifestly attributable to the acute mutual suspicions
> between the two Dominions. Though the bigger, stronger

of them, who should therefore be scrupulous to eschew any temptation to bully, she responded by unseemly military display—backed, it is said, by economic blockade—and by publicly magnifying into a major crisis an affair relatively small and silly, which could, we believe, have been suitably handled with gentler and unhurried fingers.

But the Kashmir affair is by no means small. That State ranks among this country's biggest, and fills a region of exceptional strategic importance on the map. If—as much evidence suggests—last week's alarming incursion of armed Pathans into its Western part had the Pakistan authorities' tacit support, that is disgraceful, and will constitute a lasting slur on the new Dominion's fair name. But it also, if true, displays a strange unintelligence, for it has forthwith had the effect, which might have been foreseen, and which surely the Pakistan government cannot have wanted, of catapulting the Kashmir Durbar into the arms of the Indian Union.

We view the prospects now created with profound misgiving, as must all of detached outlook who yearn for abatement of suffering and strife on this populous subcontinent. Kashmir's accession to the Indian Union, despite the undertaking about later voluntary withdrawal of the Union's troops and influence, makes no better sense than did Junagadh's to Pakistan. Both arrangements run flagrantly counter to realities. Whether India, without hazard to her own precariously re-established internal peace, and to movements of pitiable Punjab refugees, can effectively help her new protégé to restore order if the incursion has been truly formidable remains to be seen. Air transport can do much nowadays to win access to mountain-girt country. Nevertheless, her armed forces, though larger and stronger than Pakistan's, are over-stretched, and (like Pakistan's) much disorganized by partition.

The talk about plebiscites—for Kashmir and,

by unmistakable implication, for Junagadh—though theoretically attractive, may not mean much in practice. Such things need much organizing, and are difficult to complete fairly and peacefully. Last summer's, in the NWFP and Sylhet, stirred strong feeling; and those were held in what was British India, under impartial plans devised before the country was split. Such conditions no longer exist; and it is not easy to see how plebiscites in faction-ridden States such as Kashmir and Junagadh, even if honestly conducted, could be otherwise than widely suspect.

The logical outcome from an unnatural tangle obviously would be that the rulers of Junagadh, and in due course of Hyderabad, should make up their minds to join the Indian Union, and of Kashmir to join Pakistan. The present topsy-turvydom whereby each new Dominion has gained accession from a state inhabited by a majority of contrary communal composition is too brittle and absurd to endure. Meanwhile a public, tragically aware of how strongly passions are running, and of recent unprecedented carnage, can but hope for statesmanship from both Governments. Pakistan's reaction to India's forward move will be awaited with anxiety. The dismal, deep, damnable fact must be faced that the two Dominions now stand perilously poised before what, whether so declared or not, would be war—a war which neither would be able to sustain militarily or economically without ruin.

Within hours of the editorial appearing, Stephens received a summons. It was not a cordial meeting with the Governor General, as Stephens recalls in his book *Horned Moon: An Account of a Journey Through Pakistan, Kashmir and Afghanistan*: 'The Governor-General's press attaché, Mr Campbell-Johnson, telephoned; would I please come to see His Excellency? During the ensuing interview, *The Statesman* was in effect threatened with death, on the Indian Cabinet's behalf, unless it adopted a more pro-Indian line…expressing the gravest displeasure, Lord Mountbatten declared that "by this article", (I quote from my memorandum),

> [W]e had done serious public disservice. After all the trouble which he (Lord Mountbatten) and Mr Patel had taken to explain matters, they had found themselves that morning 'hit for six—yes, Sir'. Amazement had been voiced in Cabinet, by Mr Patel and others. It had been impossible for him to defend me. He had felt much embarrassed and annoyed, having previously tried hard to build up in his colleagues' minds the notion that a British-owned newspaper in the new India was needed. Did I suppose that Mr Patel, after being hit for six in such a fashion, would ever now do anything for us? And so on.

After his angry outburst, Mountbatten went on to share 'important news' with *The Statesman* editor—there was to be an inter-dominion conference about Kashmir at Lahore the next day. But that conference did not take place. In fact, it turned out to be a 'fiasco.' It was first postponed and then Nehru could not attend because he was indisposed. Sardar Patel expressed his inability to leave Delhi to attend the conference in Lahore. Stephens cheekily adds that Patel, though being busy, 'managed relatively long trips to Srinagar and Junagadh'. All this seems to suggest that the Congress leadership was averse to participating in inter-dominion jamborees where a sensitive issue could be brought up. They had got what they wanted. With Mountbatten around, things were going their way.

On 30 October, Stephens called Mountbatten's press adviser Campbell-Johnson to convey to the Governor General that he had considered the issue carefully and could not change his views about Kashmir. He also added for good measure that as long as he was editor he would 'try to uphold an inter-Dominion policy, rather than to support one side.'

The indomitable Sardar Patel could not tolerate such an affront. When Stephens exceeded limits and published an ad released by Pakistan-occupied-Kashmir (PoK) in *The Statesman*, the Iron Man of India politely asked Stephens to return home for good. I have written at length about Stephens's analysis of the Kashmir problem at Independence for a simple reason—to show that the origins of the tragedy were complex and mishandled. It will take a great deal of sagacity, statesmanship, and give and take, if both India and Pakistan are ever to come to an agreement on how the problem can be resolved or forgotten in an atmosphere of harmony.

What was the death toll in the killing fields of Jammu? There are no official figures, so one has to go by reports in the British press of that period. Horace Alexander's article on 16 January 1948 in *The Spectator* is much quoted; he put the number killed at 200,000. To quote a 10 August 1948 report published in *The Times*, London: '2,37,000 Muslims were systematically exterminated—unless they escaped to Pakistan along the border—by the forces of the Dogra State headed by the Maharaja in person and aided by Hindus and Sikhs. This happened in October 1947, five days before the Pathan invasion and nine days before the Maharaja's accession to India.' Reportedly, as a result of the massacre/migration, Muslims who were a majority (61 per cent) in the Jammu region became a minority.

Mountbatten was in control in Delhi and had news of the genocide of Muslims in Jammu filtered out of the media. Sadly, there has been precious little discussion in India about this horrible phase of history.

Maharaja Hari Singh's involvement, with the support of the RSS, is evident from a letter Jawaharlal Nehru wrote to Vallabhbhai Patel on 17 April 1949 (quoted in *Frontline* magazine):

In this (intelligence) report, among other things, a reference was made to a growing Hindu agitation in Jammu province for what is called a zonal plebiscite. This idea is based on the belief that a plebiscite for the whole of Kashmir is bound to be lost and, therefore, let us save Jammu at least. You will perhaps remember that *some proposal of this kind was put forward by the Maharaja some months back.* It seems to me that this kind of propaganda is very harmful, indeed, for us. Whatever may happen in the future, I do not think Jammu province is running away from us. If we want Jammu province by itself and are prepared to make a present of the rest of the State to Pakistan, I have no doubt we could clinch the issue in a few days. The prize we are fighting for is the valley of Kashmir. [This is what Nehru had dug in his heels for. The consequences are for all to see to this day.]

This propaganda for a zonal plebiscite is going on in Jammu, in Delhi and elsewhere. It is carried on by what is known as the Jammu Praja Parishad. Our intelligence officer reported that this Praja Parishad is financed by the Maharaja. Further, that the large sums collected for the Dharmarth Fund, which are controlled by the Maharaja, are being spent in propaganda for him.

The lid on these massacres was lifted by Ved Bhasin and a few journalists of that time. But like the collective silence over the pogrom in Hyderabad, the holocaust in Jammu has been a story hidden from public view by the machinations of the very people who covertly allowed the massacres to take place. These included many in the national leadership of the Congress party at the time. The events of Hyderabad and Jammu and Kashmir reveal the emergence in New Delhi of an establishment which was indifferent to Indian Muslims. Consider the testimony of journalist Ved Bhasin. Here I am again quoting from his paper presented at the Jammu University in 2003.

Communal tension was building up in Jammu soon after the announcement of the Mountbatten plan with the Hindu Sabha, RSS and the Muslim Conference trying to incite communal passions. Tension increased with a large number of Hindus and Sikhs migrating to the State from Punjab and NWFP and even from areas now under Pakistan's control. Trouble was brewing in Poonch, where a popular non-communal agitation was launched after the Maharaja's administration took over the erstwhile jagir under its direct control and imposed some taxes. The mishandling of this agitation and use of brutal force by the Maharaja's administration inflamed the passions, turning this non-communal struggle into a communal strife.

The Maharaja's administration had not only asked all Muslims to surrender their arms but also demobilised a large number of Muslim soldiers in the Dogra army and the Muslim police officers, whose loyalty it suspected. The Maharaja's visit to Bhimber was followed by large-scale killings.

According to Bhasin, the communal flare-up was the worst in Jammu. 'Rumours were spread about Muslims arming themselves and planning to attack Hindus to justify the communal carnage that took place later.' According to the 1941 census, the Muslim population of Jammu province was over 12 lakh; the total population was 20 lakh. Jammu district had a population of about 4.5 lakh with the Muslims accounting for 1.7 lakh. The population of the capital city of Jammu was just 50,000, Muslims constituting nearly 16,000. By September end, a large number of Muslims from the border areas of Bishnah, R. S. Pura, Akhnoor, etc. had fled to Sialkot in Pakistan. With communal riots taking place in neighbouring Punjab there was total panic in the border areas.

Bhasin reports the large-scale killing of Muslims in Udhampur district, particularly in Udhampur proper, Chenani, Ramnagar and Reasi areas. Even in Bhaderwah (about 150 kilometres from Udhampur), a number of Muslims were victims of communal marauders. According to Bhasin, the RSS played a key role in these killings, aided by armed Sikh refugees 'who even paraded the Jammu streets with their naked swords'. Some of those who led the riots in Udhampur and Bhaderwah later joined the National Conference and some even served as ministers. There were reports of Muslims massacred in Chhamb, Deva Batala, Manawsar and other parts of Akhnoor, with several of them fleeing to the other side or moving to Jammu. In Kathua district too there was the large-scale killing of Muslims and reports of women being raped and abducted.

As for the attitude of the state, Bhasin alleges that instead of preventing these communal killings and fostering an atmosphere of peace, 'the Maharaja's administration helped and even armed the communal marauders'. He goes on to say that many Muslims living outside Muslim-dominated areas were brutally killed by the rioters who moved freely in vehicles with arms and ammunition even when the city was officially under curfew. 'The curfew it appeared was meant only to check the movement of Muslims,' he says.

Terrible carnage took place later when the Muslims in Talab Khatikan area were asked to surrender.

> They were shifted to the police lines at Jogi gate, where now Delhi Public School is situated. Instead of providing them security, the administration encouraged them to go to Pakistan for safety. The first batch of several thousands of these Muslims were loaded in about sixty lorries to take them to Sialkot. Unaware of what is going to happen to them these families boarded the buses. The vehicles were escorted by troops. But when they reached near Chattha on Jammu-Sialkot road, in the outskirts of the city, a large number of armed RSS men and Sikh refugees were positioned there.

They were pulled out of the vehicles and killed mercilessly with the soldiers either joining [in] or looking [on] as idle spectators. The news about the massacre was kept a closely guarded secret. Next day another batch of these Muslim families were similarly boarded in the vehicles and met the same fate. [T]hose who somehow managed to escape the wrath of killers reached Sialkot to narrate their tale of woe...

The state administration denied it had any role in the massacres. It even feigned ignorance of any plans to change the demography of the Jammu region. But Bhasin differs:

I will just mention two incidents to show that the administration was involved to change the demographic character of Jammu. As the general secretary of the students' union, I had issued an appeal entitled 'Insaniyat Ke Naam Par', asking people to maintain communal peace and harmony in the best interests of the State and join in the efforts for providing relief to the Hindu, Sikh and Muslim sufferers of the communal orgy. We had also formed a students' peace committee. I was summoned by the then governor of Jammu, Lala Chet Ram Chopra, at his official residence at Kachi Chowni. Though polite, he warned me of dire consequences... He first warned me by saying that 'I could have put you behind bars for your nefarious activities. But since you also happen to be a Khatri like me and are also related to me, I am simply giving you advice. It is not the time to form peace committees and work for peace but to defend Hindus and Sikhs from the Muslim communalists who are planning to kill them and destabilise the situation. We have already formed a Hindu Sikh Defence Committee. You and your colleagues better support it.' Then he added, 'We are imparting armed training to Hindu and Sikh boys in Rehari area. You and your colleagues should better join such training.' When I sent a colleague to the training camp the next day he found that some RSS youths and others were being given training in the use of .303 rifles by soldiers.

Another incident that I recall is about Mr Mehr Chand Mahajan (the then prime minister) who told a delegation of Hindus who met him in the palace when he arrived in Jammu that now when the power is being transferred to the people they should demand parity. [One] of them associated with National Conference asked how can they demand parity when there is so much difference in population ratio. Pointing to the Ramnagarrakh below, where some bodies of Muslims were still lying he said 'the population ratio too can change'.

Mahatma Gandhi did comment on the situation in Jammu on 25 December 1947 and his remarks have found mention in Volume 90 of his *Collected Works*: 'The Hindus and Sikhs of Jammu and those who had gone there from outside killed Muslims. The Maharaja of Kashmir is responsible for what is happening there... Muslim women have been dishonoured.'

᷈

In recent years there has been a great outpouring of sympathy for the pitiable condition in which Kashmiri Pandits have lived in Jammu refugee camps for the past twenty-five years. The future of Kashmir is inconceivable without its Pandits. But consider another side of the story too. Swaminathan Anklesaria Aiyar wrote an article in the *Times of India* on 18 January 2015. It placed the tragedy of the Pandits in its proper perspective. Aiyar clubbed it with another ethnic cleansing in the state that is almost never mentioned. Entitling his piece 'A Tale of Two Ethnic Cleansings in Kashmir', Aiyar wrote: 'Today, Jammu is a Hindu majority area. But in 1947 it had a Muslim majority. The communal riots of 1947 fell most heavily on Jammu's Muslims; lakhs fled into what became Pakistan-occupied Kashmir. That turned Jammu's Muslim majority into Hindu majority... In sheer scale this far exceeded the ethnic cleansing of Pandits five decades later.'

Aiyar concludes: 'The tragedies of J&K constitute a long, horrific tale of death and inhumanity. It has many villains and no heroes. Both sides have been guilty of ethnic cleansing. Both claim to be victims, forgetting they have also been perpetrators. On the twenty-fifth anniversary of Azaadi uprising, the Hindu–Muslim divide is deeper and ethnic amnesia more selective than ever before. Some stories do not have happy endings.'

Given this reality, it will be very difficult to find a happy ending to the tragedy of Kashmir. Neverthless, we have no option but to try. It is to be hoped that governments in both India and Pakistan will find a way to heal the wounds that have been inflicted, on a more or less constant basis, on the region. It is beyond the scope of this book to suggest a realistic solution to the Kashmir 'problem'. In a general kind of way the panacea for Kashmir, Indo–Pak and Hindu–Muslim relations can only take place if the triangular interconnection mentioned elsewhere in the book is properly understood.

NINE

Global Error: The War on Terror

GEORGE W. BUSH'S ambassador to India Robert Blackwill's lunches and dinners were simulated sessions of a Harvard lecture room. 'Imagine I am Henry Kissinger,' the chubby ambassador would announce to his guests as he settled down, spreading a napkin over his knees, at the end or sometimes even the beginning of a meal. The circular dining table in the Ambassador's residence, which could seat a dozen or more guests, was perfectly suited to these 'panel discussions'. At one such dinner, seated next to me was Pranab Mukherjee, currently President of the Republic. The NDA under Atal Bihari Vajpayee was in power. Pranab was then an Opposition Member of Parliament. It was November 2001. Pakistan had joined the global war on terror.

Blackwill was all praise for Musharraf for having joined the war on terror. On hearing this, Pranab became fidgety. 'How can he say this?' he whispered to me.

I raised my hand: 'Ambassador, you know how we have been plagued by cross-border terrorism from Pakistan, at least since 1989. Your government has been chastising successive Pakistan governments on this score. How does a net exporter of terrorism overnight become a frontline state in America's war against terrorism?'

Blackwill looked at others around the table hoping that another question would get him off the hook.

Pranab stood up. 'You must answer this question,' he said. 'This is most important, no doubt.'

Blackwill presented the American view of the situation. 'The problems between India and Pakistan are all part of an old regional conflict,' he explained. 'Now Pakistan has joined us to fight the global war on terror.'

The reason I mention this anecdote is to show how our standoff with Pakistan has been made way more complicated by the world's (especially the Western world's) war with Islamic fundamentalism, a war in which several significant mistakes have been committed.

The history of Western conflict is largely the story of conflict between the three Semitic or Abrahamic religions: Christianity, Islam and Judaism. In the West, this conflict reached its peak with the Crusades in the eleventh century. But in India the story was different. Since the advent of Islam in India 1,200 years ago, the dominant narrative has been one of social and cultural accommodation, and occasionally, even mutual admiration.

It is an amazing coincidence that Muslim contact with India and the West began in the same year—711 CE. It was in this year that Muhammad bin Qasim's probe into India took place. He was a young general in the Umayyad's army. Another general with the Caliphate, Tariq ibn Ziyad, crossed the narrow strip of ocean between Morocco and the tip of Spain. He anchored by the giant rock which he called Jabal al Tariq (the Rock of Tariq). The British renamed it Gibraltar. North of Gibraltar, through Spain and Portugal, the entire Iberian Peninsula came under Muslim rule. This lasted nearly 800 years until Columbus set sail for the New World in 1492.

During the rule of the Umayyad Caliphate, Andalusia's capital, Cordoba, became the biggest and 'most dazzling city in Western Europe' in the tenth century, when London and Paris were small towns. Jewish, Muslim and Christian philosophers met in the city square. It became a renowned intellectual centre. It had more hamams (steam baths) for its population of about 200,000 than even some of the later and bigger Ottoman cities. This, at a time, when there was a taboo on bathing in Europe. Composer Mozart had died at thirty-six because of this taboo.

At the other end, Muhammad bin Qasim's probe which landed him in Sindh signalled the Arab world's continued interest in India. Before Islam, there had been thousands of years of trade relations between the two, punctuated by acts of piracy, to loot and to control the shipping lanes. Qasim's invasion was harsh and differed vastly from later arrivals who formed the Delhi Sultanate (1206-1526) and built the Qutub Minar in the first city of Delhi in Mehrauli. Qasim returned to Arabia after an extended and unfriendly exploration of three years. He never made India his home unlike the founders of the Delhi Sultanate and the Mughals. That is the beginning of the story of Muslims in India. During the Mughal period, India's GDP was 25 per cent of the world's collective GDP. By 1900, under the British, it had plummeted to 1.6 per cent.

A much more benign arrival, one that initiated great cultural commerce, was that of the Sufi saint Shahbaz Qalandar, in the early twelfth century, also in Sindh. To this day people across the subcontinent go into a trance listening to 'Dama dum mast Qalandar'. With the coming of the Sufis, the tone of Islam's interaction with Hinduism became softer.

The Christian-Muslim face-off was proceeding differently. When Pope Urban II ordered the First Crusade against the Muslims in 1095, one of his milder directives was 'to exterminate this vile race from our lands'. Of course, the Crusaders turned upon the Jews instead with much greater ferocity.

By contrast, Islam's experience with the Hindu civilization was wholesome and led to the greatest multicultural edifice the world has known. The pity is that today this great edifice is being chipped away by electoral politics. The war on terror is aggravating an already dismal situation. Partition and what it brought in its train has been a body blow to this history of cultural enmeshing. Also harmful has been organized Christian and Muslim proselytization. Whatever the iniquities of the caste system, conversions should not have had official sanction in a society where conversion is taboo.

By the time P. V. Narasimha Rao became prime minister in June 1991, the Soviet Union had been officially declared dead. There was no alternative for New Delhi except to lurch towards the US, which had at this stage quite suddenly become the sole superpower. This 'lurch' made practical sense but it also came with costs. Another event occurred at this time: the Gulf War or Operation Desert Storm was launched almost as a celebration of victory. Peter Arnett of CNN brought the war live from the terrace of the Al Rasheed Hotel in Baghdad to the world's drawing rooms. For the first time in history, a war was televised live.

This was an epoch-making event in the history of broadcasting. India being a recipient of these images had willy-nilly accepted the Western narrative. The televised war on terror, the weekly discovery of Muslim terrorists, was custom-made for media trials. This proceeded to divide Muslim and non-Muslim worlds and to boost communal temperatures. The atmosphere was already filled with Islamophobia on the eve of 9/11 when two passenger planes flew into New York's twin towers. The retaliatory bombardment of Afghanistan transformed the war on terror into a war without end. By participating in this war, for reasons I will explain later, the Indian establishment proceeded to alienate its own Muslim population.

India was keen to be seen in the senior league, fighting global terror. In the process, we exaggerated our own subplot that was focused on Pakistan, Kashmir and Indian Muslims. The war on terror resulted in loss of life, of course. But it has done much worse; it has separated people who have lived together for centuries. This Hindu–Muslim separation of the mind is deeper than anything preceding it. Muslims and non-Muslims have been parcelled into hostile camps. And the control on the levers of this war is America's which, alas, has no experience of Muslims. We should be guiding them; we have known Muslims since Islam's founding. After a thousand years of living together, a people are being separated to fight a war initiated by the West for its own reasons.

⌣

Indian independence coincided with the beginning of the Cold War. Since 1947, India followed a policy of non-alignment or equidistance from the Soviet and Western blocs. But, in effect, New Delhi leaned towards Moscow for a number of reasons: socialism as a credo seemed attractive to a poor nation attempting to set right the ravages of colonialism; Russia stepped in to offer a helping hand from time to time; it was geographically closer, and so on.

Pakistan, on the other hand, had remained the West's ally since 1947 because that was the pre-determined trajectory it was supposed to follow. Narendra Singh Sarila's *The Shadow of the Great Game: The Untold Story of India's Partition* explores the role played by Pakistan as one assigned to it by imperial powers. After the discovery of oil on an industrial scale in the Gulf, which the West was thirsty for, it needed a major Muslim country as a 'pliable' ally, and Pakistan more or less chose itself for historical as well as geopolitical reasons. So Pakistan was nursed along in every possible way since Indian non-alignment was declared 'immoral' by John Foster Dulles who served as Secretary of State under US President Dwight D. Eisenhower. Even Pakistan's nuclear programme was silently tolerated.

Pakistan paid its dues by allowing the US and the Saudis to help create the Mujahideen in Afghanistan. These Islamic militants would drive out the Soviets from Kabul in 1989, an event which was a precursor to the collapse of the Soviet Union. All this was not without costs, including to the US. The spare jihadi reservoir exported militancy to Kashmir, Egypt, Algeria and eventually to New York on 9/11. Zbigniew Brzezinski's remark to an interviewer in January 1998 will be remembered for its callousness. The priority, he said, was to defeat the Soviet Union and not worry about 'some stirred up Muslims'. Well, the 'stirred up' Muslims are plaguing the world today.

Ironically, Pakistan which set up vast facilities—hundreds of madrasas to train jihadists to fight the Soviets in Afghanistan—was in December 2001 forced to wage war in Afghanistan against terrorists and their support structures responsible for 9/11. It was a tough call for Pakistan. It was being called upon to fight.

⌒

With the collapse of the Soviet Union in 1990-1991, the terms of engagement, both external and internal, changed. Having won the Cold War, the West had to reorder its game plan. British Prime Minister Margaret Thatcher gave the first clue about the changed play. On a visit to Finland, journalists asked her if Britain needed her nuclear deterrent now that the Soviet Union was beaten. 'We still have a problem in the Middle East,' was her reply.

American strategists like Zbigniew Brzezinski searched for a new role for NATO now that the principal target of the alliance, the Soviet Union, was gone. The German and Japanese economies were booming. Would they come up trumps in the new global power distribution? The word 'Axis' reared its head in the minds of the allies. To forestall such outcomes, a coalition of the willing was forged after Saddam Hussein's dubious occupation of Kuwait. There was a view that US Ambassador April Gillespie in her last meeting with Saddam Hussein had virtually set him up—she signalled that the US would not react. Operation Desert Storm was launched in January 1991.

The entire build-up to the first war on Iraq was swallowed by the Indian media hook line and sinker. What provoked Saddam Hussein to occupy Kuwait? No questions were asked in India.

⌒

When the Gulf War started, I approached the Americans for a visa to cover Operation Desert Storm. I was told the war was being directed from Saudi Arabia. But the Saudis on their part said that Americans were prosecuting the war. Exasperated, I obtained an Iraqi visa and drove 1,200 kilometres from Amman to Baghdad to find myself in Hotel Al Mansour. The more favoured Al Rasheed hotel's top two floors had been taken over by CNN. The lower floors were distributed between American and British journalists. All other journalists, including the European contingent, had been left to fend for themselves.

I have dwelt on these details to give the reader a comprehensive idea of what I witnessed. Yasser Arafat happened to be Saddam Hussein's guest in Baghdad at this time. He was convinced the war would not take place and that what we were seeing was American bluster. His logic was simple: the American withdrawal from Vietnam had been precipitated by the frequency with which body bags were returning home. Iraq's flat battlefield would yield a crop of body bags on a scale that the Americans would simply not risk.

But the Americans had a different idea. They decided not to have boots on the ground at all. Operation Desert Storm was the most dazzling display of air power in history. From my fourteenth floor room I could hear the sound of a hundred giant rattles amplified a thousand times, and fireworks which exceeded Milton's description of Hell. The impact of this high-voltage coverage on the global mood was unsettling.

CNN's live coverage of the war was seen by Western audiences as an enormous triumph coming as it did on the heels of the Soviet collapse. In Arab, indeed all Muslim, societies, the images represented the humiliation of a Muslim country. Instantly, the world was divided into two sets of audiences. For the West, it was victory; for the Muslim world, humiliation.

All this impacted India. Operation Desert Storm and the birth of the global media coincided, more or less, with P. V. Narasimha

Rao taking over as prime minister and appointing Manmohan Singh as his finance minister—with clear instructions to embark on new economic policies which would tie India to the West and to the US specifically.

Only Doordarshan, India's government-funded TV channel, existed when Rao became prime minister in 1991. By 1994, TV channels were beginning to mushroom. This was to accommodate the advertising the new economic policies would generate. These channels had links with Murdoch, Reuters, CNN and so on. Live global television, as I've mentioned, was inaugurated with the coverage of the Iraq War and many Indian TV channels, which had links with the Western media, simply took their 'feed' from Western sources. The minds of our elites were soon being shaped by the BBC and CNN. This has become the norm today because the Indian media has shown a singular lack of initiative when it comes to covering or having a view on international events. The attitude seems to be—you shape the world, we will mark time with caste, cricket and shallow TV debates.

Exactly a decade after the US defeated the Soviet Union, the 9/11 attacks on the Twin Towers in New York took place in September 2001 and George W. Bush formally announced America's 'global war on terror'. The US was now the sole superpower and the sole superpower was now out to consolidate its hegemony. US Vice President Dick Cheney, Secretary of Defence Donald Rumsfeld, President of the World Bank Paul Wolfowitz, plus a powerful grouping called the neo-conservatives were aiming at full spectrum dominance. The Taliban, which had accorded hospitality to Osama bin Laden, the mastermind behind the 9/11 attacks, was hammered out of power with logistical help from Pakistan. In the process of being hammered, some Taliban and Al Qaeda fighters found sanctuary among cousins in Pakistan, where many of them had, in any case, been trained by the ISI to fight the Soviets.

After 9/11, US-India coordination deepened. Hindu–Muslim

differences coincidentally became wider. When President George W. Bush visited New Delhi in March 2006, he was billed to address a joint session of Parliament. A massive protest by Muslims at Delhi's Ram Lila grounds forced the government to cancel the event. The Bush-led war on terror cast the US President as the enemy in the minds of Indian Muslims. With the rest of India he was among the most popular US presidents ever. This contradiction became one more fault line in the deepening communal divide.

Since the post 9/11 war on terror, every fake encounter or atrocity committed by militant groups has been laid at the doorstep of the country's Muslim community. This, despite the fact that most Muslims have no association with groups like the Indian Mujahideen (IM). The former Union Minister for Minority Affairs in the UPA government, Rehman Khan, was categorical. 'Most Muslims believe IM does not exist.'

The Indian media should shoulder a fair amount of blame (due to bias as well as incompetent reporting) for the enthusiasm with which terrorism has been blamed on Muslims. But the activities of the intelligence and security agencies are even more responsible for vilifying the Muslim community and aggravating the communal divide. It has been found that nearly 90 per cent of those held for suspected terrorist activity are never charged or convicted. It is also interesting that Hindu extremist groups who have been charged with acts of terror like the Malegaon blasts (September 2006) or the bombing of the Ajmer dargah (October 2007), to name just a couple, by and large are treated more sympathetically than their Muslim counterparts by the authorities, the media, and the population at large.

In sum, the global war on terror has become the newest platform on which to build Hindu nationalism. It is no accident that thousands of angry Indian Muslim men are routinely picked up on charges of being suspected jihadis. The Jamia Teachers' Solidarity Association (JTSA), Delhi, compiled a report in 2012 entitled 'Framed, Damned, Acquitted: Dossiers of a Very Special Cell'. From hundreds of judgments in the various courts of India, the association picked up sixteen instances where cases against alleged terrorists were dismissed by the courts on various counts, including a complete lack of evidence. Those arrested were charged with being agents of various terrorist organizations and charged with 'heinous' crimes ranging from war against the state and conspiring, planning and attempting to organize terrorist strikes and bomb attacks in the country. The courts dismissed these cases because the charges turned out to be fabricated. According to the JTSA report, every accused in these cases was acquitted 'not simply for want of evidence, but because evidence was tampered with, and the police story was found to be unreliable and [incredible]'.

The report also pointed out that there was only a 30 per cent rate of conviction in suspected 'terrorist' cases because unverified secret information led the police to the accused. Independent witnesses rarely joined in the 'crackdown' and private vehicles were used in operations so there were no logs to prove that the police did conduct a raid on a particular place. Also, the time when a suspect was picked up was much earlier than when he or she was shown on record as arrested.

Take the case of forty-five-year-old Sayyed Liyaqat Shah. He was declared innocent in January 2015 by the National Investigation Agency (NIA), the nodal agency that investigates terrorism cases. All charges against him were dropped. Shah's ordeal began in March 2013 when he, accompanied by his wife and teenaged daughter, was arrested at the Indo-Nepalese border and charged with plotting attacks on targets in Delhi during the Holi festival. The suspected 'terrorist' and his family were returning from Pakistan-occupied Kashmir (PoK) under the Rehabilitation and Surrender Policy initiated by the J&K government in 2010. Under this policy, Indian citizens who had turned to militancy and had crossed the LoC could return to Kashmir once they declared their intent to lay down arms.

Prospective returnees and their families are subjected to an intensive check by RAW, IB and the J&K police before clearance is given. Shah was cleared by these agencies but was arrested by the Delhi police at Sunauli check post, an entry point on the Indo-Nepalese border. The police case was that he was proceeding to Delhi to collect an AK-56 rifle, two magazines with sixty rounds, hand grenades and maps from a guesthouse in Old Delhi. According to the police, Shah was directed there by his handler in Pakistan and the arms were to be used in the attacks that were to follow. After the case was investigated by the NIA, it fell apart. The arms, it was revealed, were planted in the guesthouse by a police informer who was absconding. The entire case was cooked up. Shah had been framed.

Why do the police target innocents? Apparently, specialist squads created to fight terror have to show results. There are rewards, by way of medals and promotions, for officers who effect arrests. The incentives have only become more attractive since the global war on terror was launched. Also thrown in are trips overseas for officers who bust terror modules and save Indian cities from potential terrorist strikes.

Suspects, we learn from the JTSA report, are picked up by the Special Cell, incarcerated, tortured, taken to court and returned to their cells without ever being charged or convicted. Years of their lives are thus lived in captivity. The men whose cases have been written about in this report were all acquitted between 1992 and 2012. Yet they suffered grievously. When they returned home their world had changed. Many parents had died of grief and the lives of families and children were ruined.

The waiting period for undertrials could be years—ten, fifteen, twenty—depending on their luck. Finally, when the case is heard, the judge often announces the acquittal of the accused because the grounds are flimsy, and clearly concocted. Acquittal does accord physical freedom but the lost years, and the normalcy of everyday life, cannot be reclaimed.

After 9/11 and 26/11 there is declining sympathy among the majority population for Muslim youth who are falsely picked up as terrorists. It is presumed that they are guilty even if there is no evidence. There is no public outcry when innocents are charged with trumped-up cases. With every such arrest more members of the community turn against the state and may even be persuaded to join militant groups or take to arms. It is a vicious circle. If injustice becomes the law, resistance becomes duty.

Simmering grievances in the ghettoized enclaves of the 'Other' tend to consolidate divisions of the mind. From cricket to the US election results—on everything Hindus and Muslims have different perceptions, sometimes diametrically opposed to each other's. This surly lack of communication creates distances of the mind, more durable than communal clashes.

Epilogue

I cannot put a date to exactly when it happened, but gradually, over many years, people around me began to identify me as 'Muslim'. This was 'new' and, I suppose, the beginning of a process which placed me with the 'Other'. Firaq Gorakhpuri has a wonderful couplet to describe the phenomenon: 'It needed prescience but we were growing lonely in a crowded world.' In 1990, the late Vinod Mehta, distinguished editor, author of *Lucknow Boy*, and a friend of at least sixty years, beginning with school, invited me to write a column for his magazine from a 'Muslim perspective'. I glared at him. Et tu, Vinod? We had grown up knowing each other's families, enjoying the same food, books, movies, played sports on the same grounds and waited on Saturdays with bated breath for the well-groomed ladies of Isabella Thoburn College to troop onto the pavements of Hazratganj. Our differences, if any, were about Jeeves and Blandings Castle—we would argue about which sequence of books was funnier. And now, as editor, Vinod was slotting me with the 'Other'. In a sense, I suppose he was following a trend because of the way things had worked out after Independence. If the country were to keep up the pretence of secularism, and equality, it needed the 'Other', although those of us who 'belonged' to this category seemed to be in short supply.

In 1972, D. P. Dhar, as head of Policy Planning for the Indo–Pak summit in Simla that year, called up the editor of *The Statesman* where I was working at the time and asked that I be assigned to the hill station because 'we must have a bright, young Muslim journalist' in the Indian contingent. Pakistan President

Zulfiqar Ali Bhutto was bringing scores and they would all be Muslim. And that is how I got the opportunity to interview Benazir Bhutto, the nineteen-year-old undergraduate from Oxford who had accompanied her father.

It was all splendid while the going was good. The thought never occurred to me then, as it does now—that there were larger implications to the way I lived my life and thrived in my chosen career. Jayaprakash Narayan, Atal Bihari Vajpayee, Inder Gujral, Pran Chopra, Inder Malhotra, Kuldip Nayar and scores of others—all extended patronage to me and quite rejoiced in it. The environments in which these worthies operated had very few Muslims. After Partition, there was a dearth of enlightened Muslims. Secularism was still invoked even though it was a declining ideal, having been much profaned.

Another reality dawned on me. In a fifty-year career no Muslim had ever helped me strategically and for a good reason: after Partition Muslims seldom reached positions from which they could dispense favours. One or two who did were cautious, averse to helping members of their community. That would open them to the charge of nepotism or communal bias.

A country emerging from layers of feudalism had necessarily developed a system of networks. For a time, caste networks ruled. Everyone was affected. The poorest Brahmin in Mustafabad or Rae Bareli was secure so long as Pandit Govind Ballabh Pant was UP's chief minister. That powerful network began to collapse as a huge churning overtook Indian society that will continue well into the twenty-first century. Groups and castes will find new levels. But given the current socio-economic condition of the Muslim, as spelt out by Sachar Committee, he is likely to be kept below the churning by his clerical leadership which strikes bargains with the political class and keeps the community mired in religion in enclaves distant from modernity.

And yet, it could have all been so different. In the course of the book I have investigated the major missteps that took place after Independence, and pointed out in some instances how matters could have been better handled. But only rarely did the political and personal will of our tallest leaders rise above electoral, sectarian considerations. And their personal ambitions. If enough people in power had decided to take a different path, things would have been radically different. Of that I am convinced, after decades of being an observer and citizen of the subcontinent.

On the ground, people would have responded positively to the idea of coming together, even if strategic or other considerations had driven them apart. Let me illustrate this with an anecdote.

I was a staff reporter with *The Statesman* when the war to liberate Bangladesh broke out in 1971. The editor, Evan Charlton, advised against my covering the Bangladesh front because the militia there could mistake me for a Punjabi. That would be the end of me. So I was sent to Chhamb in the Western Sector where there was no likelihood of an ethnic mix-up. Before I set out in my army uniform, my great aunt, Naani Ammi, took me aside. She gave me two talismans or Imam Zamins before I set off for the war front—one for me and one for Major Akhtar of the Pakistan Army, a first cousin of mine who she thought I would meet during a break in the fighting. That is how hazy the project to divide the subcontinent was in many minds. Even today I find it difficult to control my tears when I remember Naani Ammi standing in the doorway with two talismans for her grandchildren—one an Indian and the other a Pakistani.

Why have our politicians, power-brokers, ordinary citizens, failed to reach out, to bridge the divide between Hindus and Muslims. In Allahabad University, during the Babri Masjid–Ram Janmabhoomi agitation, I put a simple question to the packed audience consisting of teachers and students, almost equally divided between Hindus and Muslims. 'Have the Hindus in this audience ever seen the inside of a Muslim home?' One or two murmured 'my father knew Persian' or 'my mother cooks chicken' as evidence of his or her emancipation from religious parochialism. But, no, none of them had ever been to a Muslim home.

Likewise, the Muslims in the gathering had never visited a Hindu home. At that moment, a truth hit me between my eyes. We have lived in a state of uninstitutionalized apartheid for decades, even centuries. The segregation between people belonging to different religions has been complicated by the restrictions of caste.

As we know, caste in this country is further stratified by the clan you belong to. At the very top of society, with a few exceptions, you are segregated by class and not necessarily by caste. But, at other levels, it becomes progressively oriented towards caste.

There is little crossover and there are often atrocities perpetrated by higher castes upon lower castes.

New converts to Islam imagined they had broken away from these stratifications towards a more egalitarian system. Indeed, in the congregational system of Islam, they could all enter the mosque. As the poet Iqbal said:

Ek hi saf mein khare ho gaye Mahmud-o-Ayaz
(Mahmud of Ghazni and his slave stood shoulder to shoulder in prayer.)

The mosque, madrasa and the marketplace became centres for social mobility. But even this apparently egalitarian system could not escape stratification—albeit, larger ones: Ashraf, Ajlaf and Arzal. (Elite, weavers and middle craftsmen and the menials.) As we have seen, Sir Syed Ahmad's Aligarh Muslim University was meant only for the Ashraf, consisting of Sayyids, Pathans and Shaikhs or converts from Hindu upper castes among the Hindus.

It is against this background that my interaction with the faculty and students in Allahabad must be seen. That we have stopped 'visiting each other's homes' should not be taken literally. Although there could be much greater interaction between the two communities, especially in the cities. In rural areas there was greater interaction in public spaces. A contrasting situation comes to mind. In the South African apartheid system there were three clear-cut enclaves for whites, Indians and blacks. The separation was enforced by the state. In India, separation is enforced by ancient custom and social habit.

If there has been no culture of social interaction across caste and sub-caste lines, contacts across communal lines have been even more restrictive, except at a rarefied level where, as I've mentioned, class trumps caste and community. Yet even in north Indian Muslim enclaves, where hierarchies were determined by class, these class divisions could be overcome by a shared Urdu culture. In other words, especially up to the twentieth century in north India, familiarity with Urdu poetry, music, a knack for repartee, clear diction and witty conversation ensured entry into most social circles. Religious identity was dwarfed by personal civility and culture. It was like joining a gentleman's club in London's Pall Mall. You could be of any make or colour but you had to be 'clubbable', interesting, able to speak proper English. It was sometimes more important to be interesting than to be relevant.

In these social enclaves, as we have seen in the book, the secular turf was extensive and accommodated motifs of an infinite variety: poetry, music, folklore, diction, mythology, Brajbhasha, Awadhi, stretching down to the village fairs, where intense cultural cross-fertilization took place. This is how the tapestry of Awadh's composite culture was woven. Kashmiri Pandits and Kayasthas, enthusiastic participants in Urdu culture, were regular visitors to Muslim homes.

I have always wondered why students of our schools, colleges, universities, indeed all Indians, are not encouraged to undertake a carefully planned 'Bharat Darshan'. A Muslim who is not aware of the exquisite craftsmanship of temples at Halebid and Belur, Ajanta and Ellora and the granite wonder of Shravanbelagola is as ignorant as an Italian who has not seen St Peter's Basilica and the Sistine Chapel. For sheer control of scale, the Brihadeeswarar

Temple in Tanjore is unsurpassable. Any Indian who is not familiar with these wonders is as unfortunate as the one who is ignorant of Amir Khusro, Mirza Ghalib, Tagore or Thyagaraja. This is our collective heritage and it should be sacrilege for any Indian to demonstrate an unfamiliarity with it. Wherever Muslims have embraced the spectacle of India the result has been a flowering of composite culture. Austerities imposed by Muslim reform schools lead to cultural ghettoization. In extreme situations the Muslim goes beyond becoming the Other, he becomes a caricature.

The Muslim as the 'Other' hit home particularly hard one day in 1996 when our maid, Ganga, asked my wife to join her in the kitchen to talk about something 'in private'. The Indian cricket team was then in the quarter-finals of the ongoing World Cup. She said, 'My husband and I were watching TV last night and wondered which team you and sahib favoured.' My wife, a teacher by instinct and profession, patiently explained the story of Partition and how there were many more Muslims in India than in Pakistan.

Meanwhile Rangili, the young girl who helps Ganga, teased Jamil, our driver: 'Teri team haar gayi (your team has lost).' Jamil, never short of words, shot back: 'Agar meri team haar gayi, to teri team ka kaptaan Pakistani hai (If it is my team which has lost, then the captain of your team is a Pakistani).' The Indian cricket team captain at the time was Mohammad Azharuddin. This completely foxed Rangili, who marched off to Ganga's quarters complaining that Jamil had described the captain of the victorious Indian team as a Pakistani.

Jamil was in the dock. Ganga, who is a 'Nepali' from Darjeeling, embarked on a mock trial of Jamil. Her husband Jagdish joined in.

'But are you not a Muslim?' Rangili asked cheekily.

'Yes, but not a Pakistani,' Jamil replied.

'Muslims are Pakistanis,' Rangili persisted.

'Azharuddin is also a Muslim,' Jamil said.

My wife furnished more data. 'Azharuddin, who received an award as captain of the winning team, is a Muslim; Sidhu, the man of the match, is a Sikh; Vinod Kambli, who hit a century in the previous match, is a Christian.'

Ganga eyed my wife suspiciously, 'You mean the Hindu did nothing?'

My wife was beginning to lose patience. 'An Indian team is an Indian team. There are no Muslim or Hindu teams in our country,' she asserted.

Ganga found this illogical. 'If the Pakistani team is a Muslim team, why should the Indian team not be a Hindu team?'

Ganga's logic gave Jamil yet another opening. 'If you want a Hindu team, you cannot have Azharuddin as captain.'

Jagdish intervened aggressively, 'If having Azharuddin as a captain means that we cannot have a Hindu team, we should not have him as captain.' This angered Jamil. 'Who are you to remove Azharuddin? In fact, you should shut up because you are a Nepali.'

'But I am a Hindu', Jagdish continued.

'Does a Nepali Hindu have more rights in India than an Indian Muslim?' Jamil asked fuming.

The conversation came to an abrupt end when the doorbell rang and our friend Anup entered. For the past few days he had been drawing up plans for us to travel to Lahore to see the World Cup finals in March 1996. Provided, of course, India made it to the finals. Anup was in a state of high agitation. 'Have you seen all this?' he asked, thumping the set of newspapers on my table with the back of his hand. 'They have gone crazy in Pakistan. The country's senate has asked for an inquiry into the Pakistani defeat at Bangalore. Wasim Akram's house has been stoned. Jamaat-e-Islami says so long as the country was ruled by a woman [Benazir Bhutto], Pakistan would keep losing.' Anup paused, then continued his soliloquy. 'They are treating a cricket defeat as a national humiliation. I suppose they have nothing else through which they can define their nationalism.'

He waited for me to react then asked. 'So what do you think?'
I was busy reading the astonishing stories from Pakistan, how
the nation was in convulsions after losing the Bangalore match.
'I refuse to go to Lahore under these circumstances,' Anup said.
He said his friends at ITC, who had offered him passes for the
Lahore match, were having second thoughts themselves. There
would be a small Indian group at the Gaddafi stadium. 'They
may attack us; they may even kill us,' Anup added.

Ironically, Anup's somewhat exaggerated anxieties were set
at rest by the turn of events at Eden Gardens where India was
saved the agony of having to face hostile crowds at Lahore because
of their loss to Sri Lanka in the semi-finals. The high pedestal
of self-righteousness on which we stood after Bangalore came
crashing down after Calcutta. The Calcutta crowds were the great
leveller. They set fire to the stands at Eden Gardens. Indo–Pak
relations, which had touched rock bottom following Pakistan's
defeat, were on an even keel again. Diplomacy would have had
to struggle for months to achieve what the Sri Lankan cricketers
and the Calcutta crowds did in a day's therapeutic cricket. And
they did it so convincingly that the Pakistani overreaction in
their country was confined to the newspapers.

The final words to Anup were mine: 'Now nobody will notice
a group of Indian fans in Lahore. So, Anup, call up your friends
and hit the road to Wagah and watch some decent cricket, free of
Indo–Pak tensions.' For the record, Sri Lanka defeated Australia
in the final.

India, Pakistan and Bangladesh are permanent realities. These
cannot be wished away. The cancer that Partition left behind
cannot continue to claim hearts and minds and lives. In chapter
after chapter, we have seen how the complex triangular reality
of India–Pakistan, Hindu–Muslim, New Delhi–Srinagar must be
grasped. Tinker with any one axis and it will have an immediate
impact on the other two. And yet no concerted effort is being
made to take a holistic view of the triangle, understand it, and

order our behaviour according to its imperatives.

Never before have we had it so bad—not a day passes without someone questioning the legitimacy of the Indian Muslim, a call for us to be 'super patriots', to prove our patriotism. Even Bollywood, a religion unto itself, and an industry which, ironically, has many leading actors who are Muslims, has not been spared. Arguably the country's biggest stars—Shah Rukh Khan and Aamir Khan—both faced a furious backlash from the Hindu majority in late 2015 when they spoke out about incidents of communal tension and an increasingly intolerant environment in the country. Among the many disproportionate reactions to the actors' statements was the Hindu Mahasabha's call for them to be charged with treason.

The brutal murder of Mohammad Akhlaq, Shiv Sena activists forcing the cancellation of a concert by Ghulam Ali and the attack on an organizer of a talk featuring former Pakistani foreign minister Khurshid Kasuri are but a few of the recent signs that indicate how communal elements are gaining strength.

Alarm bells are ringing—India needs to affirm its commitment to pluralism, diversity and religious harmony and not pander to politicians—whether from the left-of-centre Congress or the right-of-centre BJP.

What can be done?

To begin with, we need the courage to accept the harsh diagnoses of actions of the past. Mistakes were made—Partition was one of them. It cannot be undone. The three entities that have grown out of it have to be nurtured, embraced and helped to flourish. Each entity must pull itself out of a negative-identity syndrome—'We are because we could not live with them.' This is an endless spiral, leading nowhere. Indo–Pak hostility generates communal hatred, leaves Kashmir unsettled. Revert to the triangle—that is the objective reality.

First, minds have to be prepared to accept that reality. Towards this end, temperatures on the Indo–Pak, Hindu–Muslim, New

Delhi–Srinagar axes have to be lowered.

TV channels which stoke cross-border tensions need to be disciplined. At the same time Pakistan will need to be reminded, in no uncertain terms, that the export of terror will not be permitted. The 'global war on terror' cannot be allowed to exploit existing fault lines in this country. As to Kashmir, we will need to negotiate carefully and sensitively to build on whatever positive trends exist to find a lasting solution to the problem of India's most sensitive state.

Of course, Indian Muslims must be freed from the clutches of their clerics just as Hindus need to turn away from communal politicians. Will any of this happen in my lifetime? The signs are not encouraging. The real maha yudh is for the soul of India. Two visions are in epic contest—a vision of a mythical communally-charged past glory versus an India of rational enlightenment that is gentler and more egalitarian. This is the basic tussle in which Muslims are being squeezed. Obviously, it is the latter framework in which all Indians, including minorities, must find their salvation.

My hope is that young politicians, untainted by 1947 and its aftermath, might be able to break the Indo–Pak logjam, transcend the hate and obscurantism and foster people-to-people contact. But this too will remain a homily like so many others: regular commerce across the line of control in Kashmir should become the order; Hindu–Muslim tensions will then fade; strategies have to be devised to defeat the hardliners on both sides who will always impede that agenda. We have heard enough of these homilies.

The reality is more challenging. The consequences of Partition are three uneasy nations. They cannot be undone. If they are to thrive and prosper, they have to progress together. India and Pakistan (for example) are also part of each other's internal politics. For every impulse to engage and harmonize, there is an equally powerful one that militates against it—for political reasons. Indian Muslims have a very human vested interest in

occasionally flocking with relatives sent to the other country—
some stark choices were imposed at the time of Partition. There
must be a similar desire on the part of at least half a generation
on the other side. A dear friend of mine in the Foreign Office,
Keviv Ujtak, says, 'Saeed Bhai, I am afraid you will have to forget
your relatives.' For all practical purposes, I have more or less
forgotten them. Some nostalgia remains. In a couple of generations
that too will go.

> Turfatar yeh hai, ki apna bhi
> na jaana, aur yun hee
> Apna, apna kehke humko
> sabse beygaana kiya

> (The irony is that you never
> considered me your own;
> You only claimed me, until
> I was a stranger to everybody.)

Acknowledgements

I would like to thank my uncle, Sayyid Wasi Naqvi, the first Congress MLA from Rae Bareli who put me through my paces in political reporting and politics; my great uncle, Sayyid Mohammad Sadiq, a brilliant lawyer who never studied files; my mother, Begum Atia Naqvi, erudite, with sharp insights; Maamujan, Sayyid Mohammad Mehdi, a ponderous thinker, a great intellectual influence on me, communist but soft on Jawaharlal Nehru; 'Aunt Agatha', Alia Imam, first woman PhD (in 1950) in the family, a firebrand tamed by circumstances; my cousin, Mushtaq Naqvi, the only litterateur Firaq Gorakhpuri deferred to. So much in this book is owed to these elders who raised me.

Aruna Naqvi jolted me out of my apathy. She made it happen. Ramesh Kumar patiently transferred onto the computer my illegibly scribbled manuscript; Ajith Pillai cut out the meandering bulges.

I must thank Saba, Farah and Zeba for their continued interest.

David Davidar for taking on the book and placing me in the reliable hands of editor Simar Puneet, who grasped the spirit of the book immediately and then edited and shuffled paragraphs with such dexterity so as to fool me entirely that what was being published was, indeed, my manuscript. Sanskrita, the original Bharadwaj from Assam, authenticated all my references.

Notes

INTRODUCTION

x   'affiliation of knowledge and power': Edward W. Saïd, *Orientalism*, Pantheon Books, 1978.

CHAPTER ONE: GROWING UP IN AWADH

16   **zamindari abolition in 1951:** Bipan Chandra, et al., *India After Independence 1947-2000*, Penguin India, 2008.

30   **Somnath was no ordinary temple:** Romila Thapar, *Somanatha: The Many Voices of a History*, Penguin, 2004; Romila Thapar, *The Penguin History of Early India: From the Origins to AD 1300*, Penguin UK, 2015.

31   **'it was soon back to business as usual':** Romila Thapar, *The Penguin History of Early India: From the Origins to AD 1300*, Penguin UK, 2015.

33   **In a manner of speaking, they had all developed the same aesthetics of Islam:** It turns out that Hazrat Moinuddin Chisti—indeed all Sufi Saints of well-established orders were Sayyids too or direct descendants of 'Ahle Bait'. An 'aalim', a religious scholar, or Ulema, which is the plural for 'aalim', in Iran, Iraq, Lebanon, or Shia pockets in Pakistan and India can easily be identified as Sayyids. Sayyid Ulema will always wear a black turban. By that reckoning, Ayatollah Khomeini, Ali Khamenei, President Rabbani and, in Iraq, Ayatollah Ali Sistani, Hasan Nasrullah in Lebanon are all Sayyid, which means that former Presidents Hashemi Rafsanjani, Mahmoud Ahmadinejad and President Hassan Rohani are non-Sayyids.

CHAPTER TWO: THE MANGOES OF MUSTAFABAD

34   **Shatranj ke Khilari (The Chess Players):** Andrew Robinson, 'Satyajit Ray's The Chess Players', *History Today*, Volume 57 Issue, 7 July 2007.

35   **Kathak maestro, Birju Maharaj, is full of stories:** S. Kalidas, 'The Last Maharaj of Lucknow', *India Today*, 21 February 2014.

46   **declining socio-economic condition of Muslims as reported by the Sachar Committee:** Vidya Subrahmaniam, 'Muslim deprivation

widespread: Sachar Committee', *The Hindu*, 1 December 2006; Tarunabh Khaitan, 'Dealing with discrimination', *Frontline*. May 2008; http://mhrd. gov.in/sites/upload_files/mhrd/files/sachar_comm.pdf accessed 10 May 2016.

46   **no follow-up has taken place on the Ranganath Misra Commission recommendations:** 'Report of the National Commission for Religious and Linguistic Minorities', Minority Affairs Ministry, http://www.minorityaffairs. gov.in/sites/upload_files/moma/files/pdfs/volume-1.pdf, accessed 10 May 2016.

CHAPTER THREE: PARTITION'S LONG SHADOW

53   **very high-profile murder of Viceroy Lord Mayo:** Ram Kapse, 'Hundred Years of the Andaman's Cellular Jail', *The Hindu*, 21 December 2005.

54   **When numbers rose from 20,000 in 1857:** Ronald Edward & John Gallagher, *Africa and the Victorians: The Climax of Imperialism*, Doubleday, New York, 1968.

54   **'Though the Mohammadan's cow-killing is made the pretext…':** Sanjeev Nayyar, 'The truth about cow slaughter in India', rediff.com, 16 October 2015.

56   **'it was [Jinnah] who warned Gandhiji not to encourage…':** A. G. Noorani, 'Assessing Jinnah', *Frontline*, Volume 22-Issue 17, 13-26 August, 2005.

57   **'the Muslim league is an important communal organization':** Rajmohan Gandhi, *Understanding the Muslim Mind*, Penguin India, 2003, p150.

57   **'Your tone and language again display the same arrogance':** Ibid.

58   **'there must be a reappraisal of reputations':** 'The Partition on India: Myth and Reality', *The Economist*, 21 April 1990.

58   **would spoil the Independence Day festivities in which he was to star:** H. M. Seervai, *Partition of India: Legend and Reality*, Second Edition, Universal Law Publishers, 2012, p168.

59   **'Jinnah may have raised the flag of Partition but now the real flag bearer was Patel':** Maulana Abul Kalam Azad, *India Wins Freedom: The Complete Version*, first published by Orient Longman 1988, p201.

60   **'is not only extremely intelligent but has a most attractive and friendly temperament':** Ibid, p198.

61   **'My only hope now is in you':** Ibid, p203.

61   **'he no longer spoke so vehemently against it':** Ibid, p203.

61   **'If even you have now adopted these views, I see no hope of saving India from catastrophe':** Ibid, p203.

63   **In his book *Guilty Men of India's Partition*:** Ram Manohar Lohia, *Guilty*

Men of India's Partition, Kitabistan, 1960.

63 **It resulted in more than 14 million people being uprooted:** 'Rupture in South Asia', report by UNHCR, www.unhcr.org, (last accessed 2 April 2016).

63 **'Hundreds of thousands of Hindus and Sikhs who had lived for centuries':** Khushwant Singh, *Train to Pakistan*, first published by Chatto & Windus, 1956.

64 **'Lord Mountbatten said to me more in sorrow than anger':** Maulana Abul Kalam Azad, *India Wins Freedom: The Complete Version*, first published by Orient Longman in 1988, p220.

65 **'He is entirely communal and has no sense of compromise or generosity':** Archibald Percival Wavell, Penderel Moon (ed.), *Wavell: The Viceroy's Journal*, OUP, 1973.

65 **'Patel was a staunch Hindu by upbringing and conviction':** Michael Brecher, *Nehru: A Political Biography*, Beacon Press, 1970.

65 **He said that the reports were 'grossly exaggerated':** Maulana Abul Kalam Azad, *India Wins Freedom: The Complete Version*, first published by Orient Longman in 1988, p232.

65 **'He [Gandhi] seems determined to blacken the name':** Ibid, p236.

65 **Patel put out a story that 'deadly weapons':** Ibid, p233.

66 **Shourie wrote three articles:** Arun Shourie, 'The man who broke up India', *The Illustrated Weekly of India*, 20 and 28 October, and 3 November 1985.

67 **H. M. Seervai took Shourie to task:** H. M. Seervai, *Partition of India: Legend and Reality*, Second Edition, Universal Law Publishers, 2012, pxiii.

67 **Nehru's deep respect for the Maulana:** In another letter to Indira from Ahmadnagar Jail, Nehru writes that the Maulana 'reminds [him] very forcibly of eighteenth century Rationalists and French Encyclopaedists'. He adds, 'Maulana has got a mind like a razor which cuts through a fog of vague ideas.'

67 **Let me quote the letter:** Mahatma Gandhi, *Collected Works, Volume 88, Mahatma Gandhi*, Publications Division, Ministry of Information and Broadcasting, Government of India, 1958.

69 **'I claim that with us both the Khilafat is the central fact':** Mahatma Gandhi, *Young India, Volume 6*, Navajivan Publishing House, 1924.

71 **According to official estimates, the massacre of Muslims that followed took the lives of more than 40,000:** Mike Thomson, 'Hyderabad 1948: India's hidden massacre', BBC, 24 September 2013; read the Sunderlal Report here: www.frontline.in/static/html/fl1805/18051140.htm.

71 **'It is to be noted that the Union armies rescued the very Deshmukhs**

and Razakar': Puccalapalli Sundarayya, *Telangana People's Struggle and Its Lessons*, Foundation Books, 1972, pp139-140.

72 'the Telangana movement can take pride in this important achievement': Ibid, p140.

CHAPTER FOUR: THE LESSONS OF MEENAKSHIPURAM

75 **S. Nihal Singh...shares this nugget in his memoirs:** S. Nihal Singh, *Ink in My Veins: A Life in Journalism*, Hay House, 2011.

76 **'Yes, I was forced by the upper-caste Hindus to run away from a system':** 'Maulana Azad on Mass Conversion', *IANS*, 10 January 2014.

78 **'If missionaries come to India only for evangelical work':** B. S. Raghavan, *Quintessence: A Look At The General Social Milieu*, ICFAI Books, 2005.

CHAPTER FIVE: THE BREAKING OF THE BABRI MASJID

88 **The status quo remained in place until 1949:** 'Timeline: Ayodhya holy site crisis', BBC, 6 December 2012.

88 **...by a mob more than 100,000 strong:** Ramachandra Guha, *India After Gandhi: A History of the World's Largest Democracy*, Macmillan, 2007, p638.

89 **In September 1990...L.K. Advani embarked on a Rath Yatra:** 'Temple Rerun: Tracing Ram Rath Yatra, 25 years later', *Indian Express*, 27 September 2015.

89 **It was in 1855, during Wajid Ali Shah's rule, that a dispute arose in Ayodhya:** Sarvepalli Gopal, *Anatomy of a Confrontation: Ayodhya and the Rise of Communal Politics in India*, Penguin India, 1993, p32.

90 **the British institutionalized the Mandir-Masjid issue:** 'Timeline: Ayodhya holy site crisis', BBC, 6 December 2012.

92 **an intelligence video of [Vajpayee's] speech in Lucknow:** 'There are sharp stones there, the ground has to be levelled', *Outlook*, 7 December 2009.

93 **the ensuing riots spread to cities like Mumbai, Surat:** Ramachandra Guha, *India After Gandhi*, Macmillan, 2007, pp582-598.

93 **caused the death of around 900 people:** Steven I. Wilkinson, *Votes and Violence: Electoral Competition and Ethnic Riots in India*, Cambridge University Press, 2006, p14.

96 **When Rajiv Gandhi visited Bhagalpur he promptly reinstated Dwivedi:** Saeed Naqvi, Sanjay Kapoor, *The Last Brahmin Prime Minister*, Har-Anand Publications, 1996.

96 **He kicked off the party's general election campaign in 1989 from Ayodhya:** Inderjit Badhwar and Prabhu Chawla, 'General Elections 1989:

Moment of Truth', *India Today*, 30 November 1989.

99   **Dayal records, 'the Deputy Inspector General...':** Rajeshwar Dayal, *A Life of Our Times*, Orient Blackswan, 1998, p93.

105   **For clarity I turned to the most important ideologue of the RSS:** An earlier version of this interview was first published in my book *Reflections of an Indian Muslim*, published by Har Anand Publishers in 1993.

CHAPTER SIX: UNHOLY RIOTS

117   **fifty-eight major communal riots in forty-seven places since 1967:** Smruti Koppikar and Saba Naqvi, 'A Beast Asleep?', *Outlook*, March 2012.

118   **According to the Justice Jaganmohan Reddy Commission report:** Pingle Jaganmohan Reddy, Nusserwanji K. Vakil and Akbar S. Sarela, *Report: Inquiry into the communal disturbances at Ahmedabad and other places in Gujarat on and after 18th September 1969*, Home Department, Government of Gujarat, 1971, p180.

118   **Jayaprakash Narayan was invited by Nehru:** Ratan Das, *Jayaprakash Narayan: His Life and Mission*, Sarup & Sons, 2007.

122   **On the morning of 27 February 2002:** 'Eleven sentenced to death for India Godhra train blaze', BBC, 1 March 2011.

125   **Modi had been made chief:** Aditi Phadnis, *Business Standard Political Profiles of Cabals and Kings*, Business Standard Books, 2009, pp116–21; V Venkatesan, 'A Pracharak as Chief Minister', *Frontline*, 13 October 2001.

126   **Among the one lakh Muslims who were moved to relief camps:** Priyanka Kakodkar, 'Sleep and the Innocent', *Outlook Magazine*, 13 May 2002; Dionne Bunsha, 'The Crisis of the Camps', *Frontline*, Volume 19 - Issue 08, 13-26 April 2002.

126   **'destroyed the grave of Wali Gujarati, Urdu's first great poet':** Asghar Ali Engineer, *The Gujarat Carnage*, Orient Blackswan, 2003, p119.

130   **This amateurish video set the Muslim world ablaze:** Michael Joseph Gross, 'Disaster Movie', *Vanity Fair*, 27 December 2012.

130   **'the desecrated page very briefly at the police station':** An earlier version of this appeared in the author's column 'Saeed's Diary', 'The Ghaziabad Whodunnit', *The Sunday Guardian*, 23 September 2012.

134   **Tension in Faizabad was palpable:** Omar Rashid, 'Faizabad violence was well-planned and targets had been selected', *The Hindu*, 1 November 2012.

135   **'Hindus and Muslims had both voted for the SP in the recent elections':** An earlier version of this appeared in the author's column 'Saeed's Diary', 'Carving Communal Constituencies: Countdown To 2014', *The Sunday Guardian*.

137 **The videos reached Mumbai too but the Congress chief minister, Prithviraj Chavan, remained silent:** Vinaya Deshpande, 'Dhule riots reflect changing nature of communal violence, says activist', *The Hindu*, 16 January 2013; Amruta Byatnal, 'In Dhule, the struggle for identity manifests as violence', *The Hindu*, 3 March 2013.

139 **Acharya Giriraj Kishore warned women journalists:** Saba Naqvi and K. S. Shaini, 'Civil Code, De Facto', *Outlook*, 30 April 2007.

142 **'First, good-looking Muslim men are identified':** Prashant Jha, 'Where Sangh spins narratives of victimhood, belligerence', *The Hindu*, 11 September 2013.

143 **'One of the most remarkable campaigns...':** Mohan Rao, 'Love Jihad and Demographic Fears', Indian Journal of Gender Studies, Sage Publications, October 2011, Volume 18, 3, pp425-430.

143 **The Hindu Janajagriti Samiti:** Ibid.

144 **U.N. Mukherji had written a book:** Ibid.

144 **'demographic common sense functioning as a trope':** Mohan Rao and Sarah Sexton, *Markets and Malthus: Population, Gender and Health in Neo-liberal Times*, Sage Publications India, 2010, p119.

145 **This was despite clarifications issued by the Census Commissioner:** Ibid, p118.

145 **Historian and scholar Tanika Sarkar notes:** Tanika Sarkar, 'Semiotics of Terror: Muslim Children and Women in Hindu Rashtra', *Economic and Political Weekly*, Vol 37, No 28 (13-19 July 2002).

CHAPTER SEVEN: A PROCESSION OF PRIME MINISTERS

153 **Shastri requested RSS supremo Guru Golwalkar:** Priti Gandhi, 'Rashtriya Swayamsewak Sangh: How the world's largest NGO has changed the face of Indian democracy', *DNA*, 15 May 2014.

154 **Atal Bihari Vajpayee was moved to describe her as Goddess Durga:** 'Remembering "Iron Lady" Indira Gandhi', *Times of India*, 31 October 2009.

159 **Mrs Gandhi returned to power with a thumping majority of 353 seats:** Gaurav Choudhury, 'Tryst with destiny to India Shining: a history of polls', *Hindustan Times*, 25 May 2014.

160 **The anti-Sikh riots that followed Mrs Gandhi's assassination:** Rahul Bedi, 'Delhi 1984: Memories of a massacre', BBC, 1 November 2009.

167 **In the general election held under his leadership:** Tom Lansford, *Political Handbook of the World 2014*, CQ Press, p628.

167 **During these thirteen days, the Enron deal was signed:** The deal was

shrouded in such corruption that playwright Lucy Prebble wrote a play, *Enron*, which was staged in London's West End and New York's Broadway to full house. Enron's CEO Kenneth Lay, a friend of President George W. Bush, died in some disgrace in 2006. There were numerous cases of corporate corruption in the US climaxing with the Lehman Brothers scandal in 2008. But in India, where most of the corruption took place, there was not even a whimper.

170 **'My opinion on the ordinance...':** 'Rahul tears ordinance and the PM', *Indian Express*, 28 September 2013.

172 **Giriraj Singh, BJP MP from Bihar:** Faizan Ahmad, 'Those opposed to Narendra Modi should go to Pakistan, BJP leader Giriraj Singh says', *Times of India*, 20 April 2014.

172 **Another BJP MP, Sadhvi Niranjan Jyoti:** 'Ramzada vs haramzada: Outrage over Union Minister Sadhvi's remark', *Indian Express*, 2 December 2014.

172 **'Wrap them in pigskin...':** 'Tathagata Roy suggests Russian treatment to terrorists, sparks controversy', *India Today*, 6 January 2016.

CHAPTER SEVEN: THE MAKING OF THE KASHMIR PROBLEM

175 **'preoccupied with his own':** H. M. Seervai, *Partition of India: Legend and Reality*, Second Edition, Universal Law Publishers, 2012.

175 **Nehru, as history tells us:** Rudranghsu Mukherjee, *The Great Speeches of Modern India*, Penguin India, 2011.

177 **'to be in flight, having been terrorized...':** Ian Melville Stephens, *Horned Moon: An Account of a Journey Through Pakistan, Kashmir, and Afghanistan*, Chatto & Windus, 1953, p119.

177 **'startled by their one-sided verdicts on affairs':** Ian Melville Stephens, *Horned Moon: An Account of a Journey Through Pakistan, Kashmir, and Afghanistan*, Chatto & Windus, 1953; Shashi Joshi, *The Last Durbar*, Roli Books Private Limited, 2007, p136.

178 **'undercurrents in his remarks seemed only to confirm my surmise':** Ian Melville Stephens, *Horned Moon: An Account of a Journey Through Pakistan, Kashmir, and Afghanistan*, Chatto & Windus, 1953.

178 **'subject to a plebiscite, this great State, its inhabitants mainly Muslim...':** Ibid.

179 **'how could anyone, however able, function...':** Ian Melville Stephens, *Horned Moon: An Account of a Journey Through Pakistan, Kashmir, and Afghanistan*, Chatto & Windus, 1953.

179 **'try to maintain an inter-dominion policy, in fairness':** Ibid.

180 **The date for the transfer of power:** Saros Cowasjee, *Studies in Indian*

and Anglo-Indian Fiction, Harper Collins Publishers, India, 1993, 29 May 2008, p79.

181 'The date I chose came out of the blue': Dominique Lapierre, Larry Collins, *Freedom at Midnight*, Simon and Schuster, 1975.

183 'Both the new Dominions have been behaving rashly': Ibid.

187 Horace Alexander's article: A. G. Noorani, 'Why Jammu Erupts', *Frontline*, Volume 25 - Issue 19, September 2008.

187 Jawaharlal Nehru wrote to Vallabhbhai Patel on 17 April 1949 (quoted in *Frontline* magazine): Ibid.

189 'Communal tension was building up in Jammu soon': Ved Bhasin, www.kashmirlife.net, 17 November 2015.

192 A Tale of Two Ethnic Cleansings in Kashmir: S. A. Aiyar, 'A tale of two ethnic cleansings in Kashmir', *Times of India Blog*, 18 January 2015.

CHAPTER NINE: GLOBAL ERROR: THE WAR ON TERROR

196 During the Mughal period, India's GDP: Angus Maddison, *The World Economy, Volumes 1-2*, Development Centre of the Organisation for Economic Co-operation and Development, 2006, p638.

196 'to exterminate this vile race from our lands': Andrew Gordon Fiala, *The Just War Myth: The Moral Illusions of War*, Rowman & Littlefield, 2008.

198 Narendra Singh Sarila's *The Shadow of the Great Game*: Narendra Singh Sarila, *The Shadow of the Great Game: The Untold Story of India's Partition*, Constable, 2007.

199 'some stirred up Muslims': 'The CIA's Intervention in Afghanistan: Interview with Zbigniew Brzezinski, President Jimmy Carter's National Security Adviser', *Le Nouvel Observateur*, 15-21 January 1998. Read the interview here: http://www.globalresearch.ca/articles/BRZ110A.html

202 'Most Muslims believe IM does not exist': Manoj C. G., 'Muslims don't believe Indian Mujahideen exists, says Rahman Khan', *The Indian Express*, 26 July 2013.

202 It has been found that nearly 90 per cent of those: Duncan Gardham, 'Only one in eight terror arrests result in conviction', *The Telegraph*, 13 May 2009.

203 Take the case of forty-five-year-old Sayyed Liyaqat Shah: Aman Sharma, 'Punish the Delhi Police Special Cell for framing Sayyed Liyaqat Shah, set an example', *Economic Times*, 27 January 2015.

Bibliography

Abdullah II, King of Jordan, *Our Last Best Chance*, Viking, 2011.

Azad, Abul Kalam, *India Wins Freedom: An Autobiographical Narrative*, Orient Longman, 1959.

Acemoglu, Daron and Robinson, James, *Why Nations Fail: The Origins of Power, Prosperity, and Poverty*, Crown Business, 2012.

Ahmad, Talmiz, *The Islamist Challenge in West Asia*, Pentagon Press, 2014.

Alawi, Amir Ahmad, *Journey To The Holy Land: A Pilgrim's Diary*, (tr.) Hasan, Mushirul, and Jalil, Rakhshanda, OUP India, 2009.

Ambedkar, B.R., *Annihilation of Caste*, Undelivered Speech, 1936.

Ahmad, Talmiz, *An Introduction of Contemporary Islamic Groups and Movements in India*, (self-published), 2001.

Appignanesi, Lisa and Maitland, Sara (eds.), *The Rushdie File*, Syracuse University Press, 1989.

Armstrong, Karen, *Holy War: The Crusades and their Impact on Today's World*, RHUS, 2001.

Asiananda, *Jinnah: A Corrective Reading of Indian History, the Third Advent*, Open University Press, 2005.

Bhagwat, Mohanrao, *Vijayadashmi Address: Corruption is on the Rise Because of Lack of Character*. (http://samvada.org/2012/news/vijayadashami-speech-by-rss-sarasanghachalak-mohan-bhagwat-from-nagpur/) accessed 11 May 2016.

Chandra, Bipan et al., *India After Independence 1947-2000*, Penguin India, 2008.

Chester, Lewis, *American Melodrama: The Presidential Campaign of 1968*, Viking, 1969.

Chomsky, Noam, *Occupy*, Penguin UK, 2012.

——, *Pirates and Emperors, Old and New: International Terrorism in the Real World*, South End Press, 2003.

Chughtai, Ismat, *Lifting the Veil: Selected Writings of Ismat Chughtai*, Penguin India, 2009.

Collier, Dirk, *The Emperor's Writings: Memories of Akbar the Great*, Manjul

Publishing House, 2011.

Cowasjee, Saros, *Studies in Indian and Anglo-Indian Fiction*, HarperCollins India, 1993.

Collins, Larry, and Lapierre, Dominique, *Freedom at Midnight*, Collins 1975.

Dash, P. L., *Caspian Pipeline Politics, Energy Reserves and Regional Implications*, Pentagon Press, 2009.

Dayal, Rajeshwar, *A Life of Our Times*, Orient Blackswan, 1998.

De Gourdon, Come Carpentier, *From India to Infinity*, Har-Anand Publications, 2012.

Desai, Ashwin and Vahed, Goolem, *The South African Gandhi*, Stanford University Press, 2015.

Dixit, J. N., *India and Regional Developments*, Gyan Publishing House, 2004.

Fiala, Andrew Gordon, *The Just War Myth: The Moral Illusions of War*, Rowman & Littlefield, 2008.

Doniger, Wendy, *On Hinduism*, Aleph Book Company, 2013.

Draper, Theodore, *A Very Thin Line: The Iran-Contra Affairs*, Hill and Wang, 1991.

Saïd, Edward W., *Orientalism*, Pantheon Books, 1978.

Engineer, Asghar Ali, *Muslims in India*, Gyan Publishing House, 2006.

Ernst, Carl W., *Sufism: An Introduction to the Mystical Tradition of Islam*, Shambhala, 2011.

Fair, C. Christine, *Fighting to the End: The Pakistan Army's Way of War*, OUP, 2014.

Fatah, Tarek, *Chasing a Mirage: The Tragic Illusion of an Islamic State*, John Wiley & Sons, 2008.

Ferguson, Niall, *Civilization: The West and the Rest*, Penguin UK, 2011.

———, *Empire: How Britain Made the Modern World*, Penguin UK, 2009.

Gandhi, Mahatma, *Collected Works, Volume 88*, Mahatma Gandhi, Publications Division, Ministry of Information and Broadcasting, Government of India, 1958.

———, *Young India*, Volume 6, Navajivan Publishing House, 1924.

Gandhi, Rajmohan, *Understanding the Muslim Mind*, Penguin India, 2003.

Gandhi, Sonia (ed.), *Two Alone, Two Together*, Penguin India, 2004.

Gayer, Laurent and Jaffrelot, Christophe (eds.), *Muslims in Indian Cities: Trajectories of Marginalisation*, C Hurst & Co Publishers, 2012.

Gayer, Laurent, *Karachi Ordered Disorder*, HarperCollins India, 2014.

Ghose, Sankar, *Political Ideas And Movements In India*, Allied Publishers, 1975.

Gilbert, Martin, *A History of the Twentieth Century*, William Morrow Paperbacks, 2002.

Gopal, Sarvepalli, *Anatomy of a Confrontation: Ayodhya and the Rise of Communal Politics in India*, Penguin India, 1993.

Goodwin, Doris Kearns, *No Ordinary Time: Franklin and Eleanor Roosevelt: The Home Front in World War II*, Simon & Schuster, 1995.

Gorenberg, Gershom, *The Accidental Empire*, Holt Paperbacks, 2007.

Gupta, Om, *Media Society And Culture*, Isha Books, 2006.

Gupta, Dipankar, *Revolution From Above*, Rupa Publications, 2013.

Guha, Ramachandra, *India After Gandhi*, Macmillan, 2007.

Hajari, Nisid, *Midnight's Furies: The Deadly Legacy of India's Partition*, Houghton Mifflin Harcourt, 2015.

Hai Mohammad, Abdul, *History of Aurangabad*, Savera Offset Printers, 2004.

Hasan, Mushirul, *Nationalism and Communal Politics in India*, Manohar Publishers and Distributors, 1991.

———, *Proceedings of the Indian National Congress*, Niyogi Books, 2013.

Haider, Niaz, *Shola-e-Awargi* (The Vagabond's Mission).

Hasan, Zoya, *Congress After India*, OUP India, 2012.

Hazleton, Lesley, *The First Muslim: The Story of Muhammad*, Riverhead Books, 2014.

Herbert, Eugenia W., *Flora's Empire: British Gardens in India*, University of Pennsylvania Press, 2011.

Hobsbawm, Eric, *How to Change the World: Reflections on Marx and Marxism*, Yale University Press, 2012.

Hossain, Syud and Chakrabartti, J. N. (eds.), *Dr. Syud Hossain: A Glimpse of His Life, Speeches & Writings*, Syud Iqbal Ahmed, 1960.

Howell, Georgina, *Gertrude Bell*, Farrar, Straus and Giroux, 1988.

Huntington, Samuel P., *The Clash of Civilizations And The Remaking of World Order*, Simon & Schuster, 2011.

Stephens, Ian Melville, *Horned Moon: An Account of a Journey Through Pakistan, Kashmir, and Afghanistan*, Chatto & Windus, 1953.

Imam, Dr Alia, *Ikeesvein Sadi Mein Science Aur Adab—Tazad Kahan?* (Science and Literature in the 21st Century—Where's the Contradiction?).

Islam, Shamsul, *Golwalkar's We or Our Nationhood Defined*, Pharos Media & Publishing, 2006.

———, *Muslims Against Partition*, Pharos Media & Publishing, 2015.

Iyer, V. R. Krishna, *Sublime Footprint*, Gyan Publishing House, 2007.

Jaffrelot, Christophe (ed.), *A History of Pakistan and Its Origins*, Anthem Press, 2004.

Jalal, Ayesha, *The Sole Spokesman*, Cambridge University Press, 1994.

Jalil, Rakhshanda (ed.), *New Urdu Writings: From India and Pakistan*, Westland Ltd, 2013.

Jamil, Javed, *Muslims Most Civilised, Yet Not Enough*, Mission Publications, 2013.

Jeffrey, Robin, and Sen, Ronojoy, *Being Muslim in South Asia: Diversity and Daily Life*, OUP India, 2014.

Kapoor, Coomi, *The Emergency: A Personal History*, Penguin UK, 2015.

Kaura, Ajīta, Zahīr,Nūr and Ali Khan, Refaqat (eds.) *Sufism: A Celebration of Love*, Foundation of SAARC Writers and Literature, 2012.

Khurshid, Salman, *A Home In India*, Hay House India, 2014.

Kibaroglu, Mustafa, *Turkey's Neighbourhood*, Foreign Policy Institute, 2008

Kumar, Amrita and Bhaumik, Prashun, *Lest We Forget: Gujarat 2002*, Rupa Publications, 2002.

Lahiri, Prateep K., *Decoding Intolerance: Riots and the Emergence of Terrorism in India*, Roli Books, 2009.

Lelyveld, Joseph, *Great Soul: Mahatma Gandhi and His Struggle with India*, Vintage, 2012.

Lewis, Bernard, *Islam in History*, Open Court, 2001.

Lohia, Ram Manohar, *Guilty Men of India's Partition*, Kitabistan, 1960.

Michael Brecher, *Nehru: A Political Biography*, Beacon Press, 1970.

Mir, Ali Husain and Mir, Raza, *Anthems of Resistance*, India Ink, 2006.

Mīr Taqī Mīr *and* Naim, C.M. (eds.), *Zikr-i Mir: The Autobiography of the Eighteenth Century Mughal poet,. Mir Muhammad Taqi 'Mir', 1723-1810*, OUP, 2000.

Mital, Ruchi, *Costumes and Attire During the Mughal Period 1526-1707*, P. Rajarshi Tandon Open University, Allahabad.

Mitta, Manoj, *The Fiction of Fact Finding: Modi and Godhra*, HarperCollins India, 2014.

Mohyeddin, Zia, *The God of My Idolatry: Memories and Reflections*, Pakistan Publishing House, 2016.

Morris, Ian, *War: What Is It Good For?*, Farrar, Straus and Giroux, 2014.

Mukherjee, Rudranghsu, *The Great Speeches of Modern India*, Penguin India, 2011.

Mujeeb, Mohammad, *Indian Muslims*, Munshiram Manoharlal, 2003.

Mukherji, Kumar Prasad, *Lost World of Hindustani Music*, Penguin India, 2006.

Nag, Kingshuk, *The Namo Story*, Roli Books, 2013.

Naqvi, Saeed, *Reflections of an Indian Muslim*, Har Anand Publications, 1993.

———, and Sanjay Kapoor, *The last Brahmin Prime Minister*, Har-Anand Publications, *1996.*

Naqvi, Zameer, *Poet of the Ages Mir Anees*, 2008.

Naqvi, Saba, *Capital Conquest*, Hachette Book Publishing, 2015.

———, *In Good Faith: A Journey in Search of an Unknown India,* Rupa Publications, 2012.

Nasr, Vali, *The Shia Revival,* W. W. Norton & Company, 2007.

Nichols, Beverley, *Verdict on India,* Read Books, 2006.

Noorani, A. G. *The Destruction of Hyderabad,* Tulika Books, 2013.

Thakurta, Paranjoy Guha et al., *Gas Wars: Crony Capitalism and the Ambanis,* 2014.

Parekh, Bhikhu C., *Rethinking Multiculturalism: Cultural Diversity and Political Theory,* Harvard University Press, 2002.

Peirce, Gareth, *Dispatches from the Dark Side: On Torture and the Death of Justice,* Verso, 2012.

Pillai, Ajith, *Off the Record,* Hachette India, 2014.

Rao, Mohan, and Sarah, Sexton, *Markets and Malthus: Population, Gender and Health in Neo-liberal Times,* Sage Publications India, 2010.

Rumi, Raza, *Delhi by Heart,* HarperCollins India, 2013.

Sachau, Dr Edward C., *Alberuni's India,* Rupa Publications, 2015.

Sardar, Ziauddin, *Mecca: The Sacred City,* Bloomsbury USA, 2014.

Scahill, Jeremy, *Dirty Wars,* Avalon Publishing Group, 2012.

Schmidt, John R., *The Unraveling: Pakistan in the Age of Jihad,* Picador, 2012.

Seervai, H. M., *Partition of India: Legend and Reality,* Emmenem Publications, 1989.

Siddique, Zafar Ahmad, *Shibly,* Uttar Pradesh Urdu Akademi Lucknow, 2005.

Singh, Khushwant, *Train to Pakistan,* Penguin UK, 2016, first published by Chatto & Windus in 1956.

Singh Sarila, Narendra, *The Shadow of the Great Game: The Untold Story of India's Partition,* Constable, 2007.

Singh, Arvindar, *Myths and Realities of Security and Public Affairs,* Prabhat Prakashan, 2011.

Singh, Jaswant, *Jinnah: India-Partition Independence,* OUP Pakistan, 2010.

Sundarayya, Puccalapalli, *Telangana People's Struggle and Its Lessons,* Foundation Books, 1972.

Singh, S. Nihal, *Ink in My Veins: A Life in Journalism,* Hay House, 2011.

Tarin, Dr Hanif, *The Truth of Terrorism,* Manas Publication, 2009.

Taseer, Aatish, *The Temple-Goers,* Viking, 2010.

Thakur, Atul Kumar (ed.), *India Since 1947: Looking Back at a Modern Nation,* Niyogi Books, 2013.

Thapar, Romila et al., *India: Historical Beginnings and the Concept of the Aryan,* National Book Trust, 2006.

Thapar, Romila, *Early India: From the Origins to AD 1300,* Penguin, 1990.

———, Romila Thapar, *Somanatha: The Many Voices of a History,* Penguin,

Index

Urdu poetry, 2, 4, 9, 19, 21, 23-26, 28, 32, 36, 42, 49, 59, 69, 73, 149, 209–210, 216

Vajpayee, Atal Bihari, 78, 80, 92-93, 125, 147, 157, 166-169, 194, 207
varna or caste-based system, xiv, 27, 133
Veda Samaj movement, 82
Virk, Major G. P. S., 91
Vishwa Bharati, 20
Vishwa Hindu Parishad (VHP), 93, 96, 97, 104, 107, 114, 127, 142, 144, 145

Wavell, Lord, 55, 65, 175, 181
Western imperialism, 156-157

Wisner, Frank, 167
Yadav, Akhilesh, 131, 133, 141
Yadav, Lalu Prasad, xiv, 121
Yadav, Mitrasen, 135
Yadav, Mulayam Singh, xiv, 106, 141
Young India, 69
Yunus, Mohammad, 120, 155-159, 180

Zafar, Bahadur Shah, 34, 38
Zaheer, Syed Sajjad, 37
zamindari, abolition of, 3, 12, 14,, 16, 38-39, 48, 148, *see also,* feudal
Ziyad, Tariq ibn, 195
Zoroastrian culture, 27